A URBAN AMERICA

POLICY CHOICES FOR LOS ANGELES AND THE NATION

Edited by

James B. Steinberg, David W. Lyon, and Mary E. Vaiana

RAND

This research was supported by RAND as a part of its program
of public service.

Urban America: Policy Choices for Los Angeles and the Nation

Edited by James B. Steinberg, David W. Lyon, and Mary E. Vaiana.

Chapter 13, Table 2: William C. Apgar, Jr., "Recent Trends in Rental
Vacancies," Working Paper 89–3, Joint Center for Housing Studies of
Harvard University, as published in Martha R. Burt, *Over the Edge:
The Growth of Homelessness in the 1980s*, © 1992, The Russell Sage
Foundation. Reprinted by permission of the Russell Sage Foundation.

Cover design by Peter Soriano.

RAND
Copyright © 1992

ISBN: 0-8330-1281-9

Published 1992 by RAND
1700 Main Street, P.O. Box 2138, Santa Monica, CA 90407-2138
To obtain information about RAND studies or to order documents, call
Customer Service, (310) 393-0411, ext. 6686

In 1948 RAND was founded "to further and promote scientific, educational and charitable purposes, all for the public welfare and security of the United States." On the basis of this charter, RAND's mission has focused on informing public policy through research and analysis. Since the mid-1960s, this research and analysis has covered a broad range of social and economic issues of concern to citizens and policymakers at every level of government. This work, carried out under the auspices of RAND's Domestic Research Division, today spans criminal and civil justice, education and human resources, health sciences, labor and population, and environment and natural resources. Funding for this research comes from the federal, state, and local governments and from philanthropic foundations and charitable gifts.

In the wake of the civil disturbances in Los Angeles during the spring of 1992, we at RAND began to consider how we might contribute to a better understanding of the forces at work today in American cities—and especially in Los Angeles—and how what we had learned over the years from our research might contribute to building better communities for tomorrow. We drew on RAND's unique assets: the expertise of our professional staff and our extensive research and policy analysis over the years on a broad range of issues affecting our cities and their inhabitants.

This collection of essays, written by some of RAND's most-distinguished analysts, represents a contribution to the local and national debate on key issues that will shape policy in the coming years.

RAND does not speak with one voice, but many; what we have in common is a commitment to professional excellence and a dedication to sound, thoughtful, and innovative public policy. We offer this volume in that spirit.

James A. Thomson

CONTENTS

ACKNOWLEDGMENTS

Many people contributed their time, intellectual energy, and good will to this book. We would like to thank the following RAND staff and consultants who reviewed the individual chapters: Beth Asch, Robert Bell, Sandra H. Berry, Jonathan Cave, Tom Glennan, Peter Jacobson, James P. Kahan, Edward Keating, John J. Kirlin, Stephen P. Klein, Arleen Leibowitz, Grant N. Marshall, Lorraine McDonnell, Bridger Mitchell, Joseph P. Newhouse, Bruce Orvis, Mark Peterson, Elizabeth Rolph, David Ronfeldt, Randy Ross, Hilary Saner, Brian M. Stecher, Susan Turner, Gail L. Zellman. Their comments sharpened the focus and refined the substance of each essay.

James N. Dertouzos and Daniel A. Relles administered the review process and kept it on track under a very tight schedule.

Allan Abrahamse and Peter Morrison provided useful tabulations of 1990 census data.

Wendy B. Anderson and Sybil Sosin of RAND's Publications Department masterminded the production process, cheerfully causing order to appear from chaos. Janet DeLand performed electronic wizardry on the files and made software incompatibilities disappear. Elise Kalfayan prepared the marketing materials.

Gary Bjork graciously found time to write the biographical sketches of the contributors.

Doris Siegel lent her computer skills, patience, and organizational talents to nearly everyone. Without her as a focal point, all the pieces would never have come together.

Judy O'Neill and her colleagues at Custom Editoral Productions copyedited and produced the book, working long hours to meet a very demanding schedule.

Financial support for this book was provided by RAND, using its own funds.

Introduction

James B. Steinberg and David W. Lyon

I

Over the years, the problems and challenges of America's cities have captured the attention of some of our most insightful social analysts and critics. Their research and commentary have challenged the national conscience and stimulated the public and government to seek new and imaginative solutions. What we now call urban policy has been shaped, not only by elected officials and civic activists, but by the timely and trenchant ideas of observers ranging from Jacob Riis, Jane Addams, and Upton Sinclair to seminal writers like Jane Jacobs, Kenneth Clark, Michael Harrington, and Daniel Patrick Moynihan, to name but a few.

The civil disturbances in Los Angeles in April 1992 brought home to this community and to the nation the serious continuing problems facing our large urban centers. With its echoes of an earlier outbreak of violence a generation ago in Watts, these events led many of us at RAND to ask ourselves some questions: What in our city and in our nation's cities has changed since the summer of 1965—and what has not? Are the problems of today fundamentally similar to those we have struggled with for decades? Has government policy—federal, state, and local—made things better, worse, or has it been mainly irrelevant? What lessons have we learned from past government programs and policies that can help us do a better job in the future? And, finally, of special concern to a place such as RAND, how has research contributed to understanding our cities' problems and to devising innovative solutions—and what crucial questions remained unanswered?

This book is the result of our questioning. We turned to 19 RAND analysts who have conducted extensive research on social policy and asked them to reflect on the current issues facing our cities and our cities' people. The book does not attempt to address systematically all the issues that properly belong on the urban agenda; rather, it focuses on three broad areas where we at RAND have developed special expertise: children, youth, and families; crime and criminal justice; and public services and social welfare. Taken together, the book's essays increase our understanding of what our cities—especially our city, Los Angeles—look like, how they work and why often they don't work, the problems their residents face, and the dynamic trends that will shape their future.

The authors offer some innovative suggestions about how we can meet the challenges of the 1990s and beyond. Equally important, they identify the limits of our knowledge and the uncertainties that face policymakers. And the prescriptions they offer transcend conventional ideological labels.

II

Despite the diversity of topics and perspectives, the following common themes emerge from these essays.

1. *The range and scope of our cities' problems have, if anything, grown over the last three decades.* As Julie DaVanzo, Georges Vernez, Paul Koegel, and Audrey Burnam show, cities now shelter a growing proportion of our nation's poor, the undereducated, immigrants, and the homeless. Lynn A. Karoly describes the widening income gap between the richest and poorest in our nation, and DaVanzo shows the scope and effects of poverty on America's children—effects that are particularly severe in inner cities such as the South Central area of Los Angeles. DaVanzo demonstrates that, in many cases, family poverty goes hand in hand with the breakup of the "traditional" two-parent family. This demographic trend is most advanced in our cities, exacerbating the problem of urban poverty and bringing with it a number of serious economic and social challenges. These changes in income and demography are placing an increasingly heavy demand on public services, ranging from public safety (Petersilia, Reuter/MacCoun, Greenwood), to health care (Tranquada/Glassman), to education (Hill).

2. *Through a series of deliberate federal and state policy decisions over the last three decades, local governments, especially the governments*

of cities and urban counties, have been forced to assume increasing responsibility for meeting these rising demands—but their financial capacity has not grown correspondingly. Local responsibility offers some important benefits, including the ability to experiment and to adapt policies and programs to unique conditions, but it also creates a serious problem because urban jurisdictions have the hardest time marshaling resources to meet the clamor for services. As Robert A. Levine and Barbara R. Williams explain, the decentralization of urban programs (after the "categorical" federal grants of the War on Poverty) was designed to strengthen local governments by giving them a greater say in program operation as well as the funds needed to help do the job. But when the fiscal squeeze occurred, the funds disappeared—first federal support, followed more recently by state cutbacks. Yet the responsibilities remained. But there are limitations on the cities' ability to pick up the tab—often self-imposed as in the case of California's Proposition 13. Preston Niblack and Peter J.E. Stan show the effects of this squeeze on urban government's resources. It is a story that will be familiar to even the most casual reader of local newspapers in California and elsewhere: broad-ranging service cutbacks in the face of constant or in some cases growing demand.

3. Many urban problems are beyond the reach of local government action. Some of the problems facing cities are attributable to *changes in federal government policy,* including immigration (Vernez); housing (Koegel/Burnam); health insurance, especially for the indigent (Tranquada/Glassman); military enlistment (Hosek/Klerman); and more broadly, trade and macroeconomic policy, which affects not only the overall levels of employment opportunities (Levine/ Williams) but also the mix of skills and regional labor demand (Karoly). Other urban challenges are attributable to *broad social changes,* for the most part beyond what any level of government can affect. These include changes in family structure and composition (here discussed by DaVanzo and Ellickson but also in a recent RAND book, *New Families, No Families,* by Frances K. Goldscheider and Linda J. Waite), drug use (Reuter/MacCoun), and attitudes toward crime and criminal sanctions (Petersilia, Greenwood).

4. The problems that cluster in our cities most immediately affect the most-disenfranchised members of society, those who have the least political clout to gain support for effective policies to meet their needs.

The essays in this book largely concern groups within our society who are either disenfranchised—children, immigrant noncitizens, the homeless—or those who do not participate effectively in electoral politics—the poor, the undereducated, the mentally ill, substance abusers, and the like. It is not surprising that, in the competition for scarce government resources, their problems often take a back seat to programs that serve broader, politically more powerful interests.

But from a broader perspective, the public has a substantial incentive to support cost-effective solutions to the problems of these groups because, at least in some cases, failing to do so imposes significant social and economic costs. Altruism and human compassion have been important motives in American social welfare policy, although in recent years two presidents have challenged the division of responsibility between the public and private sector to meet these human needs. But some of our authors suggest that government involvement in social welfare programs can be justified on a more pragmatic basis. The public as a whole would benefit directly from programs that, for example, reduce crime and juvenile delinquency (Greenwood); provide more cost-effective health care for indigents (Tranquada/Glassman); limit the multiple costs imposed on society by homelessness (Koegel/Burnam) and drug use (Reuter/MacCoun); and enhance the productivity of today's youth, who will become tomorrow's workers (DaVanzo, Ellickson, Hill). The need to find effective solutions is particularly compelling for the problems that affect children because failing to act now means more serious and more intractable problems in the future, as today's problems are replicated again in succeeding generations.

Some of the authors' diagnoses are controversial, and documentation of the societal costs of these problems (not to mention the benefits of various interventions) remains sketchy in some cases. Nonetheless, these essays present powerful arguments that the public should be prepared in its own self-interest to support well-designed programs and policies targeted at the disadvantaged.

These general observations provide the context for policy-making. What do these essays tell us about the nature of effective policy approaches or solutions?

5. *Simple solutions have often proven ineffective and wasteful because they are based on a "misdiagnosis" that ignores the multiple, linked*

causes of urban social problems. This can be seen most clearly in the chapters that deal with the problems of today's children—substance abuse, teenage sex and pregnancy, delinquency, dropping out of school, unemployment, homelessness—(DaVanzo, Ellickson, Reuter/MacCoun, Koegel/Burnam). This is also Joan Petersilia's cautionary tale about the effect of California's "lock 'em up" policy on reducing crime rates, a perspective mirrored in Peter W. Greenwood's analysis of residential strategies for dealing with delinquent youth and Peter Reuter and Robert MacCoun's discussion of the limited success of drug enforcement in breaking up street drug markets or in reducing drug use.

But in a number of cases, policy can be targeted to produce a beneficial outcome, even if it does not completely eliminate the problem. Paul T. Hill suggests ways to make urban schools work even without tackling all the problems of today's youth; Robert E. Tranquada and Peter A. Glassman offer policy options to improve access to health care in cities even under current fiscal constraints and in the absence of a thoroughgoing reform of health insurance for the indigent and unemployed; Phyllis L. Ellickson identifies several intervention strategies that can prove cost-effective, although the positive effect is likely to be limited to only a relatively small percentage of the target youth population.

6. *Preventive strategies are appealing because they offer a cost-effective approach, but our knowledge of how to prevent is limited, and we must therefore accept the need for some more costly, ameliorative strategies.* Many of our authors, such as DaVanzo, Koegel and Burnam, Ellickson, and Greenwood, contrast preventive and ameliorative strategies and not surprisingly advocate prevention as a high payoff, cost-effective approach. But they recognize that prevention is no panacea, in part because we don't always know what works, and even when we do, it is often hard to reach the target population.

7. More generally, government policy can only have a limited effect, especially if a proposed policy has to swim against broad social and economic currents. While we shouldn't simply throw up our hands, *we should have realistic expectations and develop policy solutions that work with, rather than against, underlying social forces.* This is most dramatically clear in the case of the changing American family and the controversial area of "family values." In some ideal sense, more

two-parent families, greater teenage sexual abstinence, and a clearer social stigma associated with smoking and drug and alcohol use would help to ease many problems of contemporary urban American life. These are worthy goals for political, cultural, and religious leaders to pursue. But there will be no return to the Ozzie and Harriet family, and our policies, as Ellickson shows, must deal with the consequences; if youth are going to drink, teach them not to abuse alcohol; if they are going to engage in sex, help them avoid unintended consequences of disease and pregnancy. Similarly, although we can take steps to help parents to stay together—for example, by eliminating disincentives to two-parent families as DaVanzo discusses—policy should reflect the reality that, for many Americans, one-parent families are here to stay and should focus on alleviating the poverty and other problems they face. Immigration is another example. Undocumented immigration will continue, short of enacting draconian measures, which have never been politically acceptable to the nation. Therefore, policy should be designed to help both these immigrants and the communities in which they live to deal with the consequences.

8. *Economic prosperity can alleviate some urban problems and ease the fiscal pressure on America's cities.* Economic prosperity helps both the demand and the supply side of the urban equation: with more people working, there are fewer demands on health and welfare services that are associated with unemployment and poverty. As the demand for labor increases, opportunities for the harder-to-employ increase, thus benefiting the disadvantaged everywhere, as Levine and Williams point out in their review of anti-poverty strategies over the past three decades. At the same time, economic prosperity helps fill government coffers and makes it easier to finance those services that are still needed. But when the economy turns down, the effect is multiplied in the opposite direction. Niblack and Stan illustrate the "double whammy" of local government finance in California: a growing reliance on "procyclical revenues"—for example, income and sales taxes—that drop during a recession just as needs are growing.

But even sustained prosperity will not solve all of our cities' problems nor benefit all of our cities' people. The most vulnerable are the ones who need the most help and are the last to benefit from a rising tide. A number of our authors show that even the sustained growth of the

1980s failed to reach segments of the urban community, and the benefits of growth were not equally shared, as Karoly illustrates. The changing employment mix, which is creating an increasing number of low-paying jobs without health insurance and other benefits, means that not just the unemployed but also the "working poor" are placing demands on urban social welfare services. We see this clearly from Koegel and Burnam in their discussion of the "new homeless" and from Tranquada and Glassman in their study of medically indigent working families. And even growth did not bring about the same high level of employment as in previous decades. Finally, some segments of the urban community (the mentally ill, alcohol and drug abusers, single parents of small children) are so weakly attached to the labor market that even high overall levels of employment are unlikely to help them. For these, targeted programs are the only plausible solution.

III

In preparing their chapters, we asked our authors to focus where possible on the specific characteristics and problems of the Los Angeles area. In some cases, they were able to use recently released 1990 census data, which allowed them to examine not only the greater Los Angeles area but specifically South Central. In other chapters, the authors have drawn on research and experience specific to Los Angeles and to the state of California.

What emerges from these essays is a portrait that enriches our understanding of the Los Angeles landscape, although the main characteristics will come as little surprise to residents or to policy analysts. Los Angeles shares in most of the worrisome urban social and demographic trends—only more so in many cases. In particular, Los Angeles faces especially daunting problems arising from the diverse waves of immigration that continue to bring millions here and to create a mix and range of problems that stem in part from that diversity.

The 1990 census documents a trend well known to LA residents: there is no longer a "majority" group in the county. Non-Hispanic whites make up 41 percent of the population; those of Hispanic origin, 38 percent. Blacks, including Hispanic blacks (11 percent) slightly outnumber Asians/Pacific Islanders (10 percent). This snap-shot is the culmination of three trends active since the 1980 census: an 8.5 percent decline in the non-Hispanic white population, virtually no change in the number of blacks, and a dramatic increase in Hispanics (up 65 percent) and Asians/Pacific Islanders (up 110 percent).

Immigrants accounted for more than 60 percent of metropolitan Los Angeles's population growth of three million over the last decade and 54 percent of the state's population growth. (Metropolitan Los Angeles includes Los Angeles, Anaheim, Riverside, Long Beach, and Ventura.) The percentage of foreign born has grown from 18 percent to 27 percent in the metropolitan area, the second highest (after Miami) in the nation, and has reached 33 percent in Los Angeles County, 38 percent in the city. Forty-five percent of recent immi-grant children (those in the United States for three years or less) live in California; in the Los Angeles school district, recent immigrant students make up 10 percent of total enrollment and, under current trends, will increase by about 10 percent a year. Thus immigration is having, and will continue to have, a dramatic influence on the size and composition of the student population in Los Angeles, placing increasingly heavy demands on funding for public education as well as for other public services, such as health care.

Another group generating growing demands on the community is the homeless population. Although it is difficult to place an exact num-ber on the homeless, Los Angeles vies with New York for the largest homeless population in the country. RAND research suggests that in Los Angeles the homeless population is predominantly young, un-married, male, and minority, with blacks outnumbering Hispanics. In the downtown and Westside area, women make up 16 percent of the homeless, and three-quarters of them are parents; approximately 20 percent have their children with them. More than half lived in Los Angeles before first becoming homeless and as many as 70 percent have lived in Los Angeles for more than one year. One-third had at least some college education, but a roughly equal percent had not finished high school. Not surprisingly, the homeless have high rates of mental health and substance abuse problems; crack cocaine in particular is increasingly common among them.

Part of the problem stems from the dramatic decline in low-income housing, a decline which is more pronounced in Los Angeles than the national average. The number of units renting for under $500 per month (in 1985 dollars) in Los Angeles fell from 35 percent of the market in 1974 to 16 percent by 1985. By 1985, 74 percent of poor households were spending more than half their income on rent.

Although the Los Angeles metropolitan area has shared in the national trend toward greater income and wage inequality, the income gap has grown wider in Los Angeles than the national average. Real income fell 17 percent between 1973 and 1990 for a family near the bottom of the income distribution (the 10th percentile) compared with a 9 percent drop nationally; income rose 22 percent for those near the top (the 90th percentile) compared with 12 percent nationally. The result, as Karoly notes, is that, "in Los Angeles in 1990, family income at the 90th percentile was almost 13 times higher than at the 10th, while the ratio was about 11 to 1 for the nation as a whole."

For wages, the trends in California and in Los Angeles are similar to the national pattern, with sharp drops in real wages for male workers both at the bottom and in the middle of the wage distribution; real increases in wages for women at all parts of the spectrum were evident, especially among women near the top of the wage distribution. Unlike the national and statewide pattern, however, real wages for male workers near the top of the wage distribution in Los Angeles did not rise in real terms, though the small size of the sample may affect this conclusion.

DaVanzo's research offers further insight into patterns of family poverty in Los Angeles County and in the South Central area. The poverty rate for families with children under 18 is slightly higher in the county than the national average (17 percent vs. 15 percent); in South Central, it is 38 percent, more than double the countywide rate. The poverty rate for Hispanics (24 percent) and blacks (26 percent) in the county is twice as high as for whites (12 percent) and Asians/Pacific Islanders (13 percent). In South Central, the poverty rate is similar for all races and ethnic groups, but the population of South Central is overwhelmingly black (56 percent, including Hispanic black) and Hispanic (42 percent).

In Los Angeles County, poverty rates are similar for married white and black couples (8 percent and 9 percent, respectively), half the rate for two-parent Hispanic families (17 percent). Poverty rates for single-parent families are somewhat higher for blacks (41 percent) than whites (25 percent) and are higher still for Hispanics (46 percent), roughly mirroring the statewide pattern. Asian/Pacific families fall in between for both one- and two-parent families. In South Central, poverty rates are higher for both single- and two-parent families, reaching 51 percent for female-headed black families and 64 percent for female-headed Hispanic families.

The high rate of poverty among female-headed black families has an especially large effect since, in Los Angeles County, the percentage of black female-headed households (48 percent) is three times the rate for whites (16 percent) and more than double the rate for Hispanics (19 percent). This mirrors the national pattern except for Hispanic families, which are less likely to be female headed in Los Angeles County than nationally (24 percent). In South Central, the percentage of black households that are female headed is somewhat higher than the countywide percentage (58 percent vs. 48 percent), while the percentage for Hispanics is roughly the same.

The poverty rates for black and Hispanic households in South Central are a product of different mixes of family size, educational attainment, and labor force participation. Adult blacks have a much higher rate of high school graduation (63 percent in 1990) compared with Hispanics (18 percent), although this difference should narrow over time since, for the 16- to 19-year-old age group, 72 percent of blacks and 60 percent of Hispanics were enrolled in school. However, in 1990 only 47 percent of black males over 16 were employed compared with 71 percent of Hispanics. (Part of the difference is accounted for by the higher number of blacks over 16 still in school.) The median income for Hispanic households is 12 percent higher than for blacks ($20,740 versus $18,463), but the mean size of Hispanic households is much larger (5.28 persons vs. 2.78); thus black per capita income is twice as high ($9,174 vs. $4,625).

Immigration, homelessness, and growing poverty contributed to the demand for a broad range of public services from local Los Angeles–area governments. For health care services, provided in part by Los Angeles County, the problem is compounded by the low level of workplace-based health insurance in California. Only 56 percent of working Californians receive insurance from their employers compared with 64 percent nationally. The problem is particularly acute for working Hispanics (40 percent have employer health insurance) and blacks (52 percent). Almost one-third of the county's nearly nine million residents was without health insurance at some time during 1989, the highest per capita rate among the 30 largest metropolitan areas in the country.

Local governments play a major role in meeting these demands for a wide variety of services, and in California, the role of local government is especially important: local government spending makes up about 66 percent of total state and local spending compared with the national average of 61 percent. Niblack and Stan present in detail the evolution of local government finances since Proposition 13. Following the 1978 limits on property taxes, Los Angeles County grew more dependent on state aid, which made the county especially vulnerable to statewide revenue shortfalls in recent years; by contrast, the city has turned to user fees and charges to help make up revenues lost from Proposition 13 and to compensate for the near-total elimination of federal grants in the 1980s. The county's real per capita spending has remained flat between 1977 and 1990, constraining the services traditionally provided by the county (social services, health and welfare); but the city has increased its real per capita spending steadily since Proposition 13. Although spending has increased in real terms for all major spending categories, police and fire have fallen in relative terms (from 37 to 29 percent of the budget from 1977 to 1990), while environment and housing (including sewerage and waste disposal) and interest on debt have increased their share of the budget.

This profile of Los Angeles clearly suggests that, in the coming decades, the city and the county will face, much more intensely than in the past, many of the same public service and finance problems that have long troubled the nation's older cities. For Los Angeles, many aspects of the broad sweep of domestic policy research carried out by RAND and by other institutes in the country over the last 30 years is more relevant and timely than ever.

IV

The chapters in this volume are only a small sample of findings from 25 years of RAND research on domestic policy. America's cities have always played a central role in this research—whether focused upon the behavior of urban dwellers; assessing programs designed to improve the well-being of the urban poor; or helping local and state governments come to grips with the financing, delivery, and governance of public services. Jane Jacobs characterized it best in her influential book, *The Death and Life of Great American Cities*, when she observed, "Cities are an immense laboratory of trial and error." RAND has been active in that laboratory for some time, describing the trends, learning from the trials, and helping decisionmakers minimize the errors.

In the late 1960s, the New York City–RAND Institute was created to work side by side with the city's politicians and bureaucrats in their efforts to improve the delivery of fire, police, housing, and social services. The Levine and Williams chapter recalls a federally funded effort in the early 1970s to understand and map the changing fates of St. Louis, San Jose, and Seattle. This work ultimately led to a framework for assessing the impacts of urban policies that distinguished between the consequences of policies for *people, geographic places,* and *political jurisdiction* and for analyzing how the design of policies often muddled these distinctions (this framework is discussed in the chapter by Levine and Williams). By the late 1970s, RAND was assessing the consequences of California's Proposition 13 for the quality of municipal services and was determining whether rent control was significantly changing the price and quantity of rental housing in Los Angeles—a question central to the Koegel/Burnam chapter on homelessness.

Fiscal stringency at the local government level began to hit cities hard in the early 1980s. Cleveland leaders, who were designing an economic development strategy for revitalizing their city's troubled economy, asked RAND to identify "winning" sectors of its economy to strengthen future international competitiveness and to design an information system that could be institutionalized into a permanent economic monitoring capability for the Cleveland metropolitan region. (That capability is now located at Case Western Reserve University.) During the period, RAND was also asked by the mayor of Saint Paul to design a strategy for implementing a system of "cost centers" and user fees that might relieve the property tax base. The chapter by Niblack and Stan on fiscal trends in California describes just how aggressive Los Angeles has had to be with fees and special charges to balance budgets in the late 1980s and early 1990s.

A legacy of the federal government's focus on urban poverty in the 1960s was the design and implementation of social program experimentation. The movement toward "controlled" trials of program design stemmed both from a need to build political support for new programs before they were implemented and from the recognition that little was known about whether the programs would actually accomplish their objectives without offsetting side effects. In the early 1970s, RAND was asked to lead four social experiments involving cities and states throughout the country—the Health Insurance Experiment, the Housing Allowance Supply Experiment, the Education Voucher Demonstration, and the Los Angeles Electric Pricing Experiment.

What is telling for the findings reported in this volume is the degree to which controlled experiments have become the benchmark for designing and testing programs in our nation's cities—from the findings on prevention of adolescent drug use described in Ellickson's chapter to the conclusion reached by local probation officers throughout the country that intensive supervision of probationers is not going to be an easy or effective solution to prison overcrowding (Petersilia). Although the conclusions from these controlled trials are not always encouraging, we know much more today about what works and what doesn't when confronting the issues posed by the circumstances and in the aftermath of the civil disturbances in Los Angeles.

The findings reported in this volume about Los Angeles and about urban America more generally stem from a substantial amount of ongoing analysis and modeling of demographic, economic, and programmatic trends at the national level. Income growth and distribution (Karoly); cost, quality, and access to health care (Tranquada/ Glassman); the homeless and mental illness (Koegel/Burnam); immigration reform and control (Vernez); reforming urban education (Hill); children, youth, and families (DaVanzo); reforming the criminal justice system (Petersilia, Greenwood); drug markets and street crime (Reuter/MacCoun) are topics that represent just a small sample of the work taking place in the eight research programs of RAND's Domestic Research Division. A selected bibliography of RAND research related to the problems of urban America appears at the end of this volume.

Reviewing this work at RAND in light of the Los Angeles disturbances was a sobering experience. We know more about our cities today than we did in 1965. But the portrait that emerges is disturbing: we have not only failed to meet the lofty goals for improvement of the 1960s; in many respects the problems have become more complex, more deeply ingrained, and more formidable.

Can government action help us build a better future for our cities and the people who live in them? Taken together, these essays suggest that better policies can take us at least part of the way, but only if we as a nation can sustain a sense of urgency and common commitment.

We hope that this volume will stimulate discussion, clarify issues, and help shape the policy choices facing public and private decisionmakers at the federal, state, and local level during this time of change. Most important, the events of April 1992 have served to renew and intensify RAND's commitment to the use of its research findings and recommendations for improving the health and well-being of residents of California, and of residents of urban communities throughout America.

1

Public Policy and the Inner City Across Three Decades

Chapter One

Public Policy and the Inner City Across Three Decades

Robert A. Levine and Barbara R. Williams

INTRODUCTION: PROBLEMS AND POLICIES

The April 1992 civil disturbances in Los Angeles stirred a strong sense of *déjà vu*. The arson, killing, and looting in poor minority sections of the city, the immediate trigger of police-citizen interaction, and the presumed more fundamental causes—joblessness, poverty, and discrimination—all bore clear resemblances to the Los Angeles Watts disturbance of August 1965.

This chapter is about public policy in urban areas, however, and at first glance, the policy settings for the two events differed in both positive and negative ways. On the one hand, 27 years of public policy had brought major progress in at least one area, ending legal racial discrimination and segregation and reducing their *de facto* manifestations. On the other hand, policy in the 1980s and early 1990s had retreated from the active antipoverty policies of the 1960s.

In large measure, the self-conscious "urban" policy of the 1960s was focused on the problems of urban poverty, discrimination against blacks, and inner-city economic decline. In the aftermath of the 1992 events, policies and policy proposals similar to those of the 1960s have begun to surface again.

The major purpose of this chapter is to provide a historical frame of reference for considering the problems and policies of the 1990s, starting with an examination of the parallel experiences of the 1960s. However, neither the 1960s nor the 1990s can be taken in isolation. The policies of the 1960s that emphasized reducing poverty in the inner city were colored by the suburbanizing policies that began at the end of World War II and continued through the 1950s; the retrenchment of the 1980s was, in large measure, a reaction to the decentralization of policy in the 1970s, which in turn was a response to the 1960s belief in a strong federal role. This discussion focuses on the 1960s and the 1990s, with brief looks at the roots and transitions of the post–World War II period and the 1970s and 1980s. Much of the material has been drawn from a major RAND program of urban policy research that began in the 1970s and died as part of the general retreat of the next decade.

We review the four periods leading up to today, stressing the ideas and policies of the 1960s. From this history we draw comparisons between 1992 and 1965. Finally, we use the comparisons to suggest a frame of reference for evaluating policy alternatives for the future.

The chapter sets forth no recommendations. To do that for specific cities like Los Angeles, we need to undertake specific studies to weigh programmatic or investment options against one another in the context of local political interests and other community priorities. Even where urban needs are clear (e.g., low national and regional unemployment as a *sine qua non* for other pieces of the solution), countervailing objectives not considered here (e.g., price stability) might predominate. In any case, after examining both historical and current data, we conclude that local initiatives can make improvements at the margin, but significant improvements in employment for the hard-core poor and in their children's skills and opportunities are dependent on external factors, especially strong national economic growth and the federal role in urban economic development.

V-J DAY THROUGH THE 1950s

The United States entered World War II as a nation in depression. Urban and rural areas were sharply distinguished from one another. Cities were centers of industry, commerce, and clustered residences; populated rural regions were primarily agricultural; and suburbs were upper-income enclaves with a pleasant green style of life pictured in movies like the *Andy Hardy* series. The depression had cut off the mobility that might have allowed significant numbers of Americans to move into those suburbs.

When the war ended, the attraction of the suburban life-style, plus the conversion of depression into boom, made rapid change possible. To be sure, Levittown was not Andy Hardy country, but it was far better than depression slums and hard-scrabble farms. Three major federal policies abetted this powerful economic and social tide:

- The addition of low-interest veterans' mortgages to the New Deal's Federal Housing Administration (FHA) program made home ownership easy.

- The modernization of the road and highway system, accelerated in 1956 by President Eisenhower's massive Interstate Highway program, facilitated commuting and encouraged manufacturing outside of traditional urban sites.

- The Cold War revival of the defense budget and its movement in the direction of high technology induced rapid growth in the new areas of the Sunbelt, where suburbanization was the norm even within the expanding borders of old cities.

In spite of some overtones of deliberate policy (e.g., population dispersal to enhance survival from nuclear attack), this policy thrust was primarily an effort to assist an overwhelming popular movement.

As the 1950s ended, however, two major unintended consequences were becoming clear:

- Uncontrolled sloppy suburban sprawl. [1]

- Emptying out of central cities: first, of people who could commute from their suburban homes to their city jobs; more gradually, departure of manufacturing and other jobs to urban peripheries and farther. [2]

It is the second of these phenomena with which this chapter is concerned. For, together with another less policy-related economic change, the mechanization of agriculture in the South, "inner cities" were becoming segregated centers of poverty, inhabited increasingly by blacks displaced from farming. The response, as the 1960s began, was a much more conscious urban policy, focusing on poverty and race.

THE 1960s

The War on Poverty [3]

The origins of the War on Poverty were at least as rural as they were urban. Campaigning in the West Virginia primary in the spring of 1960, President John Kennedy had been genuinely shocked by the poverty he saw. That, plus the increasing number of confrontations stemming from civil rights attempts to break racial barriers—at that time still mostly in the South—sensitized the new chief executive to several powerful writings that had raised poverty to a high level of consciousness, at least among liberal intellectuals.

Notable among these examinations were Michael Harrington's book *The Other America: Poverty in the United States* and a long *New Yorker* article by Dwight McDonald, both of which concerned urban poverty as much as rural. [4,5] These two works were stirred together with other elements, including the "Culture of Poverty" concepts that anthropologist Oscar Lewis had derived from observing poor families in Latin America, and several quite urban and frequently radical pilot programs, particularly the Ford Foundation's Gray Areas project and a number of efforts sponsored by the President's Committee on Juvenile Delinquency. The latter came under the aegis of the president's brother, Attorney-General Robert Kennedy. New government programs for manpower training and welfare reform also contributed to the stew, as did a quantitative analysis of poverty by the President's Council of Economic Advisers.

After President Kennedy's death, the new president, Lyndon Johnson, cooked all these ingredients, plus his own early experiences with poverty and his dedication to racial equality, into a new dish, the War on Poverty. As headquarters for this war, the Economic Opportunity Act created a new agency reporting directly to the president, the Office of Economic Opportunity (OEO), so named to stress its central slogan, "A hand up instead of a handout." To lead the agency, Johnson appointed Kennedy's brother-in-law Sargent Shriver, a dedicated believer in the cause.

OEO requested and received a first-year appropriation of $1.5 billion, which in 1991 dollars would be about $6 billion—not a small sum for a new office outside any cabinet department. With this appropriation, the agency ran a diverse set of efforts and was formally or informally responsible for a broader range. The programs under its formal responsibility stressed youth training, including the Job Corps; a variety of minor urban and rural small business development efforts; a volunteer "domestic Peace Corps," and the Community Action Program (CAP).

CAP, the identifying center of the War on Poverty, was many things. It was a set of local programs designed and managed, not by elected officials (except in Chicago, where few had the temerity to buck Mayor Richard Daley), but by selected or newly created agencies that were supposed to stress "maximum feasible participation" of the poor people being assisted, a key concept of the Economic Opportunity Act. CAP was also a set of pilot demonstrations that bred programs still in being today. They include Head Start, Legal Services, and an urban impact program known by the names of its authors, Senators Robert Kennedy and Jacob Javits. The Kennedy-Javits program continues to provide a model for focusing broad public and private resources on small urban areas. It was also a seedbed for many of the radical ideas of the early 1960s. Because of its radicalism and its setting up of alternative political power centers challenging local governments under the banner of "maximum feasible participation" (even, for a short time, in Chicago), it was immensely controversial.

Radicalism and controversy were toned down enough by the end of OEO's first year (1965) that they did not kill the agency, although they came close. Radical confrontation, however, left lasting legacies, not only of its own programs and advocates but of its antithesis, created by political dialectic: an attempt to return power to official urban governments. That will be discussed below.

Much of OEO's indirect responsibility for informally coordinating government antipoverty efforts as a whole was picked up by its planning staff, made up largely of economists. In 1965 this group produced a Five-Year Anti-Poverty Plan, proposed by Shriver to the White House, that centered on a proposal to substitute for the existing welfare system a negative income tax (NIT), which would provide financial incentives for recipients to obtain jobs and for welfare families to stay together; job training, supported by a large-scale program of public jobs similar to the New Deal's Works Progress

Administration (WPA); education (a major ongoing poverty program outside of OEO provided federal aid to improve the education of poor children in schools with insufficient resources); and CAP as the local coordinator and catalyst of many of these efforts.* The whole plan, the training and job programs in particular, depended on what was thought of as tight "full employment"; if jobs were seeking workers throughout the economy, then even the hardest-to-employ could find positions. All of this was estimated to require a $10 billion annual expenditure increase over the 1965 level across the federal government (about $40 billion in 1991 dollars). Only about $3.5 billion of this would have gone to OEO. In addition to its planning and coordination efforts, this staff initiated a new kind of social experimentation, designed with controls that would make possible rigorous evaluation of results. The initial experiment concerned the proposed NIT.

Under the constraints of political and fiscal reality, as well as the burgeoning Vietnam War, few elements of the antipoverty plan were ever tried. In addition to the OEO-generated programs that have lasted until now, however, both the grand ideas of the plan and the smaller programs of the agency have provided an intellectual and experiential frame of reference for examining the very similar proposals of the 1990s.

The Long Hot Summers

In the early evening of August 11, 1965, Los Angeles police in Watts, a central part of South Central's black ghetto, arrested a young man for reckless driving. Precise subsequent events have been disputed, but the result was a confrontation between police and population and a six-day civil disturbance that resulted in 35 deaths and $40 million in damage.

Watts was the first in a four-year series of civil disturbances. In the summer of 1966, major disturbances took place in Chicago and Cleveland; in 1967, in eight cities, notably Newark and Detroit; in April 1968, in Washington and Baltimore, triggered by the assassination of Martin Luther King.

These events spawned two major official reports, both of which set forth findings on causation, together with policy proposals both to better control future disturbances and to correct their fundamental causes. By the end of 1965, a commission appointed by California Governor Edmund G. (Pat) Brown and headed by former CIA Director John McCone presented the 101-page "McCone Report" on the Watts disturbance. [6] In the spring of 1968 (the report was written before the Washington and Baltimore disturbances), the National Advisory Commission on Civil Disorders, appointed by President Johnson, published the more comprehensive "Kerner Report," named after the commission's chairman, Governor Otto Kerner of Illinois. [7] That report focused on the disturbances of 1967, but it drew from the entire series up until that time.

The McCone Report is useful for the analysis of this chapter both because of its policy recommendations and because of its specificity to Los Angeles, which makes it possible to compare 1965 and 1992. To begin with, in 1965 the violence was confined to Watts, a small section of South Central. It was black civilians versus white police: the population involved was all black; the Los Angeles police force at the time was only 4 percent black.† Civilian whites, many of whom were Jewish, were involved primarily as victimized store owners. Hispanics entered the report only peripherally because essentially they had not entered the events.

The McCone Report warned that "the existing breach" between the black and white communities, "if allowed to persist, could in time split our society irretrievably." It centered its discussion of causation on the migration of "totally untrained" blacks from the South and their consequent frustration in finding jobs and stable living conditions, but it also stressed three "aggravating events": the "angry exhortations" of civil rights leaders; the repeal by referendum a few months before of California's Fair Housing Law; and the publicity given federal antipoverty programs that "did not live up to their press notices." [8]

More specifically, the commission asserted that "the three fundamental issues in the urban problem of disadvantaged minorities are: employment, education, and police-community relations." [9] The primary policy recommendations were:

- An "emergency literacy program" in designated "emergency schools" in the area.

- Opening a job-training and placement center in Watts.

- An independent inspector-general in the Police Department, with a staff of officers and civilians to investigate complaints; an expanded community relations program; and hiring more blacks into the department.

- Improved mass transit for the area.

- A new hospital in South Central.

- An accelerated urban renewal program.

- A city Human Relations Commission. [8]

In one form or another, these recommendations were all adopted.

The still well-known identifying sentence of the Kerner Report was "Our nation is moving toward two societies, one black, one white, separate and unequal," an observation not dissimilar from the "irretrievable breach" of the McCone Report. [7] The Kerner Commission put the fundamental blame on "white racism," with the disturbances of 1967 catalyzed by:

> Frustrated [black] hopes. . . . A climate that tends toward approval and encouragement of violence. . . . The frustrations of powerlessness. . . . A new mood . . . among Negroes [and the fact that] to some Negroes, the police have come to symbolize white power, white racism and white repression. [7]

More specifically, the Kerner Report listed a number of grievances, in rough order of the intensity with which they were felt:

1. Police practices.

2. Unemployment and underemployment.

3. Inadequate housing.

4. Inadequate education.

5. Poor recreation facilities and programs.

6. Ineffectiveness of the political structure and grievance mechanisms.

7. Disrespectful white attitudes.

8. Discriminatory administration of justice.

9. Inadequacy of federal programs.

10. Discriminatory consumer and credit practices.

11. Inadequate welfare programs. [7]

The Kerner Commission came up with a broad range of recommendations, including:

- Local task forces, grievance committees, and participation mechanisms. (This, two and a half years after the initiation of CAP.)

- Police grievance mechanisms, community programs, and recruiting of blacks.

- Better preparation and training for disturbance control and arrest and trial procedures.

- Federal action to provide two million new jobs, half of them public, supported by training and antidiscrimination programs. (The OEO planners had recommended provision for four million public jobs.)

- School desegregation and increased federal support for a variety of education programs.

- Welfare reform (albeit less radical than NIT).

- Federal open housing laws and substantially increased public housing. [7]

Unlike McCone's specific and limited local recommendations, most of Kerner's national recommendations, including those on jobs, education, and welfare, went unadopted, at least in the scope at which they were recommended. The police recommendations, which were primarily to local authorities, were seldom implemented anywhere.

The Importance of External Factors

Focusing on antipoverty and urban policies in the 1960s tends to obscure a central fact: social change is frequently far more dependent on nonpolicy factors, operating in an open society through political machinery and market mechanisms, and on seemingly unrelated policies that directly affect the choices of households and businesses. Our discussion of the 1950s mentioned three of these:

- The attraction of the suburbs.

- The postwar economic boom.

- The inadvertent urban policy based on mortgages, roads, and defense spending.

By the end of the 1960s, there were two additional external factors:

- *The Vietnam War.* The Vietnam War diverted federal funds from the War on Poverty and the cities, distracted President Johnson's attention, and deeply divided the American body politic, frustrating the healing strategies of the War on Poverty and the Kerner Commission. The Vietnam War also had a major though less-recognized positive effect, however—tight employment.

- *Tight employment.* In 1969 the civilian unemployment rate dipped to 3.5 percent because the war accelerated already expansionary economic policies. True, an economy hot enough to reduce unemployment to that extent was an inflationary economy. Nonetheless, *high employment did more to promote urban prosperity and reduce poverty than all the government programs put together.*

The Johnson Administration Reaction

Lyndon Johnson's enthusiasm for Shriver's War on Poverty cooled fast. It was not only the diversion of Vietnam, although one tragedy of that war was that it pulled the president's attention from where his heart was. Merle Miller quotes Lady Bird Johnson as saying, shortly after LBJ took up the reins: "I do hope there are not too many problems in foreign affairs matters during Lyndon's administration," and

Miller adds " . . . that was his hope as well. Why couldn't those foreigners leave him alone to build his domestic paradise?" [10, p. 358]

In any case, CAP confrontations and the consequent reactions of Democratic governors and mayors, frequently transmitted through Vice President Hubert Humphrey, soon convinced Johnson that the paradise would not be built around OEO. The president was quoted as saying that CAP was "being run by kooks and sociologists."‡ And the urban disturbances cemented his conservatism about political procedure and process, although they may have strengthened his dedication to long-run social objectives.

OEO's budget, which had started out at $1.5 billion a year, never went above $2 billion, and the economists' grandiose plans were never taken seriously. OEO's focus shifted from the independent action implicit in "maximum feasible participation" to a renewed stress on cities and city governments as such.

Even as early as 1965, the cities' political reaction to CAP produced a competing program under HUD, Model Cities. (The name was changed from its original Demonstration Cities out of concern that some would misinterpret the program's goal as promoting more "demonstrations" in cities.) Model Cities provided federal money and coordinating authority directly to city governments. Since CAP also had coordinating authority, the last years of the Johnson administration saw a lot of infighting over who was to coordinate whom. However, by the end of the administration, the pattern was clear: the president and the secretary of HUD would set, and the mayors would administer, national urban policy. The states, while not ignored, were not a crucial link in the chain. The cities had a lot of leeway in setting policy priorities, but since the Vietnam War was on, not much money went with the other powers.

The Changeover to Nixon

In its first years, the Nixon administration changed course but by no means reversed it. To the gratified surprise of many of those who had fought the poverty/urban wars, it even tried some new directions.

President Nixon did not abolish OEO; indeed, he appointed a strong new director, former Illinois Congressman Donald Rumsfeld. The agency knew its place—it no longer fought the good fight in the corridors of Washington—but its new orientation was useful, focusing in particular on the kind of social experimentation that had been started by OEO's earlier planners.

Behind the new thrust was a Nixon White House staffer, Assistant to the President Daniel P. Moynihan, a Democrat. As assistant secretary of labor in the Johnson administration in the mid-1960s, Moynihan had published a study called *The Negro Family*, which placed the deterioration of those families at the heart of America's racial problems: a broken black family was likely to be a welfare family; its male children were more likely to be on the streets than in school or jobs; its female children were in danger of heading future broken families. [11] However, most black leaders took this study as an accusation that "blamed the victim" for discrimination, a fact that poisoned relations between that leadership and Moynihan as he proceeded in later years through several ambassadorial posts to become senator from New York.

As part of the battles surrounding *The Negro Family* and the early excesses of CAP and its predecessor Gray Areas and Juvenile Delinquency programs, Moynihan had not only come to dislike CAP but to contrast what he called an "employment strategy" against poverty to his perception of CAP's social radicalism. [12] When he came to the White House, however, he saw as the best immediate chance for progress, not major employment programs in the hot economy, but rather welfare reform (an "income maintenance" strategy). Moynihan convinced President Nixon to propose a new system patterned roughly on the NIT. To bolster the proposal, Moynihan turned to the experiment that had been begun by OEO's planners in the previous administration, but ironically, the early results did not seem to support the hope that built-in incentives would turn welfare recipients into workers. That interpretation was disputed by many of the experimenters, but it was accepted by enough Congressmen that the proposal died.

The NIT experiment was the first of several social experiments carried out in the first years of the new administration. Although some criticized the experiments as substitutes for action, these efforts, plus major improvements in other areas of income support for the poor, gave Nixon's first term a progressive cast that few had expected.

The national scope of the experiments and the welfare improvements, however, plus the gradual phasedown of CAP, weakened the connections among antipoverty programs, inner-city efforts, and urban policies that had grown during the 1960s. As a result, the 1970s saw policy move away from a focus on poverty in the central cities toward two separate strategies: antipoverty efforts divorced from any specific location and urban policy as such.

THE 1970s

As policy from the 1970s turned from large-scale activism toward experimentation and concern with governance, policy analysis played an increasing role. The experiments spawned a significant body of new social science research at, among others, the University of Wisconsin Institute for Research on Poverty and the Urban Institute (both of which had been created by the Johnson administration), the Mathematica Corporation, the Manpower Demonstration Research Corporation, and RAND. In this chapter, we focus our brief discussion on RAND's work. RAND researchers were extensively involved in experiments dealing both with poverty and nonpoverty urban issues and with other problems on which the studies and policies of the 1970s increasingly focused.

Poverty

When Congress failed to adopt NIT, the Nixon/Moynihan income maintenance strategy turned in more pragmatic directions. The two most important changes were an expanded food stamp program, which had about three million recipients when Nixon assumed office in 1969 and more than 16 million when President Ford departed in 1977; and Supplemental Security Income (SSI), which essentially ended poverty among the aged. Congress initiated a third important antipoverty effort, the nutrition program for pregnant and lactating women, infants, and children (WIC).

Other antipoverty attempts were largely limited to experimentation. RAND played a major role in three of the four major strands of inquiry.

- The NIT experiment, which in spite of its early effects in inadvertently helping kill the Moynihan welfare reform, provided important information throughout the first half of the decade about the effectiveness of the job-seeking and family-preserving incentives supposedly built into the tax. Mathematica and the Poverty Institute were the leading analysts for these studies, though many organizations, including RAND, used the data they had gathered. [13]

- The Education Voucher demonstration, which offered parents the opportunity to choose among public schools for their children. [14] Confined by strong public school administrators and teachers in California to a study of choice within the public school system, the demonstration yielded only modest evidence of sustained diversification in schools' curricula or the exercise of parental choice toward entering children in schools outside their neighborhoods. Effects on schools and students were small, but the experience is still reflected in various voucher proposals.

- The Housing Allowance Study, which gave eligible families the money to find and maintain adequate housing. [15] Both the "supply experiment" conducted by RAND and the "demand experiment" conducted by the Urban Institute underscored the ability of low-income households to find and maintain adequate housing with the additional financial support offered. However, the studies concluded that, in the absence of strongly enforced requirements about housing standards, recipients would use the financial support as general income support, exercising preferences other than bringing their housing fully up to code. The experience here is still built into housing policy under the Section 8 program, which provides housing subsidies to the poor, albeit in a more-regulated pattern than simply providing vouchers.

- The Health Insurance Study, which examined the effect of varying copayments and deductibles in family health insurance policies. [16] It showed that requiring copayments could reduce the demand for health care and costs to employers without harming health status. In the period immediately following publication of the findings, the number of major employer health plans with deductibles for hospitalization more than doubled. Data from this experiment still inform the debate over alternative health care plans.

President Carter tried to revive an NIT-based welfare reform program similar to the Nixon and Moynihan proposal; like them, he failed in the Congress, which found it too radical and conjectural. By the end of the decade, the variety and scope of antipoverty programs, with the exception of food stamps and SSI, stood about where it had been at the beginning. Indeed, by the Census Bureau's count, the percentage of the population in poverty had gone up slightly, from 12.5 percent in 1971 to 13 percent in 1980. The major reason was the economic stagflation of the 1970s, due in part to repeated oil supply/price problems, another demonstration of the dominance of macroeconomic factors.

Urban Policy

By the 1970s, central cities, especially in the Northeast and Middle West, were beset by problems left in the wake of powerful population shifts to the suburbs and the Sunbelt. Economic growth and decline mirrored population movements, as subsidies to new investment, such as the preferential tax treatment of capital gains, encouraged plants and businesses to locate where land for new construction was cheap and appreciating.

Moreover, suburban sites accommodated land-hungry "horizontal" manufacturing processes, which replaced the vertical processes reflected in the multistory manufacturing plants of the early 20th century. Additionally, suburban sites provided access to highways for truck transport, more flexible and adaptable than rail or water, and also provided parking lots for workers' cars.

The outmigration from central cities was selective, leaving behind those who were poorer, less educated, and more vulnerable to unemployment. Declining municipalities were faced with relatively higher demands for services at the same time that their tax bases were eroding. As a result, the fiscal problems of the cities began to mount in the 1970s, primarily in the East and the Midwest. New York

City's 1975 financial crisis was a precursor. It was ultimately ended with the help of the federal government because that was where the money was. In California, on the other hand, the combination of a fat state treasury, with local property taxes that mounted rapidly because of increasing values and assessments, led an irate electorate to pass Proposition 13, which cut property taxes so that the state then had to become the underwriter of local finances.

Nixon's New Federalism fit nicely with the new definition of the urban problem. Convinced that cities and states should craft their own solutions, urban policymakers in the federal government turned to revenue sharing as an appealing way to reduce the fiscal burdens of states and localities and to close out the more targeted categorical programs of the 1960s. General Revenue Sharing became law in 1972, and the next several years saw a consolidation of programs: in 1974 the Community Development Block Grant Act brought together seven programs including Model Cities; this became the central vehicle for city governments to promote development and other objectives. Mayor Tom Bradley of Los Angeles used it to develop the city's moribund old downtown area; some complained that he had moved the urban problems rather than solving them. Though not trivial, these programs were small potatoes compared to the powerful market forces that drained some cities of their more affluent residents and caused others to grow almost uncontrollably.

In an attempt to build a more systematic understanding of urban growth and decline, RAND initiated an Urban Policy Analysis program in 1972 with case studies of three cities with very different growth profiles: San Jose, one of the 10 most rapidly growing cities in the United States at the time; St. Louis, one of the 10 most rapidly declining; and Seattle, a city with an economy in decline but population and services more intact than one would expect. [1,2,17]§ Although the different problems and political agendas of each city limited comparisons, what was evident was the tendency of local decisionmakers to view their problems as relatively unique, to accept local responsibility for solving them, and to look for financial help from the modest urban programs sponsored by the federal government.

To help cities look beyond these programs to the more powerful motivators of business and household decisions, RAND analysis distinguished among the intended and unintended effects of urban policies on the problems of *people,* of *geographical places,* and of *political jurisdictions.* People problems (e.g., poverty, educational deficits, unemployment) had been stressed in the 1960s. Place problems developed when, for example, high rents, crime, and congested traffic reduced the competitiveness of some urban locations. Jurisdictional problems are exemplified by those described earlier: a growing disparity between the demand for public services and resources available to the authorities responsible for providing the services.

The results of the analysis frustrated federal policymakers. An administration that sought to return problem solving to cities was not pleased to hear that the problems of those cities stemmed largely from forces beyond their control, including federally initiated policies. The equivocal results of programs meant to redress various urban problems added discouraging news. For example, tax breaks used to lure businesses into an area tended to attract firms that might have located there without them and/or bring in employees from elsewhere; income supplements and social services tied to particular locations tended to hold needy people there instead of helping them move to locations with more jobs. For local policymakers who wanted tourniquets for their hemorrhaging tax bases and specific new ideas for better services at lower costs, RAND's national analyses were too general to be very helpful.

In 1977 priorities shifted once more. The Carter administration sought a new paradigm for urban policy. Research that had focused on macroeconomic forces and unintended federal policy effects on urban jurisdictions received sudden prominence. HUD sponsored its first major contracts for research on urban finance and development questions. "Intended" and "unintended" federal policy impacts made their way into the language and then into HUD decisions. [18] In 1978 President Carter delivered an urban policy message that, among other things, affirmed his intent to sponsor a "conscious" urban policy that would require the federal sponsors of all new major policies to submit "urban impact statements" and would give top priority to efforts that offered more jobs for the unemployed. Before that could happen, however, the electorate chose another president, who sought to reduce the overall federal role in domestic policy. Urban policy vanished from national priorities, almost overnight.

THE 1980s

The story of the 1980s is the shortest of all. The Reagan administration philosophy was to reduce sharply the federal role; what they did reflected what they said, even though from David Stockman's account, the administration shrank from full implementation of its intended cutbacks. [19] By the time that President Bush succeeded President Reagan, the macroeconomic and budgetary consequences of the decade's first eight years had greatly narrowed any possibilities for deliberate poverty or urban policy; the administration had neither antipoverty or urban programs nor the funds to support them. The social and economic effects of these years have been carefully monitored by the Urban Institute. [20]

The macroeconomic flows of the Reagan administration were governed by massive policy changes and tides. Income taxes were cut drastically; defense budgets went up sharply. Outside of policy control, health costs spiraled, and although much of the additional spending was on the poor through Medicaid and part of Medicare, the cost increases did not bring about commensurate improvement in the health care of the poor. Social security pensions also rose substantially; some of that went to the poor but most did not.

Explicit antipoverty and urban programs had always been part of a fiscal residual—sardines swimming in the wake of whales. The program declines of the 1980s can be exemplified by two changes:

* From 1979 to 1989, total public spending—federal, state, and local—on labor training and services, considered by the planners of the 1960s to be the key to reducing urban poverty, fell from 0.3 to 0.1 percent of gross domestic product (GDP). Most other antipoverty expenditures also declined, although less sharply; the net decrease in the relevant categories was 0.1 percent of GDP, about $5 billion 1990 dollars. To calibrate this, defense spending increased from 4.9 to 5.7 percent of GDP, health from 3.1 to 4.1 percent, slightly more than $100 billion for the two.

* Federal contributions to urban renewal and community development, the category that subsumed all the categorical and noncategorical federal urban programs of the 1970s, had increased from $6.6 billion 1990 dollars in 1973 to a peak of $8.3 billion in 1980, but by 1990 they had gone down to $3.6 billion. For Los

Angeles, the flow of actual federal dollars under this heading dropped from $315 million in 1979 to $156 million in 1992.

All of this was but a ripple on a wave of unemployment that put further pressures on the poor and on cities. The national unemployment rate, which had dropped to 3.5 percent in 1969, increased to an average 6.7 percent from 1974–1980 under the stagflation that dominated the 1970s. The average for the 1980s, however, went even higher, to 7.2 percent. In 1989 the rate fell to a low for the decade of 5.4 percent, but then it rose in the first years of the 1990s to well above 7 percent as the economy stagnated. The Los Angeles metropolitan area was somewhat better off in the 1980s—as goes the defense budget, so goes Southern California, but that factor had been sharply reversed by 1992.

In conjunction with the decline of poverty and urban policy in the 1980s was a lack of interest in research. The Reagan administration took the view that they were elected to reduce the federal role, so it showed little interest in what worked best among a set of alternatives. The RAND urban program expired for lack of sustenance; among the efforts of the 1970s, only the health insurance effort continued to attract federal dollars and attention because health costs remained a significant problem for the federal budget as well as for consumer and business pocketbooks. RAND's two opportunities for specifically urban analysis in the 1980s came from St. Paul and Cleveland, cities that were trying self-help to fight off downward economic forces. In St. Paul, the mayor wanted to offer public services modeled on private sector practices of staffing and financing; in Cleveland, the business community wanted to understand the relative strengths of the local and regional economies to focus investment. These efforts reflected the new political environment of the 1980s: decreasing federal support left cities to their own devices and local leadership, which could not, however, restore funding levels.

1992: WHAT HAS CHANGED SINCE 1965?

The first years of the 1990s seemed a continuation of the 1980s but the April 1992 Los Angeles civil disturbances revived sharp memories of the 1960s and Watts in 1965 in particular. This section and the next present a picture of some of what has changed and what has not. This section presents an overview, divided into four categories:

- Factors that have remained relatively unchanged between 1965 and 1992.

- Factors that have improved.

- Factors that have deteriorated.

- Other changes, that have neither improved nor impaired the urban landscape.

The final section then focuses on policy, deriving lessons from the past to help choose alternatives for the future.

Similarities Between 1965 and 1992

Both disorders started in Los Angeles's South Central black area (but, as discussed further below, 1992 was multiethnic, with more Hispanics arrested than blacks, and participants and victims of all races). Both involved large-scale violence, looting, and arson. Most victims of both were members of the rioting groups or business owners of other groups. Both were triggered by incidents in which Los Angeles police were perceived to have acted brutally toward black men. In 1992, as in 1965, the Los Angeles black community was very sensitive to police racism, which the Kerner Report had stressed as a key factor nationally. Neither in Los Angeles nor in most other cities had the grievance procedures recommended in the 1960s been implemented.

Underlying the trouble in both cases was the persistence of black/white inequality and black poverty; in 1992 Hispanic poverty played a major role in spreading it. All of this was manifest in particular in the lack of employment and employment opportunities. At the time of the 1990 census, more than 40 percent of 16- to 19-year-old young men in South Central were either unemployed or outside the labor force. (Unfortunately, no comparable figure is available for 1965 or 1970.)

Journalistically, the 1960s phrase "culture of poverty" had been replaced by "the underclass," but the pictured syndrome was similar—

neighborhoods characterized by poverty, unemployment, bad schools, welfare, crime, early pregnancies, and female-headed households.

Improvements from 1965 to 1992

By 1992 legal discrimination and segregation had disappeared (with minor "private club" exceptions), and the "disrespectful white attitudes" reported by the Kerner Commission were less endemic. There was more contact between black and white middle classes, and less tendency among whites to attribute the "underclass" culture to all blacks.

More concretely, significant numbers of blacks had achieved major economic progress. Jobs were available to those who were educated and trained; affirmative action had assisted the process. The effects of this crucial change are illustrated in Figure 1, which graphs the proportions of families in the 1970 census and households in the 1990 census with incomes below the levels specified by the horizontal axis.[#] In 1970 more than half of Los Angeles County blacks lived in South Central; by 1990 only about a third lived there. The left part of the figure shows that, in 1970, blacks in and out of South Central had much lower incomes than whites. (The income distribution for blacks in and out of South Central were so close that they cannot be graphed separately.) However, by 1990, as the right side of the figure shows, the blacks who lived outside South Central had an income distribution about as close to whites throughout the county as to blacks in South Central. By 1990 many blacks were able to seize opportunities to live and work beyond earlier geographic and social boundaries. The downside of this change was the creation of two *black* societies, separate and unequal, leaving the worst-off blacks behind in South Central as a tinderbox for trouble.

Hispanics are not charted because their area of concentration, although overlapping that of the blacks, had very different boundaries. Their income distribution in 1990 was similar to that of blacks, although fewer Hispanic households had incomes below $15,000 and fewer above $25,000.

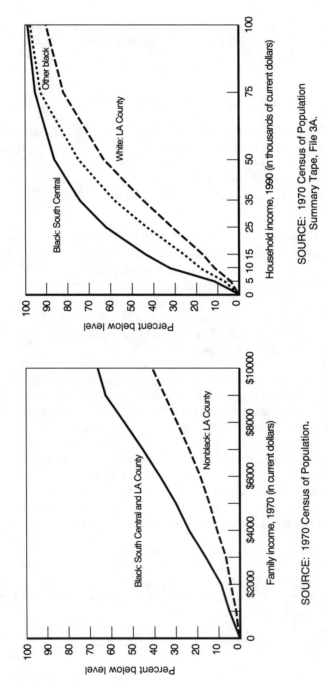

Figure 1—Income Distributions, 1970 and 1990

By 1992 minorities had achieved fairer representation, at least as compared to 1965, in politics and in key public services. The 45-*person* California congressional delegation had four black members, roughly commensurate with the relative population, as compared with one member in 1965. In 1992 the delegation also had three Hispanics and two Asian-Americans. By the end of 1991, almost 14 percent of the Los Angeles police force was black, as compared with 4 percent in 1965; by 1991 Hispanics outnumbered blacks. Blacks were represented in all superior ranks except the top three positions; in mid-1992, after the disturbances, Willie L. Williams, a black man, was installed as police chief.

In a number of ways, the black community in South Central was more stable in 1992 than in 1965. Black residents were no longer new migrants from the South; most had been in the area for many years, though transient Hispanics were replacing blacks in parts of the area. Overall, home ownership in South Central was about 40 percent, higher than the city as a whole, but some notorious public housing projects still exist and do not seem to be improving; and in reception areas for new Hispanic immigrants, housing seems at least as bad as it was in Watts in 1965. Consumer facilities, pinpointed as a problem in 1965, were substantially better in most of the area until many were burned out in 1992. Community leaders played a calming role in 1992, in contrast to the "angry exhortations" noted by the McCone Commission.

Except for police grievance procedures, most of the McCone recommendations had been implemented well before 1992. In addition to the improvement in consumer facilities, mass transit had been greatly improved and so had recreational opportunities. A major hospital had been built, although by 1992 the quality of health care was declining because of underfunding.

Deterioration from 1965 to 1992

The 1992 disturbances were in themselves worse than those of 1965: more people were killed, more property was damaged, and the unrest was spread over a wider area within Los Angeles and, indeed, went outside the city itself to other municipalities such as Long Beach and Compton.

Beyond this, however, a number of fundamental conditions were significantly worse in 1992. In particular, the national economic picture was dominated by recession and high unemployment. The 1992 economy was significantly worse in Southern California than elsewhere, due particularly to the decrease in defense jobs.

In the late 1960s, it was hoped that desegregation would solve the education problems of South Central, but the promise of desegregation never materialized, and the entire school system deteriorated badly, with minority schools at the forefront of this decline.

By all measures, the black family was much worse off in 1992 than when Moynihan wrote about it. Nationally, numbers of female-headed families and welfare were all up (not disproportionately among blacks, but because the black statistics were higher to begin with, the increase brought them to very high levels). Half the children aged 6 to 17 in South Central were in one-parent families.

Drug addiction and youth gangs existed in 1965, but the 500 plus–page Kerner Report contained no index references to gangs, and only two peripheral ones to drugs. The McCone Commission did contend that organized gangs had spread the violence once the disturbances had started but found no evidence that they had helped start it. [8] By 1992 drugs and the drug trade and youth gangs—the two generally supposed to be closely associated with one another—were considered central phenomena in South Central. Gangs helped spread the violence. More important, however, drugs and gangs were essential parts of the culture from which the disturbances sprang.

Other Changes

By 1992 the Hispanic population of Los Angeles County had overtaken the black population in numbers, had replaced blacks in some parts of South Central, and was well intermixed with them in others. The disturbances, after their beginning, were as much Hispanic as they were black. Perhaps surprisingly, blacks and Hispanics participated side by side; there was virtually no evidence of a clash between the two communities. The more contentious ethnic issues seemed to be between blacks and Asian-Americans, who mostly live outside South Central but own many businesses inside.

CAP and other antipoverty programs that the McCone Commission said "did not live up to their press notices" were gone by 1992. Activism remained, still sometimes encouraged by private foundation support, but the officially encouraged core provided by CAP had disappeared. The urban renewal recommended by McCone had taken place but not necessarily in directions desired by all. Of the Los Angeles Community Redevelopment Agency, under which renewal programs had been concentrated for many years, a local assemblyman summed up the attitude of many by saying that "the community fears the CRA." [21]

POLICIES AND IDEAS

It is difficult to net out the differences between 1965 and 1992. Are things better or worse? Possibly better on balance, because of the fading of overt and much covert racism, but the disturbances themselves indicate that matters are still far from satisfactory.

The central question, however, is not better or worse than the past, but how can policy assist in bringing Los Angeles and other American cities toward stable progress against inner-city poverty? The first part of this section compares the policies, concepts, and programs of the 1960s to those now developing. The final portion suggests a frame of reference for policy analysis to assist in choosing policy alternatives.

Looking Backward from the 1990s to the 1960s

Comparisons between the policies, concepts, and programs of the two decades can be grouped into five categories:

- Those that have lasted because they are seen as having worked.
- Those that have faded but are now being revived in the hope that their time may finally come.
- Those that dimmed and remain dim.
- Those that were largely ignored and are still being ignored.
- Those that have become significantly more relevant since 1965.

Looking first at *what has lasted,* far and away the most important set of policies are those subsumed under civil rights. In the 1960s the combination of a civil rights movement that would not accept defeat, a president who felt this mission deeply, and a Supreme Court that tended to activism on rights finally moved the American conscience as well as law to full incorporation of racial equity. Some allege that efforts have retreated in the last decade, but the basic philosophy is firmly embedded in law, politics, and even most practices. Minority political representation has improved and is improving further under legislative and judicial pressures; the same is true in the crucial area of police force composition.

Among antipoverty policies, some specific OEO programs have lasted because they were popularly adjudged as successful: Head Start, Job Corps, Legal Services. The food stamp program has been expanded and SSI for the aged initiated. The WIC nutrition program still exists but is chronically underfunded in many states, including California. Medicaid, on the other hand, together with its big brother, Medicare, has sopped up so much public money because of rising health care costs that it puts pressure on all other federal spending. Finally, the Earned-Income Tax Credit, written into the income tax laws in 1987, provides a small-scale NIT by giving "tax refunds" to working poor people who in fact owe no taxes.

As for urban policies, a few grant programs for cities (e.g., for urban transit) have lasted, albeit on a sharply decreasing scale. The idea behind urban impact programs, focusing resources on urban poverty areas, embodied in CAP's Kennedy-Javits program in the 1960s, has continued in many forms, including most recently "enterprise zones."

Other concepts come under the heading of *having faded but being revived—ideas whose logic has seemed obvious but whose implementation has proved difficult.* Hope is reviving that their time will come. Few of them have been retranslated back into policy, but they form part of the menu for future policies. For example, the police grievance procedures recommended by the McCone and Kerner commissions were never implemented; similar recommendations were made by the 1991 Christopher Commission on the Los Angeles police. [22]

Perhaps the most important of the reviving ideas, however, is simply that both combating poverty and helping cities are appropriate objectives for national policy and that the two goals are closely related. Political leaders again talk of "a hand up instead of a handout," the slogan that was central to the War on Poverty; but as in the 1960s, matters are much more complicated. In particular, policymakers are again focusing on the welfare/jobs nexus: the attempt to provide both incentives and opportunities for people to get off the assistance rolls and into employment. Current efforts echo the early antipoverty plans—a combination of the NIT, training, and public jobs, is returning—albeit with fewer public jobs and more coercion for welfare recipients to work. The welfare/family relationship, also stressed in the NIT proposals, is also coming back. And "family policy" is enjoying a revival. Although its meaning is obscured by the controversies of the 1992 political campaign, it recalls the Moynihan Report of 1965.

The CAP concept that Moynihan abhorred, that the recipients of assistance programs should help control these programs, is also now returning under the name "empowerment." Whether this will shape the relationship between urban and antipoverty programs as it did in the mid-1960s, however, is doubtful. The political lessons that put CAP into disrepute have not been forgotten.

Other 1960s concepts have *faded over the intervening years and still seem dim.* For instance, housing programs for the poor are seldom mentioned: homelessness is not synonymous with "houselessness." The issues of health care for the poor are seen simply as a part of the overwhelming national health care and cost problem.

Decreasing inequality as such has become an objective seldom mentioned; if a rising tide raises all boats, a falling tide concentrates the attention of each population segment on its own distance from the mud flats. Desegregation has also faded; the legal concept is triumphant and complete, but it has been largely abandoned as a practical solution for other problems, particularly for education in large cities. The educational effects of desegregation have been thrown into question, and in any case, "white flight" has made it almost impossible within boundaries of existing school districts.

One fundamental concept was *largely ignored by policymakers in the 1960s and is still being ignored today.* The crucial dependence of training and job programs for the poor upon high national and local levels of employment, stressed by a few economists including OEO's planners in the 1960s but ignored by most urban and antipoverty policymakers (perhaps because Vietnam was making employment very tight anyhow), has not revived. Indeed, most policy economists today, in and outside the government, focus on the objective of wiping out inflation, even at the cost of relatively high unemployment, which has a disproportionate effect on the "least employable" who are concentrated in America's cities. The merits of price stability versus rapid economic growth are outside the scope of this discussion, but for the particular set of objectives examined here, growth and low unemployment are clearly necessary preconditions.

Finally, although there is nothing new under the sun, several policy areas have become *much more relevant to central inner-city problems than they were in 1965*. Drug policy is one of these; as noted, the 1960s reports hardly mentioned drugs. And the role of Hispanic and Asian immigrants, both as change agents over the long run and as participants and victims of the disturbances in the short, means that national immigration policy has become highly relevant.

A Policy Frame for the Future

The discussion of the policies and policy ideas of the past as they have come up to the present suggests a framework for examining alternatives for the future. A basic premise for this framework is the assertion that *although not every urban problem stems from antipoverty and distress in the inner city, enough do that poverty policy and urban policy must be reconnected*. Certainly that is true for Los Angeles.

Within this broad urban/poverty area, most of the policies that have been discussed in this chapter and form part of the general discourse fall into four general categories:

- Policies to improve employment opportunities for inner-city poor.

- Policies to change the "environment" of the inner cities.

- Policies to improve policing practices.

* Restructuring of financing.

This chapter ends with some specific suggestions that stem from the previous discussion. However, for the most part, the conclusions highlight what we still need to know in each of the categories.

Employment opportunities. The suggestions begin with the central-ity of *high employment* in urban areas. How close the jobs have to be to the inner city itself is conjectural and will vary city by city, but in-sufficient jobs in the area will always translate into no jobs for the hardest to employ. Thus, the most important suggestion is that, *if national policy is serious about solving urban/poverty problems, then it must focus more clearly on solving national unemployment prob-lems.* Given sufficiently high levels of overall employment, issues needing further exploration include the appropriate combinations of training programs and job-providing programs as in the antipoverty plans of the 1960s; incentives to work and coercion to work for wel-fare recipients; and attractions to training and legitimate jobs for those now in illegitimate jobs. Some training programs have been evaluated as effective over the years, and they can provide a starting point while further investigation, and perhaps new experimentation, is carried out. [23]

In addition to high employment and jobs as such, educational reform is clearly a necessary part of the longer-run solution to unemploy-ment in the inner cities. In addition to being at least as conjectural as any other category of policies, however, effective educational reform will be long run. And since improving and stabilizing inner cities cannot wait on educational success, educational improvement can-not be the first order of business.

Inner-city environment. Certain problems that by now seem en-demic to inner cities challenge even the most optimistic problem solvers: a second and third generation of individuals and families that remain mired in early childbearing, low educational achieve-ment, poor job skills, and for whose males jail is a more common ex-perience than full-time employment. For these residents, specific problems may be harder to address because they have assumed a kind of hopeless normality. To the extent that job programs can at-tract young men and women (not excluding the possibility of finan-cial coercion through welfare reform), jobs "with a future" may go a long way to breaking the gang/drug culture. Specific reforms that might be effective need more exploration, but reversing antijob incentives in welfare is an obvious starting point. So is removing the incentive that provides welfare only to mothers without a father in residence; perhaps also revising the presumed incentive for welfare mothers to have additional children, although that is very controversial. The revival and full funding of the WIC program for maternal and child nutrition is very important. [24] Beyond that, what combination of direct family support, day care, education, exhortation, drug withdrawal programs, "empowerment," "enterprise programs," and effective policing will work and how well is impossible to say. Even more than educational reform, changing attitudes and expectations is likely to be both necessary and slow.

Policing practices.   Policing may be the area where needs are the clearest.   The recommendations of the 1991 Christopher Commission were quite specific and, as noted, similar to those of 1965. The 1965 recommendations to bring many more members of minorities onto police forces were implemented, but the events from the King beating of 1991 to the 1992 civil disturbances have indicated that, while necessary, police integration was not in itself sufficient to prevent repetition of events similar to those of 1965. The grievance and community relations recommendations of 1965 were not implemented, and although there is reason to hope that the Christopher recommendations will be, neither the reforms nor their effectiveness in changing police/community interactions is guaranteed.

Restructuring of financing.   As the federal government reduced its role in the l980s, states replaced it, cities found new sources of revenue, or they did without. In the 1990s, however, recession has led to a virtual collapse of many states' ability to act as underwriters; in California, the depth of the recession has made the state's Proposition 13–imposed role as provider of last resort impossible to maintain. (See Chapter Ten.) With this failure, cities, including Los Angeles, have been forced to orchestrate their own help. They have turned to their own business communities. Certainly cities boasting a strong, unified business sector that provides either direct support to services—for example, help to local schools—or lobbies to broaden access to financing for new business through changing tax, loan, or regulatory policies appear to be better off than those that do not. But business capabilities are invigorated or dampened by national economic trends. In our view, local initiatives can make improvements at the margin, but significant improvements in employment for the hard-core poor and in their children's skills and opportunities are dependent on strong national economic growth and the assumption of a federal role in urban economic development.

Meanwhile the gaggle of decisionmakers who must ultimately be involved in solutions is extensive—county welfare services, independent school districts, state regulatory agencies, to name only a few. Matters may have reached the point at which the federal government, the states, and the localities may be forced to think about a more radical restructuring of taxation, financial responsibility, program implementation, and overall governance. In the 1950s, federal policies not designed for their specific urban effects, plus market forces, configured the cities. In the 1960s, federal policies administered by federal bureaucrats, CAP authorities, and, ultimately, city governments tried to change the inner cities. In the 1970s, the feds provided money without much policy direction; in the 1980s, the money dried up. For the 1990s, it has been suggested as one example that both responsibilities and funds be decentralized to the states. [25] Other combinations are possible; none has yet been proven.

WHAT EFFECTS WHOM, WHERE?

Jobs, inner-city social problems, policing, and financial restructuring all concern the substance of urban/poverty policy. Crossing all these substantive categories, there remains the "process" issue of *people, places,* and *jurisdictions.*

All programs have indirect effects that are often not anticipated. Programs aimed at helping people (e.g., those that expand education or training opportunities) have the best chance of providing that help—but quite possibly by enhancing mobility in ways that may harm places or specific political jurisdictions (e.g., the move of the best-educated and -trained blacks out of South Central between 1970 and 1990). Programs that aim to increase the attractiveness of an area may be quite successful, but they may not benefit the original residents: if a program works, property values may rise, employees may be attracted from elsewhere, and current residents may grow even more disadvantaged. Or, as has happened in sections of Los

Angeles, downtown development may simply force out former residents. In reality, both people and place programs are needed in order to improve what everyone wants—the neighborhoods people live in and the opportunities they have.

And, finally, policies and processes must be implemented by jurisdictional authorities. Between the upper-level complexities of our federal system and the local jumble of municipalities, counties, and special districts, particularly endemic in California, who is to do what and who is to pay for it?

NOTES

*For whatever reason, the Five-Year Anti-Poverty Plan tended to slight health care, in spite of the fact that the administration was just beginning the Medicaid/Medicare revolution.

†Blacks were underrepresented in every way. Politically, for example, one of California's 38-man (accurate usage) delegation to the U.S. House of Representatives was black. There was also a Hispanic.

‡What he actually said is still unprintable, even in this more liberal age.

§Though we focus in this chapter on RAND's urban research, many other scholars and institutions were engaged in urban analysis during this period. Important examples include Chinitz, Benjamin, ed., *Central City Economic Development*, Cambridge, Mass.: Abt Books, 1979; Gorham, William, and Nathan Glazer, eds., *The Urban Predicament*, Washington, D.C.: The Urban Institute, 1976; Hochman, Harold M., *The Urban Economy*, New York: W. W. Norton and Company, 1976; Leven, Charles L., *The Mature Metropolis*, Lexington, Mass.: D.C. Heath and Company, 1978; and Nathan, Richard P., et al., *Monitoring Revenue Sharing*, Washington, D.C: The Brookings Institution, 1975.

#The distinction between families and households is a technical one. Although not trivial, it has little bearing on the kinds of comparisons made here. Neither does the fact that the income levels for each of the two years are in terms of dollars of that year. The issue being examined is comparison of income attributions for each of the two years.

REFERENCES

1. For an example, see Alesch, Daniel J., and Robert A. Levine, *Growth in San Jose: A Summary Policy Statement*, Santa Monica, Calif.: RAND, R-1235-NSF, 1973.

2. See Williams, Barbara R., *St. Louis: A City and Its Suburbs*, Santa Monica, Calif.: RAND R-1353-NSF, 1973.

3. Most of this section is summarized from Levine, Robert A., *The Poor Ye Need Not Have with You: Lessons from the War on Poverty*, Cambridge, Mass.: MIT Press, 1970, Chapter 4.

4. Harrington, Michael, *The Other America*, New York: Macmillan, 1962.

5. McDonald, Dwight, "Our Invisible Poor," *New Yorker*, January 19, 1963, p. 82ff.

6. Governor's Commission on the Los Angeles Riots, *The Need for Leadership*, Los Angeles, 1965.

7. *Report of the National Commission on Civil Disorders.* Citations here are from the *New York Times* edition, New York: Bantam Books, 1968.

8. "Report on Watts," *Facts on File*, 1965, p. 447.

9. *New York Times*, December 7, 1965, p. 26.

10. Miller, Merle, *Lyndon: An Oral Biography*, New York: G. P. Putnam's Sons, 1980.

11. Office of Policy Planning and Research, U.S. Department of Labor, *The Negro Family: The Case for National Action*, March 1965.

12. Moynihan, Daniel, *Maximum Feasible Misunderstanding*, New York: The Free Press, 1969, p. 99.

13. See Cogan, J. F., *Negative Income Taxation and Labor Supply: New Evidence from the New Jersey-Pennsylvania Experiment*, Santa Monica, Calif.: RAND, R-2155-HEW, 1978.

14. See Bridge, R. Gary, and Julie Blackman, *A Study of Alternatives in American Education: Family Choices in Schooling*, Santa Monica, Calif.: RAND, R-2170/4-NIE, 1978.

15. See Lowry, I. S., *Experimenting with Housing Allowances: The Final Report of the Housing Allowance Supply Experiment*, Cambridge, Mass.: Oelgeschlager, Gunn and Hain Publishers, Inc., 1983.

16. See Brook, R. H., et al., *The Effect of Coinsurance on the Health of Adults: Results from the RAND Health Insurance Experiment*, Santa Monica, Calif.: RAND, R-3055-HHS, 1984; and Manning, W. G., et al., *Health Insurance and the Demand for Medical Care: Evidence from a Randomized Experiment*, Santa Monica, Calif.: RAND R-3476-HHS, 1988.

17. See Rainey, R. B., Jr., et al., *Seattle's Adaptation to Recession*, Santa Monica, Calif.: RAND, R-1352-NSF, 1973.

18. See Glickman, Norman J., ed., *The Urban Impacts of Federal Policies*, Baltimore, Md.: John Hopkins University Press, 1980; and Vaughan, Roger J., Anthony H. Pascal, and Mary E. Vaiana, *The Urban Impacts of Federal Policies: Vol. 1, Overview*, Santa Monica, Calif.: RAND, R-2206-KF/HEW, 1980.

19. Stockman, David A., *The Triumph of Politics*, New York: Harper and Row Publishers, 1986.

20. Palmer, John L., and Isabel V. Sawhill, eds., *The Reagan Experiment*, Washington, D.C.: The Urban Institute, 1982; and Palmer, John L., and Isabel V. Sawhill, eds., *The Reagan Record*, Cambridge, Mass.: Ballinger Publishing Company, 1984.

21. *Los Angeles Times*, August 29, 1992, p. B1.

22. *Report of the Independent Commission on the Los Angeles Police Department*, July 9, 1991.

23. See Gueron, Judith M., Edward Pauly, with Cameran M. Lougy, *From Welfare to Work: A Manpower Demonstration Research Study*, New York: Russell Sage Foundation, 1991.

24. See, for example, General Accounting Office, *Early Intervention: Federal Investments Like WIC Can Produce Savings,* GAO/HRD 92–18, April 7, 1992.

25. Rivlin, Alice M., *Reviving the American Dream: The Economy, the States and the Federal Government,* Washington, D.C.: The Brookings Institution, 1992.

2

Children, Youth, and Families

Chapter Two

The Widening Income and Wage Gap Between Rich and Poor
Trends, Causes, and Policy Options

Lynn A. Karoly

INTRODUCTION

Soon after the civil disturbances in Los Angeles in April 1992, the *Los Angeles Times* reported that many city and county residents failed to share in the prosperity of the 1980s. [1] Census Bureau data revealed that the poverty rate for the city grew from about 11 percent in 1969, to 13 percent in 1979, to slightly more than 15 percent in 1989. Moreover, in South Central Los Angeles, one of the areas most affected by the disturbances, the 1989 poverty rate of 30 percent exceeded even the 27 percent level of 1965, the year of the Watts disturbance. [2] At the same time, income for the median household in the state of California and the county of Los Angeles grew about 17 percent after adjusting for inflation during the 1980s, with even higher rates of growth in more prosperous communities.

Although these data provide a context for analyzing and understanding the problems of South Central and Los Angeles as a whole, the phenomenon of increasing disparities in income is not limited to Southern California or even to the entire state. Although the size of the economic pie expanded between 1983 and 1990, a period marking the longest peacetime expansion since World War II, there is evidence that the gains were not equally shared. In particular, a number of recent studies point to a growing income gap between families and individuals at the bottom and the top of the income ladder. This pattern holds for the country as a whole as well as for many smaller geographic areas; the pattern applies to family incomes and also to workers' wages. Furthermore, the data indicate that the rise in income disparity during the 1980s continues a trend that began at least a decade earlier.

While these trends in the distribution of income are of national importance, they are particularly relevant for urban areas such as Los Angeles. Issues of poverty, the underclass, homelessness, and joblessness are inextricably linked to the factors that shape the income distribution in our society. Understanding the nature and possible causes of significant changes in the income distribution provide an important context for analyzing a variety of problems that confront urban areas and urban residents in this country. Finding realistic, effective solutions also depends critically on understanding the factors that shape the distribution of well-being in urban areas and in the United States as a whole.

In this chapter, my aim is to summarize the significant changes in the income distribution over the last two decades and to identify potential explanations for these trends. In the next section, I describe how the distribution of family incomes and workers' wages have changed during the past 20 years. Because the distributional changes apply to the United States as a whole, I focus primarily on national trends in income distribution, but I also show, when possible, how national patterns are reflected in Los Angeles and in the state of California. In general, these comparisons suggest that as the nation goes, so goes California and Los Angeles.

The observed distribution of income is the result of a complex set of factors, including the opportunities individuals face, their decisions given those opportunities, and a set of public and private institutions that help determine how society's output is allocated across families and individuals. Under the heading "Explaining the Rise in Income and Wage Disparities," I discuss the importance of a number of factors that could affect the distribution of family income and wages. These include the impact of tax and transfer policies; the effect of changes in family composition; and supply, demand, and other factors affecting the labor market. Although research has yet to fully untangle the role of the various factors that have affected the income distribution in the last two decades, the discussion of potential causes demonstrates that no single factor explains the rise in inequality. Changes in family structure, the increased labor force participation of women, and the rise in wage inequality all appear to have contributed to the greater dispersion in family incomes. The most important factors that can explain the rise in wage inequality include changes in industry structure, the increased globalization of the economy, declining unionization, and technological change.

Finally, the concluding section considers what we can expect for the future and what policy measures are available to reverse the increasing dispersion in incomes and wages. The policy options include traditional redistributive measures, such as macroeconomic policies and tax and transfer measures. Less traditional options include government policies that respond to the structural shifts in the economy.

DISTRIBUTIONAL TRENDS

Discussions of income distribution are often controversial. Words like "inequality," or "disparities," or "dispersion" can be defined objectively; but for some, they imply value judgments that one distribution is more equitable than another. In this section, I focus on what the data show about changes in income distribution without invoking normative judgments. Given the significant changes in income inequality, it is worth devoting some attention to describing the shape of the income distribution in the United States and how that distribution has changed over time.*

A Parade of Dwarfs and a Few Giants

Jan Pen once proposed that we view the income distribution as a parade, where each individual or family marches in order of their incomes, starting with the poorest and ending with the wealthiest. [3] The income of the marcher would be identifiable, not by a placard, but by the marcher's height: the person with average income would reach the average height of the population (say 5'10"), while the height of all earlier and later marchers would be proportional to their incomes. The spectacle would last just one hour, so that every six minutes, one-tenth of the population would pass by.

Consider the view from the grandstands if Pen's parade were held today using data for incomes in 1990. Each marcher represents a family in the U.S. population (including married couples, families with children, and single adults). The income measure for each family will be the annual pre-tax money income of the family (this includes items such as wages and salaries, self-employment income, Social

Security, unemployment insurance, welfare payments, and interest and dividends but excludes taxes and in-kind payments and transfers such as food stamps and medical insurance).

As the parade begins, the first participants to file by would actually have negative height because the families would report that losses from self-employment or other business ventures outweighed any positive income receipts. Within the first minute, the marchers' heads would be above ground, but their heights would be miniscule. Gradually the heights (and incomes) would increase, yet the procession would consist of dwarfs for some time. For example, 6 minutes after the start of the parade (the first 10 percent of the marchers), the marchers' heights would be just over 12 inches: families at the 10th percentile of the income distribution had a total income of about $6,200 in 1990, less than one-fifth of the average income. And, after 15 minutes (one-quarter of all families), the marchers would just begin to exceed 2 feet in height (corresponding to $13,000 in 1990). Even halfway through the parade, we would still be waiting for the person of average height to pass: the median family had approximately $26,400 in 1990, about 78 percent of the average family income of $33,800.

With 23 minutes remaining, we finally see marchers of average stature. In the remaining time, the marchers' heights increase: with 15 minutes to go, the participants stand 8 feet tall (corresponding to family incomes of about $46,000); with 6 minutes left and 10 percent of the marchers to go, we see people more than 12 feet tall (representing an income of about $70,000). Yet, even with only 3 minutes left in the parade, we have yet to see anyone of truly exceptional height: a family positioned at the 95th percentile of the distribution had about $90,000 in 1990, less than 3 times the average income. It is not until the last minute that the true giants begin to appear, standing more than two stories tall. Then, in the last seconds of the procession, as in Pen's parade, we see "figures whose height we cannot even estimate: their heads disappear into the clouds and probably they themselves do not even know how tall they are." [3, p. 53]

Trends over Time: More Dwarfs and Giants

While Pen's parade demonstrates the disparities in today's income distribution, the sight of the procession may not be too alarming: we know that incomes are not equally distributed in this country and that some families have exceptionally high incomes. What has garnered the attention of academics, policymakers, and the public is how the parade has changed over time. Based on my own research and a number of other studies, there is considerable evidence demonstrating an increase in dispersion in the distribution of family income in the last two decades. [4] In terms of our parade, this means that there are more dwarfs compared with previous processions and more giants.

One way of summarizing how the shape of the income distribution has changed over time is by examining the trends in the real (inflation-adjusted) incomes of families at the same point in the income distribution. Figure 1 shows the trend in real family income for families at three points in the income distribution: namely, the 50th

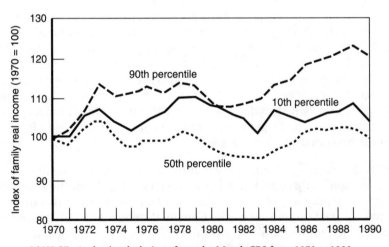

SOURCE: Author's tabulations from the March CPS from 1970 to 1990.

**Figure 1—Trends in Real Family Income
at Three Percentiles of the Income Distribution**

percentile, or median family; the 90th percentile, reflecting the experience of wealthier families; and the 10th percentile, representing the experience of lower-income families. This figure shows how both the level and shape of the income distribution are changing over time. All incomes are indexed to equal 100 in 1970. If there is no real growth in income at any point in the distribution, the trend line will be flat. An upward trend indicates real income growth; a downward trend, a decline in real income. If incomes are growing at the same rate at all points of the distribution, the shape of the distribution would remain unchanged and the trend lines for each percentile would move together. In contrast, if incomes at the top of the distribution are growing faster than they are at the bottom, the trend lines diverge.

Figure 1 confirms a growing gap between families at the top and bottom of the income distribution. At the median, real family income was stagnant over the 20-year period from 1970 to 1990, declining 5 percent in real terms between the 1973 peak (equal to $27,700 in 1990 dollars) and 1990. Likewise, family income at the 10th percentile, after peaking in 1973, fell 9 percent in real terms, from about $6,650 in 1973 to $6,100 in 1990. In contrast, real income at the top of the distribution, the 90th percentile, grew about 12 percent in real terms since 1973. Looking over the two decades between 1970 and 1990, a family at or below the median had about the same income in 1990 as a similarly situated family 20 years earlier. At the same time, a family at the top of the distribution in 1990 has seen real income gains of 20 percent compared to a family at the same position in the income distribution two decades ago. Even the economic recovery that began in 1983 did little to improve the economic fortunes of families at the bottom of the income scale.

This growing dispersion in the income distribution among families is significant in three respects. First, it is a change from the historical pattern of growing average incomes and a more equal distribution of income. Data prepared by the Census Bureau since 1947 show that inequality among families, after declining to a postwar low in 1967–1968, reached a postwar high in 1989. [5]

Second, the shifts in the shape of the income distribution imply a substantial redistribution of income, from income recipients at the bottom to those at the top. One way of quantifying the magnitude of the redistribution implied by an increase in inequality between year 1 and year 2 is to ask how much income would have to be transferred from families below the median to those above the median in order to achieve the observed increase in inequality? The increase in inequality between 1970 and 1990 is equivalent to taking the 1970 income distribution and transferring nearly $2,000 from every family below the 1970 median ($26,266 in 1990 dollars) to every family above the median. [6] While this represents only a hypothetical redistribution, it illustrates that the rise in inequality implies a substantial transfer of income among families over the last two decades.

Third, the rise in inequality through the 1980s occurred despite the longest peacetime economic expansion in the postwar period. Conventional wisdom holds that the distribution of income becomes less equal during economic downturns since families at the bottom of the distribution are more likely to face income losses during a recession. Periods of economic growth, in turn, tend to be years when the distribution becomes more equal. Although the sharp increase in inequality between 1980 and 1984 is consistent with the back-to-back recessions in 1980 and 1981–1982, the continued rise in inequality through 1989 suggests that more fundamental factors than the business cycle were at work.

The Impact on Los Angeles and Minorities

What do these trends at the national level imply for families in California or Los Angeles? The data indicate that the pattern of a growing gap between low- and high-income families is reflected, if not amplified, in the state of California and in the Los Angeles metropolitan area. Figure 2 shows the percentage change in real family income between 1973 and 1990 (the period of increasing inequality among all families) for the 10th, 50th, and 90th percentiles. The percentage changes for the United States as a whole reflect the trends shown in Figure 1 for the 1973 to 1990 time period. When we look separately at California and Los Angeles, we see a similar pattern. In each case, as in the national data, incomes grew fastest at the 90th percentile and slowest at the 10th percentile, indicating an increase in income dispersion. In Los Angeles, in particular, the differential rates of income growth between 1973 and 1990 are striking,

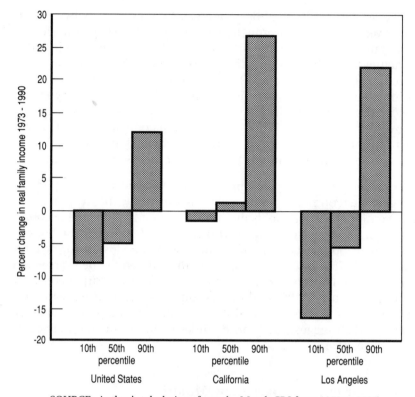

SOURCE: Author's tabulations from the March CPS from 1973 to 1990.

**Figure 2—Trends in Real Family Income,
United States, California, and Los Angeles**

with real income declining 17 percent at the 10th percentile and rising 22 percent at the 90th percentile. As a result, in Los Angeles in
1990, family income at the 90th percentile was almost 13 times
higher than at the 10th; the ratio was about 11 to 1 for the nation as a
whole.

The increasing inequality in family incomes is repeated when we
look separately at families of different race/ethnicity. [4] Figure 3
shows the percentage change in real family incomes between 1973
and 1990 at the respective 10th, 50th, and 90th percentiles of the income distribution among white, black, and Hispanic families. Again,

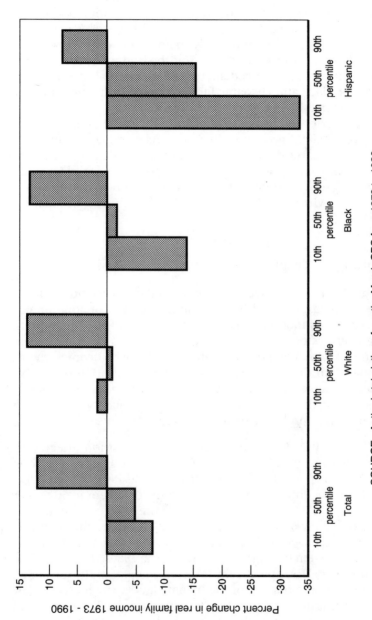

SOURCE: Author's tabulations from the March CPS from 1973 to 1990.

Figure 3—Trends in Real Family Income, by Race/Ethnicity

for families in each group, income dispersion increased over the period: incomes grew fastest at the top of the distribution and slowest at the bottom. Since black and Hispanic families have lower incomes on average (i.e., they are more likely to be in the lower ranks of the overall income distribution), families at the bottom of their respective distributions experienced sharp declines in real incomes. For instance, for black and Hispanic families at the 10th percentile, real incomes declined 14 and 34 percent, respectively—a sharper decline than that experienced by white families at the same percentile (who actually saw a slight growth in income). As a result, inequality increased to a greater degree among families headed by minorities compared with white families. A similar analysis for families of different ages and with different compositions shows that inequality increased for virtually all groups of families during the last two decades. [4]

Accounting for Taxes and Transfers

Until now, we have focused on changes in the distribution of family income before taxes and without including the value of nonmonetary transfers such as food stamps or medical insurance. Since the tax and transfer system overall is progressive, redistributing income from families with high incomes to those with lower incomes, there is less disparity in the post-tax, post-transfer distribution of income. However, because the redistributive impact of taxes and transfers declined during the 1980s, the rise in income inequality is even larger when a more comprehensive measure of income is used. [6]

During the 1980s, two major pieces of tax legislation affected the post-tax distribution of income. The Economic Recovery Tax Act (ERTA) of 1981, passed within a year of Ronald Reagan's inauguration, reduced the top marginal tax rate from 70 percent to 50 percent and phased in a 23 percent reduction in the marginal tax rates in other income brackets. One consequence of ERTA and of later increases in Social Security payroll taxes was to reduce the progressivity of the tax system during the first half of the 1980s. Later, the 1986 Tax Reform Act (TRA) specifically targeted changes in the tax code to benefit those at the bottom of the income ladder (by increasing the personal exemption, standard deduction, and the Earned-Income Tax Credit). Despite a further reduction in top marginal tax rates, most analysts have concluded that the tax system became slightly more progressive as a result of TRA. Nevertheless, the net impact of tax changes during the 1980s was to contribute to the rise in inequality. [6] Since the redistributive impact of cash and noncash transfers remained essentially unchanged during the 1980s, tax and transfer policy as a whole contributed to the rise in inequality over the decade. [7]

Another Parade: Workers and Their Wages

Given that about 80 percent of family income is derived from the labor market, changes in the wage structure are linked to the overall distribution of income. In the last two decades, there have been equally dramatic changes in the distribution of wages among workers. Again, as in the parade of family incomes, the parade consisting of workers with heights defined by wage and salary income now contains more dwarfs and more giants. Since the 1970s, there has been an increase in dispersion in the wage distribution for men, a trend that accelerated during the 1980s. Among women, the rise in wage inequality is a more recent phenomenon, starting in the 1980s. This pattern holds for annual wage and salary income, weekly wages, and hourly wages. Since inequality increased among all workers as well as full-time year-round workers, the rise in wage dispersion cannot be attributed to changes in the proportion of part-time part-year workers. [4]

To illustrate these trends, Table 1 shows the percentage change in real weekly wages between 1973, 1979, and 1990 for all male workers at three points in the distribution for the United States, California, and Los Angeles. For men, wage dispersion increased between 1973 and 1990, with the sharpest increase occurring since 1979. Between 1973 and 1990, weekly wages, after adjusting for inflation, declined 22 percent at the 10th percentile, while wages grew 9 percent over the period at the 90th percentile. Even the median male worker saw real wage declines on the order of 10 percent since 1973. Thus, wage growth for men was positive only in the upper segments of the distribution.

Table 1

Percentage Change in Real Weekly Wages, by Sex and Area

Period	United States			California			Los Angeles		
	10th	50th Percentile	90th	10th	50th Percentile	90th	10th	50th Percentile	90th
Men									
1973–1979	-6	-1	0	6	-4	3	4	-4	-3
1979–1990	-17	-9	10	-23	-6	5	-22	-16	3
1973–1990	-22	-10	9	-18	-11	8	-19	-19	0
Women									
1973–1979	9	-1	5	15	-1	2	6	-4	-4
1979–1990	4	9	19	6	9	25	9	10	33
1973–1990	14	8	25	22	8	28	15	6	28

SOURCE: Author's tabulations from the May and monthly CPS from 1973 to 1990.

Women differ from men in that wage dispersion actually declined between 1973 and 1979, as wages grew fastest at the 10th percentile compared with the 90th percentile (9 percent versus 5 percent). The compression of the wage distribution was reversed during the 1980s, with a 19 percent increase in real wages at the 90th percentile compared with only 4 percent at the 10th percentile. Despite the rise in wage dispersion among women, at each point in the distribution, real wages were higher by 8 to 25 percent in 1990 compared with 1973, a sharp contrast to the real decline in male wages.

Changes in the wage distribution for men and women in California and Los Angeles tend to mirror national patterns. One difference is that real wages have not risen in Los Angeles for men at the top of the wage distribution since 1973. The data suggest, consequently, that there has been a smaller rise in wage dispersion in Los Angeles compared with the nation. In addition, in both the state and the Los Angeles metropolitan area, wage dispersion among men appears to have declined between 1973 and 1979 due to faster wage growth at the 10th percentile of the distribution compared with the 90th percentile. (These differences may not be statistically significant due to the smaller sample sizes available for California and Los Angeles.)

One of the more striking changes in the wage structure in the last decade is the growing wage gap between more- and less-educated workers. Figure 4 illustrates this phenomenon for men by showing the trend in real median weekly wages for three groups: high school dropouts, high school graduates, and college graduates. Between 1973 and 1979, real wages declined for all three groups, although the larger drop in median wages for college-educated workers indicates a decline in the college premium during that period. Since the late 1970s, the trend in real wages has been dramatically different for the three groups. While the real wages of the median high school graduate or dropout continued to decline up to 20 percent, the median college graduate's real wages have grown by 10 percent since 1979. Wage differentials between those with more and less years of work experience also expanded during the 1980s. For many groups, such as younger less-educated workers, the absolute and relative fall in wages has been accompanied by a reduction in employment opportunities, evidenced by higher unemployment rates. Thus, for example, young black high school dropouts now face reduced prospects in

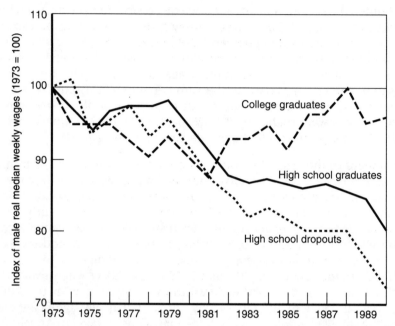

SOURCE: Author's tabulations from the May and monthly CPS from 1973 to 1990.

Figure 4—Trends in Median Real Weekly Wages for Men, by Education

the labor market both in terms of the likelihood of securing employment and in the economic rewards for work.

Trends in Income Mobility

Thus far, in order to assess how the distribution of income has changed over time, I have relied on a series of annual snapshots, or cross sections, of how incomes or wages are distributed across families or workers. In the context of Pen's parade, our cross-sectional data mean that in each successive year a family or worker may appear at different points in the procession—for example, at the head of the parade in one year or bringing up the rear in another. Thus, the trends shown in Figure 1 do not reflect changes in income for the same families over time but for families at the *same position* in the income distribution.

The alternative approach is to follow the *same families* over time to measure their movement within the income distribution. This approach can also be used to study the distribution of income measured over longer time periods, such as a decade or a lifetime. Thus, we could imagine a parade where heights are measured by a person's annual income averaged over his or her lifetime. By tracking incomes for the same families or individuals, we can also obtain a picture of the amount of mobility within the income distribution.

Some recent studies using data that follow the same families over time have produced findings that are consistent with the cross-sectional data showing a rise in family income inequality. First, studies using a more permanent measure of family income (e.g., measured over a 10-year period instead of a single year) also show a growing inequality since the 1970s. [8] This means that, after smoothing out annual fluctuations in income, there is still more disparity in today's income distribution compared with 10 or 15 years ago. These findings suggest that if we could measure income over an individual lifetime, we would also see a rise in inequality.

Second, while analyses based on following the same families over time show that there is considerable mobility within the income distribution, the data indicate that some of the upward paths were less well traveled during the 1980s. For example, one study found a reduction in the proportion of individuals who attained a middle class level of income; that is, fewer people climbed up from the lower ranks and more people slipped into them. [9] The risk of downward mobility was higher for blacks, households headed by women, and those with less than a high school education. At the same time, a higher fraction of individuals moved into the upper income category, while fewer dropped out. The study concluded that education was the single most important factor in increasing the chances of upward transitions and in reducing the likelihood of downward movement.

EXPLAINING THE RISE IN INCOME AND WAGE DISPARITIES

While evidence of rising income and wage disparities in the last two decades is well documented, the debate continues about the causes of the trends. Identifying the factors producing these trends is an important first step toward determining if policy can attenuate or reverse the trends (assuming we decide that is a desirable goal). For example, if changes in the income or wage distribution are associated with the baby boom, a demographic phenomenon largely beyond the control of policymakers, there may be little room or justification for intervention. On the other hand, changes in the income distribution may themselves be the direct result of policy changes, in which case the distributional impact of these policies needs to be recognized and quantified.

In the remainder of this section, I will discuss a number of possible explanations for the rise in family income inequality and wage inequality. Among the potential explanations for increases in family inequality, I consider the role of fiscal policies adopted during the 1980s as well as changes in family composition, including the rise in female-headed households and increased labor force participation of women. I also discuss a number of supply, demand, and institutional factors that may have affected workers and their wages over the last two decades. Explanations for the rise in wage dispersion include the effect of the baby boom, immigration, deindustrialization, international competition, technological change, and declining unionization. Because the determinants of the distribution of income and wages are complex, research into the causes of the rise in inequality is far from complete. Additional study is required before a full accounting of the relevant factors is possible.

The Impact of Fiscal Policies of the 1980s

One of the ways in which government policy affects income distribution is through tax and transfer policy. As noted above, the distributional changes of the 1980s were accompanied by substantial revisions to the tax code in 1981 and later in 1986. At the same time, real transfer spending declined during the decade, particularly for programs targeted at low-income families. These changes have led some to suggest that fiscal policies may have directly altered the income distribution by changing post-tax, post-transfer incomes. These policies may also have indirectly altered the distribution by changing pre-tax, pre-transfer incomes. For instance, some analysts have claimed that the rise in family income inequality during the 1980s was caused by the sharp reduction in marginal tax rates for high-income taxpayers, inducing them to work more, report more income, shift compensation toward cash forms, and realize more capital gains.

A review of the evidence in support of a direct or indirect role for fiscal policies provides mixed results. [6] First, the direct impact of tax and transfer policy was in the direction of increasing inequality due to a decline in tax progressivity and reductions in transfer programs. Even so, the rise in pre-tax income inequality explains about 80 percent of the increase in post-tax inequality in the last decade. In other words, only 20 percent of the increase in post-tax inequality can be explained by the declining progressivity of the system. Estimates of the possible behavioral responses to tax policy changes during the 1980s are not large enough to account for, and are often inconsistent with, the observed rise in income dispersion. The rise in inequality also predates the tax changes during the 1980s, so the modifications in fiscal policy cannot be the only culprit.

The Effect of Family Composition Changes

The period of rising income dispersion has been accompanied by significant changes in family structure that can help explain the distributional trends. Single individuals and female-headed families represent a growing share of all family units. For instance, today approximately one in six families is headed by a woman compared with just one in 10 families 20 years ago. At the same time, traditional husband-and-wife families with a working wife, once in the minority, now make up more than 60 percent of these families. The number of younger and older families have also both increased, in part reflecting the influx of postwar baby boomers into the family ranks. These various demographic factors could be expected to increase the number of low-income and high-income families.

A number of studies have examined the impact of these compositional changes. In one analysis, I estimated that about one-third of the rise in inequality between 1967 and 1987 can be explained by shifts in household composition toward single-parent families and single individuals. [4] However, the changing age composition of families played no role in the growing income disparities over the period. The contribution of an increase in the number of working wives is not clear. On the one hand, studies generally concur that wives' earnings tend to equalize the distribution of income among married-couple families, with little change in this equalizing effect over time. At the same time, the data also suggest that the earnings from secondary earners or family spouses may have contributed to the rise in income disparities among all families. [6] Although the effects of these compositional changes appear to be substantial, they do not fully account for the rising income disparities among families.

Supply, Demand, and Other Factors Affecting Labor Markets

As noted above, the largest component of family income is derived from the labor market. Compared to other sources of income, the rise in wage inequality, especially for family heads, had a significant impact on income inequality. For instance, in a hypothetical world with no increase in wage inequality among family heads between 1980 and 1985, the rise in income inequality would have been about 30 percent lower. [6]   What factors can explain the significant changes in the wage structure over the last two decades? A number of explanations have been offered, including supply-side changes such as the baby boom and immigration; demand-side factors like deindustrialization, international competition, and technological change; and changes in wage-setting institutions such as unions.

The baby boom. One of the most significant demographic changes to take place in the last two decades was the entry of baby boomers into the labor market during the 1970s. The entry of this large group of workers could be expected to affect the wage distribution in two ways. First, since younger workers earn lower wages on average compared with more-experienced workers, the influx of a large number of inexperienced workers into the labor market could increase the number of lower-wage workers. At the same time, if younger workers are not as productive as older workers, the relative increase in the supply of younger workers would be expected to lower their relative wages. While the baby boom can help explain the trend toward greater wage inequality during the 1970s, it does not appear to have contributed to the trend during the 1980s. In the last decade, the proportion of younger workers in the labor market declined, which should have improved their relative wages. In fact, recent changes in the age structure of the work force slowed the rise in inequality. If the age composition of the labor force had remained unchanged over the last two decades, the rise in wage inequality would have actually been higher. [4]

Immigration. Another supply-side factor affecting the labor market is the influx of legal and undocumented immigrants into the work force. It is estimated that nearly 12 million legal immigrants, plus an additional 5 to 6 million undocumented immigrants, have entered the United States since 1970. In 1991, the Los Angeles metropolitan area was the favored destination for new arrivals, attracting 14 percent of all legal immigrants. Since immigrants earn lower wages on average, their increased numbers in the labor market could have an impact similar to the baby boomers: increasing the number of low-wage workers and reducing the relative wages of lower-skilled workers.

Based on research to date, the impact of immigration on the national or regional wage distribution is uncertain. Typically, studies of how new immigrants affect a local or regional labor market find evidence of only a small negative impact, if any, on the wage structure. For instance, one study of 24 cities in the United States during the 1980s found weak evidence of a relationship between the share of immigrants in the labor force and the level and shape of the wage distribution. [10] In contrast, another recent analysis estimated that the increased flow of immigrants during the 1980s explains a large fraction of the decline in relative wages of high school dropouts, the group of workers most likely to be affected by an influx of lower-skilled workers. [11] However, this study did not evaluate the impact of immigration on the overall level of wage inequality.

Deindustrialization. Some have argued that the growth in service sector employment in relation to the manufacturing sector has contributed to increasing wage dispersion. Since manufacturing jobs pay higher wages on average compared with the service sector and since wage dispersion is higher in service industries, it is possible that the continual growth of the service sector and the loss of manufacturing jobs may have contributed to rising wage inequality. Indeed, there have been significant shifts in the industrial distribution of employment in the last 20 years. The share of manufacturing employment has declined from 30 percent to less than 20 percent, while the share of employment in service industries has steadily increased so that now three out of five workers are employed in this sector.

Despite the significance of these shifts, the contribution of deindustrialization is not exceptionally large, explaining about 10 to 20 percent of the growth in wage inequality on average. Even in areas with the largest declines in manufacturing, such as the rust-belt states, the contribution does not exceed 25 percent. [12] The finding that wage inequality has increased *within* most industries explains why sectoral shifts alone do not account for the changing wage structure.

International competition. During the period of rising wage inequality, foreign competition had an increased effect on the U.S. economy. Over the last two decades, trade has doubled its share of gross domestic product (GDP), rising from 8 to 16 percent. Also, during the 1980s, the U.S. trade deficit worsened dramatically after years of more-balanced trade. When the trade deficit peaked in 1987, imports exceeded exports by 40 percent. Increased competition from abroad has a variable impact on the demand for U.S. workers with different characteristics. For example, lower-skilled and less-educated workers are concentrated in exporting and in import-competing industries, such as automobiles or consumer electronics. These workers are in industries with declining demand, which reduces their relative wages. In contrast, nontraded goods and services industries with little foreign competition, such as professional services, employ a more-educated and highly skilled work force. In essence, the increased openness of the economy means that lower-skilled workers in the United States find themselves competing with equally skilled workers in other countries who have access to similar technology but are paid lower wages. One study that quantified this effect found that a substantial part of the relative wage losses of high school dropouts, and a somewhat smaller share of the relative growth of wages for college graduates, is attributable to the trade patterns of the 1980s. [11] But here again, research has yet to determine with any certainty the specific contribution of international competition to the overall rise in wage inequality.

Technological change. It is harder to assess whether technological change contributes to rising inequality. Throughout the last two decades, the increased use of technology, from computerization to automation, has changed the workplace. Manufacturing is moving away from old-style production techniques and is employing methods that permit rapid changes in production lines and the use of other flexible manufacturing processes. Advances in data processing and telecommunications are transforming the service sector as well.

The effect of new technologies on workers and their wages is uncertain. On the one hand, technological change may displace jobs previously performed by lower-skilled workers. New technologies often require greater skill, thereby enhancing the demand for and the productivity of more-skilled workers. At the same time, changes in technology may reduce the skill content of other jobs, creating greater dispersion in the skill requirements of the work force. However, the fact that we have seen a substantial rise in the economic benefits from increased education suggests that the demand for skills has been rising, perhaps as a consequence of technological change. This hypothesis finds support in a recent study that found that workers who use a computer on the job earn about 10 to 15 percent more than otherwise similar workers. [13]

Deunionization. In addition to supply and demand forces, the structure of wages is determined by a number of institutional factors, most notably unions. In their role as wage-setting institutions, unions both raise average wages and reduce wage dispersion among organized workers. There is also evidence that they help to reduce the overall degree of wage inequality. During the last two decades, the United States, like a number of other industrialized countries, has experienced a decline in the fraction of the work force that is unionized. In the early 1970s, nearly one in three workers was a union member; today the figure is fewer than one in six. Despite these trends, the decline in unionization rates can explain only some of the rise in male wage inequality, on the order of 10 to 20 percent. [14] This is because wage inequality has increased for both unionized and nonunionized workers. Thus, even if the entire work force had been unionized, wage inequality would have still increased.

Research thus shows that no single factor caused the rise in income or wage dispersion. Instead, the trends appear to result from a number of demographic, economic, and policy factors. Despite the efforts of a number of researchers, we do not yet have a complete systematic accounting of the various factors that have contributed to the rise in income and wage inequality. As a result, there is a considerable gap in our understanding of the causes of the trends. This makes it difficult to determine the appropriate policy response, if any.

IMPLICATIONS FOR THE FUTURE AND POLICY OPTIONS

Regardless of what caused the trends, the two-decade rise in income and wage dispersion in the United States is troubling. If the growing inequality had been accompanied by real gains for families and workers across the income scale, the trends might be less alarming. What gives particular rise for concern is that growing disparities go hand-in-hand with stagnating family incomes and workers' wages at the midpoint of the distribution and below. Moreover, among men in the labor market, even the median worker is worse off in real terms compared with previous years. The distributional trends are particularly relevant for urban areas like Los Angeles, where many of the causal factors, such as the loss of manufacturing jobs, declines in unionization rates, or the increased number of female-headed families, are even more prevalent. These patterns of income and wage growth have implications for other areas of social concern because they are linked with such issues as the rise in poverty, patterns of residential segregation, and trends in the homeless population.

Given what we know about the direction of the trends and their potential causes, what can we expect for the future? There are two factors that suggest that the trends are not likely to be rapidly reversed. First, although the time series indicate that the level of inequality grew more slowly in the later part of the 1980s, the current recession is likely to cause a further increase in income and wage dispersion. Second, many of the factors most strongly linked to the trends in inequality represent fundamental changes in the structure of the economy rather than short-run phenomena. For instance, future workers will still compete in a global economy, and technological advances are likely to continue to change the skill content of jobs.

There is a possible role for other factors in altering the future course of income and wage trends. Demographic changes in the coming decade, namely the baby bust that is following the baby boom, may help improve the relative position of younger families and workers. In addition, the rise in returns to education in the 1980s may encourage an increase in educational attainment. Indeed, data on school attendance show a rise in college enrollment rates among recent high school graduates, reversing a downward trend in the 1970s. An increase in the supply of college graduates will tend to dampen the current gap in wages between more- and less-educated workers.

If the trend toward more inequality in the distribution of income and wages continues, what measures are available to policymakers to counteract this trend? There are several options that invite consideration. One approach is to promote policies that encourage strong economic growth, with the expectation that all families and individuals will gain from actions that encourage job creation and high-output growth. However, although macroeconomic policies that brought about economic growth led to a more equal distribution of income in the past, the lesson of the 1980s is that there is no guarantee all will benefit from high-growth policies. As indicated earlier, the recent rise in inequality continued throughout the 1980s despite the long economic expansion. The importance of shifts in the structure of the economy, outlined in the previous section, suggests that macroeconomic policies alone are not an adequate solution.

An alternative and more direct redistributive tool available to policymakers is change in the progressivity of the tax system. To what extent can tax policy counteract the trend in pre-tax income inequality? One recent study indicates that the answer is very little. [15] Simulations of substantial changes in the tax code, including increasing the top marginal tax rate from 28 to 50 percent and doubling the Earned-Income Tax Credit, produce only a modest impact on the post-tax distribution of income. This is because much of the rise in inequality results from changes in the distribution of private incomes, such as wages and capital income.

Although these simulations suggest that there may be little opportunity to use the tax system to redress the rise in pre-tax income inequality that has taken place since the 1970s, policymakers can use the tax and transfer system to shore up the incomes of families and individuals at the bottom of the income distribution. Thus, changes such as those embodied in the 1986 Tax Reform Act, which removed about 5 million poor persons from the tax rolls, provide a way of increasing the well-being of those at the bottom of the income ladder even if they result in a small reduction in overall inequality.

If the indirect and direct redistributive tools do not offer solutions, a third approach is to use public policy to address the structural changes that have occurred in the economy over the last two decades. Such policies would be designed to alter the opportunities available to individuals and families or the choices they make given those opportunities. For example, public assistance programs could be reformed to reduce dependency and encourage low-income families to become self-sufficient through job training and enhanced employment opportunities. Industrial policies and strategic trade policies could be used to influence the composition of the economy and the mix of skills required of the work force. Education and training policies could be designed to encourage investments in the skills of the labor force, whether through tax and other incentives to businesses or by targeting incentives to individuals. These types of policy options are, by their nature, more controversial and less certain in terms of their impact. They are controversial because they entail a more activist role for government in order to influence the private decisions of individuals and firms in the economy. Their impact is less certain because they only indirectly alter family incomes and workers' wages, and their effect may not be felt for years after their implementation. In my view, such remedies deserve serious consideration due to the significance of the distributional changes and the likely ineffectiveness of traditional redistributive policies.

Whether we as a nation care about growing inequality may depend on the nature and degree of mobility among individuals and families. Further analysis is needed to fully understand changes in income and wage mobility over the last two decades. Annual data reveal a growing gap in each successive year over the past two decades between families and workers at the top and bottom of the distribution. Despite the greater degree of inequality, there is still considerable mobility within the income distribution, but that mobility is contingent to a greater extent today on family structure and one's education. Americans may be willing to tolerate a higher level of inequality than in other industrialized countries or even than our own historical experience, provided there is reasonable opportunity for upward movement through the income ranks. This is the essence of the American dream, a promise that families and individuals can better themselves during their lifetimes and that one's children and grandchildren can exceed one's own standard of living. Whether this promise is something of the past or continues today will remain the subject of debate for some time to come.

NOTES

I would like to thank Thomas K. Glennan, Randy L. Ross, James B. Steinberg, and Mary E. Vaiana for their comments on an earlier draft of this chapter.

*In the discussion of trends in income and wage inequality, the results for family incomes were based on tabulations from the March Current Population Survey (CPS) for 1970 to 1990. Trends in wages were based on tabulations from the May CPS for 1973 to 1978 and the monthly CPS files for 1979 to 1990. These two sources of CPS data provide information on a cross section of over 50,000 households or 100,000 individuals annually and can be used to study trends in income and wages over time.

REFERENCES

1. Clifford, Frank, "Rich-Poor Gulf Widens in State," *Los Angeles Times,* May 11, 1992, p. A1.

2. Hubler, Shawn, "South L.A.'s Poverty Rate Worse Than '65," *Los Angeles Times,* May 11, 1992, p. A1.

3. Pen, Jan, *Income Distribution,* London: Allen Lane, 1971.

4. Karoly, Lynn A., "The Trend in Inequality Among Families, Individuals, and Workers in the United States: A Twenty-Five-Year Perspective," in Sheldon Danziger and Peter Gottschalk, eds., *Uneven Tides: Rising Inequality in America,* New York: Russell Sage Foundation, 1992; and Santa Monica, Calif.: RAND, R-4206-RC, 1992.

5. U.S. Bureau of the Census, *Money Income of Households, Families, and Persons in the United States,* Current Population

Reports Series P-60, Washington, D.C.: U.S. Government Printing Office, various issues.

6. Karoly, Lynn A., "Trends in Income Inequality: The Impact of, and Implications for, Tax Policy," Paper presented at the conference on "Tax Progressivity," Office of Tax Policy Research, University of Michigan, August 1992.

7. U.S. Bureau of the Census, *Measuring the Effect of Benefits and Taxes on Income and Poverty: 1979 to 1991*, Current Population Reports Series P-60, No. 182-RD, Washington, D.C.: U.S. Government Printing Office, 1992.

8. Slemrod, Joel, "Taxation and Inequality: A Time-Exposure Perspective," in James M. Poterba, ed., *Tax Policy and the Economy*, Vol. 6, Cambridge, Mass.: MIT Press, 1992.

9. Duncan, Greg J., Timothy M. Smeeding, and Willard Rogers, "The Incredible Shrinking Middle Class," *American Demographics*, Vol. 14, No. 5, May 1992, pp. 34–38.

10. Butcher, Kristin F., and David Card, "Immigration and Wages: Evidence from the 1980s," *American Economic Review*, Vol. 81, No. 2, May 1991, pp. 292–296.

11. Borjas, George J., Richard B. Freeman, and Lawrence F. Katz, "On the Labor Market Effects of Immigration and Trade," National Bureau of Economic Research Working Paper No. 3761, June 1991.

12. Karoly, Lynn A., and Jacob Alex Klerman, "Using Regional Data to Reexamine the Contribution of Demographic and Sectoral Changes to Increasing U.S. Wage Inequality," Paper presented at the 1992 Population Association of America Annual Meeting, June 1992.

13. Krueger, Alan B., "How Computers Have Changed the Wage Structure: Evidence from Microdata, 1984–89," National Bureau of Economic Research Working Paper No. 3858, October 1991.

14. Freeman, Richard B., "How Much Has De-Unionisation Contributed to the Rise in Male Earnings Inequality?" in

Sheldon Danziger and Peter Gottschalk, eds., *Uneven Tides: Rising Inequality in America,* New York: Russell Sage Foundation, 1992.

15. Gramlich, Edward M., Richard Kasten, and Frank Sammartino, "Growing Inequality in the 1980s: The Role of Federal Taxes and Cash Transfers," in Sheldon Danziger and Peter Gottschalk, eds., *Uneven Tides: Rising Inequality in America,* New York: Russell Sage Foundation, 1992.

Chapter Three

Families, Children, Poverty, Policy

Julie DaVanzo

INTRODUCTION

In the United States today, more Americans live in poverty than at any time since Lyndon Johnson declared the War on Poverty in 1964. After declining slightly in the 1970s, poverty rates have once again climbed to 1960s levels (Figure 1). But unlike the 1960s, when the elderly had the highest rate of poverty, now children experience the greatest, and growing, rates of poverty (Figure 2). Children under 18, who comprise just over one-quarter of the U.S. population, accounted for 40 percent of the poor in 1990. One child in five is now living below the poverty line.

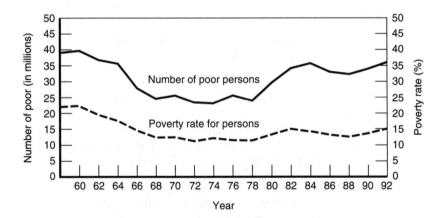

SOURCE: U.S. Bureau of the Census, *Poverty in the United States: 1990*, p. 60, no. 175.

Figure 1—Percentage of the U.S. Population Living in Households with Incomes Below the Poverty Line, 1959–1991

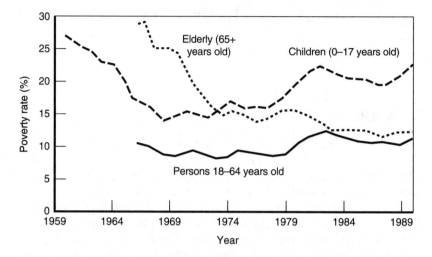

NOTE: Data for 18+ before 1967 are not comparable with data for later years.

SOURCE: U.S. Bureau of the Census, *Poverty in the United States: 1990,* Current Population Reports, Series P-60, Nos. 175 and 181, Washington, D.C.: U.S. Government Printing Office, 1991.

Figure 2—Poverty Rates for Children, the Elderly, and Other Adults, 1959–1991

Poverty, especially childhood poverty, is considerably more prevalent in inner cities, such as South Central Los Angeles. According to the 1990 census, nearly 40 percent of households with children under 18 in South Central Los Angeles were poor, more than double the rate for Los Angeles County or California as a whole (Table 1).

There are many forces at work in our society that have contributed to the rise in poverty in recent years. Broad economic developments, including overall levels of employment, changes in the mix and location of jobs in our economy, and changes in tax policy, affect the distribution of income, an issue explored in depth by Lynn A. Karoly in Chapter Two of this book. Other public policies, including the quality of public education, health, and social services, also play a role. A large literature has grown up examining the causes and consequences of poverty in general, and for children in particular.

Table 1

Percentage of Families with Children Under Age 18 That Were Poor, by Race and Ethnicity, 1990

Race/ Ethnicity	South Central LA (%)	LA County (%)	State of California (%)	United States (%)
White	38	12	10	
Black	38	26	25	
Asian/PI[a]	43	13	15	
Hispanic	40	24	23	
Total	38	17	14	15

[a]PI = Pacific Islander.

SOURCE: Census of Population, STF-3A (P123, P124A, P124B, P125), 1990.

Living in poverty has a demonstrably adverse affect on the lives of children. Over the years, studies comparing children living in households under the poverty line with those above it have shown that their futures are much bleaker: they are more likely to die at an early age, be victims of child abuse, or suffer serious illnesses; they are more likely to drop out of school or, if they finish high school, less likely to continue their education. Children in poverty are more likely to become pregnant as teens, become unwed mothers, and to remain poor as adults, perpetuating the cycle. Their poverty is not only a threat to their own well-being: children in poverty are more likely to engage in delinquent activity. (For a review of the evidence, see [1] and references therein.)

This chapter looks at what we know about the characteristics of children in poverty in our cities and the nation, focusing on the relationship between poverty and family structure. It then examines some of the policy choices now under discussion to address the problem of child poverty.

THE RELATIONSHIP BETWEEN FAMILY STRUCTURE AND CHILD POVERTY

Several characteristics distinguish families in poverty. The heads of poor families are more likely to be young, members of a minority, recent immigrants, and to have low education. One particularly notable characteristic is that more than half of the families in poverty are headed by a single parent, in most cases (over 90 percent) a female. Indeed, nationwide nearly 60 percent of poor families with children are female headed compared with only about 20 percent of nonpoor families. More generally, female-headed households are much poorer than two-parent households: the 1991 median income of female-headed households with children under age 13 ($13,012) was less than one-third that of married-couple households with children ($42,514).

The absence of a second parent, especially the male parent, greatly increases the likelihood that a family will be poor, regardless of race or ethnicity. As Table 2 shows, for black and white families with two

Table 2

Percentage of Families with Children Under Age 18 That Were Poor, by Family Type and Race and Ethnicity, 1990

	Married Couple (%)	Male Householder (%)	Female Householder (%)
South Central LA			
White	30	40	63
Black	14	36	51
Asian/PI[a]	42	36	49
Hispanic	32	40	64
Total	25	39	54
LA County			
White	8	16	28
Black	9	25	41
Asian/PI[a]	11	19	30
Hispanic	17	27	46
Total	11	22	37
California			
White	5	15	30
Black	8	24	43
Asian/PI[a]	12	19	33
Hispanic	16	26	47
Total	8	19	36

[a]PI = Pacific Islander.
SOURCE: Census of Population, STF-3A (P123, P124A, P124B, P125), 1990.

parents, the risk of being poor is roughly comparable, and small; for Los Angeles County, only 8 percent of white two-parent families and 9 percent of black two-parent families are in poverty. The comparable figures for California as a whole are 5 percent for whites, 8 percent for blacks. By contrast 28 percent of white female-headed and 41 percent of black female-headed Los Angeles County families are poor; figures for the state are comparable. A higher percentage of Los Angeles County Hispanic families with two parents are in poverty (17 percent, twice the rate for blacks and whites), but for Hispanics, too, the absence of a male parent is associated with much higher poverty rates (46 percent). This pattern holds for the state as well as for the county.

The picture is somewhat different in South Central Los Angeles. In South Central, families are substantially more likely to be in poverty regardless of whether the family has two parents or only one. In addition, the poverty rate for married couples with children is somewhat closer to the single-parent poverty rate. For example, black female-headed families are more than five times more likely to be in poverty statewide than black families with two parents; but in South Central, they are only three and a half times more likely to be in poverty. The poverty rate for black married-couple families in South Central is much lower than that for all other race/ethnic groups. Bear in mind, however, that the number of whites and Asians in South Central overall is very small.

The greater risk of poverty faced by female-headed households is one of the main reasons why, overall, more black families are poor; this is because proportionally more black families are female headed, approximately triple the white rate for South Central, Los Angeles County, California, and the United States (Table 3). In 1991 over half of all black children under age 18 in the United States lived with their mothers only compared with just over one-quarter of all Hispanic children and only one-sixth of all whites (Figure 3). The situation is different for Hispanic families, however; while the percentage of Hispanic families with children that are female headed is only slightly higher than the rate for whites, the poverty rates were double in Los Angeles County and in California. This suggests that such factors as immigrant status or education, much more than family structure, help explain high poverty rates for Hispanics, which are

Table 3

Percentage of Households with Children Under Age 18 That Are Female Headed, by Race and Ethnicity, 1990

Race/Ethnicity	South Central LA (%)	LA County (%)	State of California (%)	United States (%)
White	17	16	16	16
Black	58	48	44	50
Asian/PI[a]	26	10	10	12
Hispanic	20	19	19	24
Total	39	20	18	21

[a]PI = Pacific Islander.

NOTE: Data for the United States refer to all own children, of any age, not just those under age 18.

SOURCE: Census of Population STF-3A (P019, P020, P021) and STF-1C (P019, P020), 1990.

about the same as for blacks in the county and the state (Table 1). (The data in Table 3 refer to *households with children*, whereas those in Figures 1–4 have *children* as their units of observation. The latter data are not currently available for smaller units of geography, such as South Central.)

If present trends continue, the problem of childhood poverty can be expected to grow, to the extent that risk of poverty continues to be greater for female-headed families. Over the last three decades, the proportion of households that are female headed has grown from 8 percent in 1960 to 22 percent in 1991 and has increased for all racial and ethnic groups (Figure 4). This trend is the result of changes in the rate both of divorces and of births to unmarried women. The divorce rate more than doubled from 1960 to 1979, then tapered off slightly in the 1980s. Out-of-wedlock births increased by more than five times from 1960 to 1988 (from 5 percent of all births to 27 percent). The rate of nonmarital childbearing is highest for blacks (65 percent in 1989), followed by Hispanics (36 percent), whites (19 percent), and Asians and Pacific Islanders (12 percent), but it has increased in the past 30 years for all groups. Divorce and separation rates are also higher for blacks, [2] although the racial differences in

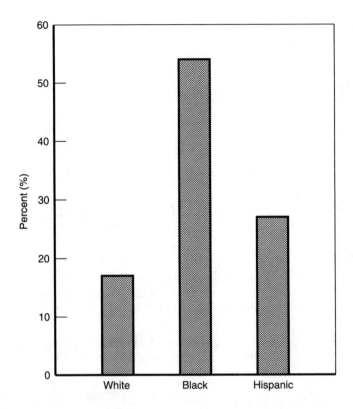

SOURCE: U.S. Bureau of the Census, *Marital Status and Living Arrangements: March 1990*, Current Population Reports, Series P-20, No. 461, Washington, D.C.: U.S. Government Printing Office, May 1992.

Figure 3—Percentage of Children Under Age 18 Living with Mother Only, by Race and Ethnicity, 1991

marital disruption are smaller than those in out-of-wedlock childbearing. The high rate of nonmarital childbearing for blacks is the main reason why so many black children live in female-headed households—in 1991, 58 percent of black children who lived in mother-only households lived with a never-married mother compared with 20 percent for whites and 33 percent for Hispanics.

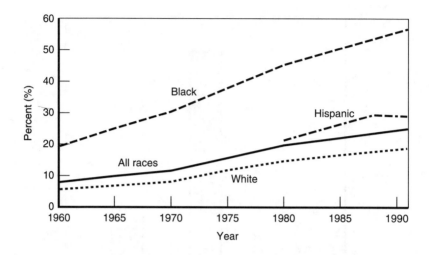

NOTE: Data are unavailable for Hispanics before 1980.
SOURCE: U.S. Bureau of the Census, *Marital Status and Living Arrangements: March 1990,* Current Population Reports, Series P-20, Nos. 450 and 461, Washington, D.C.: U.S. Government Printing Office, May 1991, 1992.

Figure 4—Percentage of Children Under Age 18 Living with Mother Only, by Race and Ethnicity, 1960–1991

Why are children in female-headed households more likely to be poor? The income difference is, not surprisingly, primarily due to the loss of economic support from absent fathers, who generally earn more than mothers. Female-headed households also have lower income because single mothers have lower wage rates than married fathers and work fewer hours on average.

In principle, child support from absent fathers could make up the difference, but in reality, child support is low and unreliable. In 1982 child support and alimony payments accounted for only 10 percent of the income of white single mothers and 3.5 percent of blacks. [3] Less than 60 percent of American women with children under 21 from an absent father had a child support award. Of these, one in five did not receive any payment and less than half received the full payment due. [4] Blacks (35 percent) and Hispanics (41 percent) are considerably less likely to receive child support than whites (68 percent), though these differences are primarily attributable to socioeconomic status rather than to race/ethnicity. Fathers of children born out of wedlock are much less likely to pay child support than those who were married to the child's mother. Yet much of the increase in single parenthood is due to increases in out-of-wedlock childbearing.

Public assistance programs are designed to help poor families, especially single-parent families with children. In 1985–1986, 46 percent of poor children in the United States and 52 percent of poor children in California received Aid to Families with Dependent Children (AFDC). But AFDC alone is insufficient to bring a family above the poverty line, though benefits have been higher in California than in the rest of the nation. In 1987 the maximum annual cash benefit in California for a single parent with two children was 84 percent of the poverty line.* However, the figure is 99 percent if we add the maximum food stamps benefit; furthermore, AFDC participants are eligible for Medicaid, which provides health care benefits that are often superior to those that would otherwise be available to low-income families. Although AFDC alone might not be sufficient to bring a family above the poverty line, the value of the package of AFDC, food stamps, and Medicaid often exceeds the income that would be available to poor households from work at a low-wage job, especially after they pay for child care, medical insurance, transportation, and other work-related expenses.

Although we have focused on the association between poverty and female-headed households, it is important to recall that not all female-headed families are poor and not all poor families are female headed. While the vast majority of poor black families were female headed (four out of five in South Central, Los Angeles County, and California), between one-third and one-half of nonpoor black families in these areas were also female headed (Table 4).

At the same time, there are many two-parent families in poverty. In South Central, one-quarter of all married-couple families with children are poor. Although only 8 percent of all two-parent families in California are poor, they still account for a significant percentage of those in poverty: approximately half of all poor white and three-fifths of all poor Hispanic households with children in California are *not* female headed. Thus the growth of female-headed households,

Table 4

Percentage of Households with Children Under Age 18 That Were Female Headed, by Poverty Status and Race/Ethnicity, 1990

	Nonpoor Families (%)	Poor Families (%)	All Families with Related Children Less Than Age 18
South Central LA			
White	10	30	18
Black	46	81	60
Asian/PI[a]	26	32	29
Hispanic	12	34	21
Total	31	59	42
LA County			
White	14	42	18
Black	39	79	49
Asian/PI[a]	9	25	11
Hispanic	14	38	20
Total	16	46	22
California			
White	13	51	17
Black	35	78	46
Asian/PI[a]	9	26	11
Hispanic	14	41	20
Total	15	50	20
United States			
Total	20	57	25

[a]PI = Pacific Islander.
NOTE: Poor examples are those with incomes below the federal poverty line.
SOURCE: Census of Population, STF-3A (P123, P124A, P124B, P125), 1990.

especially among blacks, is a factor in rising childhood poverty, but attempts to develop policy directed at childhood poverty must consider a number of other factors in addition to family structure.

We now turn to the choices available for addressing the problem of childhood poverty.

STRATEGIES FOR HELPING CHILDREN IN POVERTY

The preceding sections suggest three general approaches to helping alleviate the adverse consequences of poverty on children and families. First, since there is a correlation between female-headed households and poverty, we could adopt policies designed to increase the relative number of two-parent families. Second, we could take steps to lift children and their families out of poverty by increasing their money incomes. Finally, we could accept that many children will grow up in poverty and take steps to mitigate the worst consequences associated with it.

Strategies to Increase the Relative Number of Two-Parent Households

An increase the relative number of two-parent households would likely reduce family poverty and the adverse consequences associated with poverty and also any adverse consequences of growing up in a single-parent family, regardless of income. Children who grow up in mother-only families are more likely to have problems in school (absences, behavior problems, and higher rates of dropping out); they have lower earnings in young adulthood and are more likely to be poor; and they are more likely to commit delinquent acts, engage in violent criminal behavior, and to use drugs and alcohol. Furthermore, girls who grow up in female-headed households are more likely to become single mothers themselves, repeating the cycle. (For a review of the evidence regarding the consequences of growing up in a mother-only family, see [3] and references therein.) These differences appear regardless of racial or ethnic group. The lower incomes of female-headed households appear to account for some, but not all, of these adverse emotional, physical, and socioeconomic consequences. The poorer outcomes may also be due to less overall parental time to help children and to monitor and supervise their activities; the lack, specifically, of a father figure (e.g., in enforcing discipline and expected behavior); or the family conflict that led the family to break up or the stress experienced following a divorce.

Policies under this approach fall into two broad categories: measures to keep married couples together and those that reduce the number of births to unmarried women.

Measures to keep families together. High divorce rates seem to be a fairly well-entrenched social phenomenon not much affected by government policy. Higher incomes for men may increase marital stability, though greater economic opportunities for women could have the opposite effect by reducing women's economic dependence on men. On the other hand, higher wages for women could help relieve the poverty risk for female-headed families, thus possibly improving outcomes. Tougher divorce laws could theoretically reduce the likelihood of divorce, but the effects would probably not be large, and the notion bucks the long-established trend toward easier and less costly divorce. Marriage and family counseling and pre-divorce mediation may improve the prospects of a couple staying together, but the government can play only a limited role in fostering the use of such services.

Measures to reduce births to unmarried women. There are a number of policies that could reduce births to unmarried women. Studies have found that family planning programs, school-based clinics, and access to abortion can reduce teenage fertility (e.g., [5]). Other approaches to reduce births to unmarried women include providing skills and better economic opportunities to women at risk of early childbearing, making men more financially responsible for children they father (thus increasing the incentives for them to avoid pregnancies), and reducing the government assistance to children born out of wedlock and to their families. Studies have shown that pregnant teenagers who receive AFDC and Medicaid benefits are more likely to continue their pregnancies and keep their babies, although a decision to remove these benefits could have serious adverse costs on those who carry through the pregnancy even without benefits. These adverse consequences may outweigh the deterrent effect of this approach.

Extending AFDC benefits to poor two-parent families (as some states, including California, have done) could reduce the number of single-parent families by eliminating any incentive for the couple to split up in order to qualify for welfare. Studies have estimated, however, that such incentives account for no more than 10 to 15 percent of the changes in family structure in the last several decades. [6] Nonetheless, extension of welfare benefits to married couples with children can help reduce child poverty since a number of poor children live in two-parent families.

For women who give birth while unmarried, improved adoption services could perhaps reduce the number of single-parent households; currently very few women put their babies up for adoption, and those who do are disproportionately relatively affluent whites.

Some, for example, Moynihan, [7] and W. J. Wilson, [8] have suggested that low incomes and lack of employment opportunities for black men have contributed to the rise of female-headed households because women see little benefit from marrying a man with poor economic prospects; if so, greater job opportunities could increase the number of two-parent families.

Finally, government can play a hortatory role, as Vice President Quayle has done, in challenging the social acceptability of out-of-wedlock childbearing, although there is no clear evidence that such efforts are effective.

Strategies to Lift Families Out of Poverty

A different policy strategy assumes that lack of economic resources is a major factor inhibiting family functioning and child well-being and that low incomes, rather than family structure per se, is the key problem. The goal of this strategy is to increase the financial resources available to poor families with children, with specific policies attempting to address the reasons *why* these families are poor. Furthermore, as noted above, poverty tends to lead to situations— marital separations and out-of-wedlock childbearing—that result in single-parent households; thus, increasing income may also reduce the number of single-parent households.

Increase child support by noncustodial parents. A number of states, including California, are experimenting with mandatory child support to be withheld automatically from the paycheck of the noncustodial parent and are establishing simple rules for determining levels of child support. There has also been discussion of using the Internal Revenue Service (IRS) to help collect payments from non-paying fathers. These approaches raise a number of practical problems, including the feasibility and administrative burden of trying to keep track of noncustodial parents. Given their potentially high geographic mobility, cooperation and coordination among the states is needed.   There are also potential problems with self-employed fathers.

The Family Support Act of 1988, which mandated stronger state child support enforcement programs, attempts to deal with some of these problems.   It requires automatic withholding of child support, periodic review of support orders, improvements in states' efforts to establish paternity, and better efforts to track and monitor support payments within and across states.   It also authorized a demonstration project to provide education, training, and job services under the Job Opportunities and Basic Skills Training (JOBS) program to noncustodial parents who are unable to pay child support because they are unemployed.   Some states (e.g., Wisconsin) have experimented with making the parents of unemployed teenage fathers responsible for supporting their grandchildren, but this policy has proven to be difficult to enforce.

Increase the earnings of mothers heading families.   Female-headed households have lower incomes not only because they lack the father's income but also because single mothers have lower wage rates than married fathers and work fewer hours on average.   Early welfare programs deemed mothers of young children "unemployable" and heavily "taxed" their earnings if they worked by reducing welfare benefits for each dollar earned; however, it is now much more socially acceptable for mothers of young children to work outside their homes, and many current government programs strongly seek, through a variety of mechanisms, to encourage work and discourage welfare dependency.

The Family Support Act of 1988 requires each state to set up JOBS programs that include job search, work experience, and education and training for welfare mothers.   Failure to participate in these activities can result in a loss of welfare benefits.   The program is also supposed to provide child care support and transportation to eliminate these obstacles to work and to provide child care and Medicaid benefits for a year to those leaving welfare for jobs.   This provision recognizes that health care is an important benefit that may make many women hesitant to leave welfare, especially since their postwelfare jobs may not necessarily include health insurance coverage.   Under the Act, states are required to give JOBS priority to groups at highest risk of long-term welfare dependency (e.g., parents under age 24 who have not completed high school).

JOBS was modeled in part after Greater Avenues to Independence (GAIN), a welfare-to-work, or "workfare," program that began in California in 1985. A recent evaluation of GAIN suggests that the program can increase earnings of welfare recipients and save government money but that it is, not surprisingly, least effective where jobs are scarce and in areas, like Los Angeles County, where the welfare population has little education or recent job experience. While the ideas behind programs such as GAIN seem to be steps in the right direction toward reduced welfare dependency and increased economic self-sufficiency, current funding levels do not enable GAIN and similar programs in other states to reach a large portion of the eligible population.

Reduce taxes on families with children. In recognition of the private costs and social benefits of raising children, several policies have sought to increase the disposable income available to families with children. Some of these policies, for example, the Earned-Income Tax Credit, which was increased substantially in 1990, benefit low-wage workers with children. Other proposals have not been restricted to families in which at least one parent works, and some, in the attempt to have a more universal appeal, have proposed tax credits for all families with children, regardless of income or family structure. For example, the National Commission on Children, chaired by Senator Jay Rockefeller, last year recommended a $1,000 per child tax credit (refundable to those who owe no taxes) for *all* families. One rationale for such a policy is that the dependent exemption for children has not kept up with inflation and has declined dramatically as a percentage of per capita personal income (from 42 percent in 1948 to 11 percent in 1990); furthermore, a tax credit is more progressive than an increased exemption, whose value increases with income. However, the estimated cost of such a program is $40 billion per year. Given this hefty price tag, some feel that such a program should be a substitute for, rather than a supplement to, welfare; however, in that case, poor children would not be helped any more than those not in poverty.

Strategies to Limit the Adverse Consequences of Poverty

There are a number of reasons to consider tackling the problems of children and youth directly rather than working through income strategies. First, there is no guarantee that increased family incomes will go to benefit the child, although evidence suggests that parents do spend a significant portion of increased income on their children. Second, lack of income per se may not be the only reason why some parents are having difficulty raising children. For example, they may lack information about services that may benefit their children or may lack adequate parenting skills. In addition, direct programs may have "externalities"—benefits to society beyond the benefits to the individual, such as drug programs that reduce crime or health services that improve public health. These "external" benefits would justify providing the service even if individuals would not necessarily spend their own money to obtain it. It was for these types of reasons that food stamps and Medicaid were added as complements to AFDC several decades ago.

Child care and early childhood education programs. Organized, publicly subsidized child care programs free a single parent to work. However, these programs may have additional benefits: in the absence of such programs, some children are left with older siblings, neighbors, or even alone ("latchkey kids"), which can be harmful to the child's development and lead to future problems in school.

Resource-intensive early education programs such as Head Start are known to be cost-effective: every dollar invested is estimated to save $6 in lower costs for special education, repeated years of school, welfare, and crime. [9] And since participants seem to be more likely to finish school and have jobs and are less likely to become pregnant as teenagers, they are less likely to become the head of a poor family themselves or to need the types of remedial education that JOBS programs provide. It is unclear, however, whether less-intensive programs with higher child-to-staff ratios or staff with less training would be as cost-effective.

More generally, improved public education opportunities and stay-in-school programs could significantly affect the future prospects for children in poverty. One approach to this problem is discussed by Paul T. Hill in Chapter Five.

Health care. Programs such as prenatal care and childhood immunizations have been shown to be cost-effective. For example, each dollar spent on prenatal care through the Women, Infants, and Children (WIC) program is estimated to save $3 in hospital costs that would have been spent treating health problems that prenatal care could have prevented. [9]

The types of jobs available to low-income parents often lack health care benefits altogether or provide benefits inferior to those available through Medicaid; this may reduce the incentive for some families to leave public assistance. It is for this reason that, as noted above, JOBS programs offer Medicaid coverage for a year after the family leaves the welfare rolls, but there remains the question of how such families will cover their health care needs after this transition period.

Programs to improve parenting skills. We have already noted that some policies designed to help families and children have focused on women who are at risk of having *economic* difficulties in raising children—for example, pregnant and parenting teens and single mothers—and have attempted to provide them with improved employment prospects. Some government, community, and school-based programs also recognize that such women may have other difficulties in raising children and attempt to strengthen their parenting skills, for example, through parent education or home visitation programs. Deficient parenting skills appear to be more important than family structure per se in explaining juvenile behavior problems and delinquency. [10]

Other school-based programs. Schools, including many in Los Angeles, are increasingly being called on to provide other services that in the past were typically provided or arranged by families. These include school breakfast and lunch programs, after school child care for primary school students, "character" (ethics) education, family life education, health and family planning services, and child care for parenting students. However, this diversification of effort may detract from schools' ability to provide the best possible education for their students.

ISSUES IN THE CURRENT POLICY DEBATE

The growing number of children in poverty has stimulated interest in developing more effective policies for addressing the causes and consequences of this trend. But efforts to design and implement policy options at the national, state, and local levels of government have encountered some long-standing, troublesome issues.

1. It is very expensive to expand family and child support benefits to all worthy families, and regardless how eligibility rules are designed, all levels of government today are facing budget constraints unprecedented in the postwar period. At the same time, the potential political support for programs that benefit young children is declining. The share of families with young children has fallen; hence, there are fewer voters with a direct interest in supporting such programs.

2. One policy that has been popular politically because of its potential to increase the income of female-headed families without costly government participation is better enforcement of child support. If successful, this program can increase the income available to children, potentially reduce welfare payments to them, may increase fathers' roles in childrearing, and possibly even serve as a deterrent to the fathering of children out of wedlock. However, efforts to craft and implement mandated child support programs face enforcement challenges, especially among fathers who were never married to the mother of the household.

3. Welfare reform efforts of the 1980s, such as the Family Support Act of 1988, sought to eliminate features of earlier programs that discouraged work and were perceived to encourage welfare dependency. The Act included job training efforts and support services, such as child care, to ease the transition from welfare to work. However, these provisions have proven to be costly and have not been adequately funded. In addition, programs emphasizing job training and employment for welfare mothers have been successful for only the most employable, and program success has been highly contingent on the health and richness of local labor markets.

4. Recent welfare reform proposals put less emphasis on training and supportive services and more emphasis on reducing the costs of public assistance. These proposals have been frequently combined

with efforts to modify the behavior of the welfare poor. For example, California's welfare reform initiative, Proposition 165, combines a gradual reduction in welfare payments with disincentives (e.g., no extra benefits for children born while the mother is on welfare) for creating new welfare families and/or expanding existing families. Some argue that such incentives will encourage more responsible behavior; however, others see such proposals as punishing children for their parents' behavior; and they worry that, without provisions to improve participants' job skills, such programs do little to address the underlying causes of poverty.

States such as Wisconsin that have experimented with similar types of behavior modification incentives have sometimes found them difficult to enforce. [11] And as in past welfare reform efforts that require thorough and timely case monitoring, enforcement would no doubt be a formidable challenge to the California and similar plans.

5. In general, programs that attempt to change family structure as a way to reduce poverty are unlikely to have much effect. Family structure is certainly correlated with poverty—female-headed households are more likely to be poor—but causality is not well established. For example, both in Los Angeles County and in the state as a whole, Hispanic children are nearly as likely to be poor as blacks, yet they are much less likely than blacks to live in female-headed households. Furthermore, poverty increases the likelihood of divorce and out-of-wedlock childbearing, both of which increase the number of female-headed households.

There are substantial drawbacks to a strategy of trying to increase the number of two-parent families by reducing divorce or by en-couraging unmarried women to marry the fathers of their children. First, we don't know much about how to keep families together; it is especially unclear whether policy can have much effect in the face of what seem to be well-entrenched demographic trends. Second, it is not apparent that children who currently live in single-parent families would be better off if their families were two-parent families, holding other factors, especially income and the relationship between the mother and the father, constant. A number of studies have concluded that marital discord has a stronger relationship with delinquency and aggression than parental absence. [10] Third, this approach does nothing to deal with the problem of poverty and its associated consequences in two-parent families. Finally, there is a deep debate about the appropriateness of using government policy to favor particular family choices, as the recent debate on "family values" in the 1992 presidential campaign has so vividly shown.

6. A policy that *does* affect family structure and child well-being is family planning, which has been shown to be a very effective strategy for reducing the number of unplanned pregnancies. [5]   Children whose births are planned tend to be healthier and require less public assistance throughout their lives. If pursued aggressively, family planning programs might well lead to fewer abortions, fewer out-of-wedlock births, and fewer people in poverty. But, few programs are more controversial and more likely to generate diametrically opposed views than those having to do with the choice of childbearing.

7. One of the most successful programs to ameliorate the consequences of poverty is Head Start. It is cost-effective for society, highly beneficial to the students and their families, and more likely to lead a participant out of poverty as an adult. However, Head Start is a costly program and therefore serves only a fraction of the children eligible in the country. Because of its high cost, some are arguing for less-intensive, lower-cost ways of giving special attention to low-income children.

As Robert A. Levine and Barbara R. Williams argue in Chapter One, reducing poverty in America is still tied fundamentally to the health and strength of the nation's economy. Any solution to poverty requires an economy in a growth mode that will provide the upward mobility so long associated with the United States. America's changing family structure and its association with poverty constitute only one part of a much bigger picture.

NOTES

This chapter draws on a paper, "American Families: Trends and Policy Issues," by Julie DaVanzo and Omar Rahman, to which the reader is referred for additional details and specific references. The contributions of Dr. Rahman are gratefully acknowledged, as are the data extractions for Los Angeles and California from the 1990 census prepared by Allen Abrahamse and the very helpful suggestions of Lisa Greenwell, David Lyon, Lorraine McDonnell, Jim Steinberg, Mary Vaiana, and Gail Zellman. Special thanks are due to Christina Andrews for her assistance in preparing the graphs and tables and to Gloria Gowan for typing the manuscript.

Poverty statistics were based on a definition originated by the Social Security Administration in 1964, modified by federal interagency committees in 1969 and 1980, and prescribed by the Office of Management and Budget. The income cutoffs used by the Census Bureau to determine the poverty status of families and unrelated individuals included a set of 48 thresholds arranged in a two-dimensional matrix consisting of family size cross-classified by presence and number of family members under 18 years old. The average poverty threshold for a family of four persons was $12,674 in 1989.

*By contrast, two-thirds of the states in the United States had AFDC grant levels that were less than 50 percent of the poverty line. Furthermore, nationally, average inflation-adjusted AFDC benefits per recipient have fallen since 1968 and total inflation-adjusted benefits per recipient from AFDC, food stamps, and Medicaid have fallen since the mid-1970s. California, however, is one of only four states in which state law requires that AFDC benefits keep up with inflation, although this law has been partially suspended on several occasions and large cuts in benefits are under consideration.

REFERENCES

1. Wald, Michael, John W. Evans, and Marc J. Ventresca, "Economic Status," in Michael W. Kirst (project director) et al. (23 authors), *Conditions of Children in California*, Berkeley, Calif.: Policy Analysis for California Education (PACE), 1989, pp. 49–61.

2. Castro-Martin, Theresa, and Larry L. Bumpass, "Recent Trends and Differentials in Marital Disruption," *Demography*, Vol. 26, No. 1, February 1989, pp. 37–51.

3. McLanahan, Sara, and Karen Booth, "Mother-Only Families: Problems, Prospects, and Politics," *Journal of Marriage and the Family*, Vol. 51, August 1989, pp. 557–580.

4. U.S. Bureau of the Census, *Child Support and Alimony, 1987*, Current Population Reports, Series P-23, No. 167, Washington, D.C.: U.S. Government Printing Office, 1990.

5. Hayes, Cheryl, ed., *Risking the Future: Adolescent Sexuality, Pregnancy, and Childbearing*, Vol. 1, Washington, D.C.: National Academy Press, 1987.

6. Moffitt, Robert, "Incentive Effects of the U.S. Welfare System: A Review," *Journal of Economic Literature*, Vol. 30, March 1992, pp. 1–61.

7. Moynihan, Daniel Patrick, *The Negro Family: The Case for National Action*, Washington, D.C.: U.S. Department of Labor, March 1965.

8. Wilson, William Julius, *The Truly Disadvantaged: The Inner City, the Underclass, and Public Policy*, Chicago: University of Chicago Press, 1987.

9. Children Now, *California: The State of Our Children, 1989*, Los Angeles, Oakland, and Sacramento, Calif.: Children Now, 1989.

10. Loeber, Rolf, and Magda Stouthamer-Loeber, "Family Factors as Correlates and Predictors of Juvenile Conduct Problems," in Michael Tonry and Norval Morris, eds., *Crime and Justice: An Annual Review of Research*, Vol. 7, Chicago and New York: University of Chicago Press, 1986, pp. 29–149.

11. Kosterlitz, Julie, "Behavior Modification," *National Journal*, Vol. 24, No. 5, February 1, 1992, pp. 271–275.

Chapter Four

Helping Urban Teenagers Avoid High-Risk Behavior
What We've Learned from Prevention Research

Phyllis L. Ellickson

INTRODUCTION

Over the last two decades, negotiating the passage to adulthood has become increasingly perilous for American children. Compared with the children of the 1950s, today's youth are substantially more likely to suffer from poverty and economic hardship and to live in households where only one parent is available to meet their emotional and physical needs. As teenagers, they are also more likely to engage in high-risk activities that threaten their current and future well-being.

Drug use, while down from its peak in the 1980s, still attracts millions of American teenagers. Cigarettes and alcohol are by far the most popular drugs *and* the most lethal, causing more deaths in America than all other drugs combined. [1] While most teenagers know about smoking's harmful effects, about one in five teenagers smokes daily by the senior year of high school and is well on the way to a long-term smoking career. About 30 percent engage in bouts of binge drinking, thereby contributing to the high rate of alcohol-related motor vehicle accidents among teens, and 16 percent have used one or more illicit drugs. [2,3]

Drug use often contributes to violent behavior, and increasing numbers of teenagers are either the perpetrators or the victims of violence. [4] While not confined to particular geographic areas, the incidence and devastating effects of violence are particularly serious in the urban core; homicide is now the second leading cause of death among young black males and the third leading cause among all adolescents. [5,6]

This is a sexually active generation, a reality that generates its own set of risks. AIDS, the spectre of the late 20th century, has become an increasingly ominous threat. More than half of American high school students have had sexual intercourse, and more of them are beginning sex at younger ages. [5,7]   Unfortunately, the great majority of these students do not use condoms consistently, putting them at risk for AIDS, other sexually transmitted diseases, and pregnancy. Each year one million teenagers become pregnant in the United States, and increasing proportions of those who give birth are unwed. [8] Although the number of teenage AIDS cases is currently low, about 20 percent of all AIDS cases were probably contracted during or just after high school. [9] As heterosexual sex becomes a more common mode of transmission, the risk of AIDS will threaten the lives of even more of our young people.

As the public health community has recognized, it is these high-risk behaviors—not disease in the traditional sense—that constitute the greatest threats to adolescent health and well-being. [10] While high-risk behaviors afflict kids from all socioeconomic levels and ethnic backgrounds, they pose the most severe threats to poor children—who may lack both the resources and the reasons to reverse a downward slide. Restricted educational and employment opportunities make the urban poor particularly vulnerable to the attractions of sex, drugs, and violence and thus to their long-term consequences—teenage parenthood, job and marital instability, emotional distress, accidental injury, disease, and death.

What do we know about ways to keep kids from going off track? In the last decade, researchers at RAND and elsewhere have carefully assessed the effects of intervention programs designed to prevent or deter high-risk behavior among young teens. Most of these programs have been based in the schools and have targeted young adolescents in middle or junior high school. Most have also sought to delay or prevent kids from beginning a *specific* problem behavior (e.g., drug use, sexual intercourse) or, for those who have already started, to keep them from progressing to frequent involvement. The programs have typically focused on changing the child—helping teens develop the motivation to avoid high-risk behavior as well as the skills needed to do so.

As a result of these studies, we have learned a lot about what works—for which kids and under what conditions. We have also learned about the limits of programs that focus solely on changing children's behavior without altering their social and economic circumstances. The following discussion summarizes the results and lessons of recent prevention research, derives policy implications from those lessons, and suggests potential strategies for improving our success rate.

WHAT WE'VE LEARNED FROM PREVENTION RESEARCH

We are beginning to compile evidence about promising strategies for deterring high-risk behavior, but we have a much clearer idea about what does not work. Two approaches popular in the past have had little success: (1) the information approach, which stresses the negative consequences of drug use, precocious sexual activity, or other high-risk behaviors; and (2) the general skills approach, which helps children acquire a more positive self-image by improving their skills in decision making, communication, and problem solving. [11]

These programs failed because they were based on faulty assumptions—that knowledge alone is enough to alter behavior or that a *general* sense of competence and self-esteem will help kids reject *specific* risky actions. [12] They also failed to address the central reasons for initiating various problem behaviors—because your friends or other important people are doing it and you think it will get you things you want.

The next generation of programs was more solidly rooted in an understanding of why and how kids choose to engage in dangerous or deviant behavior. Taking a broad psychosocial approach, these programs zeroed in on notions that "everyone's doing it" and helped teens develop strategies for resisting social pressure to take health-compromising chances. The social influence model, described below, lies at the core of the most promising programs. While a few researchers have used it to postpone adolescents' sexual activity, it has been most frequently applied to drug use. Several observers have also suggested using it to reduce the risk of AIDS. [13,9] However, most of our information about the model's effectiveness comes from evaluating its effect on drug use; hence the following discussion emphasizes drug prevention programs.

How the Social Influence Model Works

This model recognizes that adolescents are especially vulnerable to social pressures. In their desire to appear grown up, they tend to emulate what they see as adult behavior, including drinking, smoking, and using other drugs. Accordingly, drug prevention programs based on the social influence model try to help adolescents recognize pressures—both internal and external—to use drugs, to help them develop counters to pro-drug arguments, and to teach them techniques for "saying no" in pressure situations.

The social influence model explicitly recognizes that teaching children how to resist drugs is not enough—programs must also *motivate* them to resist. [11,14] Social influence programs try to do this by helping kids understand the consequences of drug use, by undermining the belief that "everyone uses," and by reinforcing group norms against use. Because adolescents tend to be present-oriented and unconcerned about serious harm in the distant future, the programs emphasize how drugs can affect them now, in their daily lives and social relationships.

The original versions of the social influence model were applied to smoking prevention among junior high students, focusing largely on the external influences that push adolescents to use drugs, especially pressures from family, peers, and the media. [14] Newer versions also stress internal pressures—subtle influences an adolescent may not even be aware of, such as the desire to be accepted, to look "cool," to be part of the crowd. [15] Life Skills Training adds strategies for improving general personal competence; other variants seek to buttress school-based curricula with assistance from parents, community organizations, and/or the media.

Results from Programs Based on the Social Influence Model

Smoking prevention programs report modest success. Results from multiple programs (mostly for junior high students) suggest that tobacco prevention programs based on the social influence model can moderately reduce smoking. Those reductions, which typically range from 20 to 50 percent, last for one to two years after kids receive the program. Follow-up booster lessons help to extend effects, [16] but many early programs did not have boosters. Follow-up lessons in high school are particularly rare. Not surprisingly, therefore, program effects usually disappeared during high school. [17,18]

About 5 to 10 percent of all students who participate in antismoking programs are actually helped—they are less likely to start smoking or to be current or frequent smokers than students who do not get the lessons. [19] This estimate, derived from examining multiple antismoking programs, tells us the proportion of students that prevention programs are likely to affect. Combined with data on the size of treatment reductions, it rounds out the information we need to accurately assess program effectiveness.*

Smoking prevention programs have been "particularly effective in delaying the onset of tobacco use and less successful in targeting high-risk and minority youth." [20] Because most of them have been tested in communities that are largely white and middle class, we do not know much about their effectiveness with minorities and children of low socioeconomic status. However, two recent studies reported significant reductions in smoking among urban black youth and Hispanic students. [21,22] Several have also reported "boomerang" (negative) effects for previous smokers.

Programs focused on other substances have mixed results. Given the success of the social influence approach to smoking prevention, a number of investigators have applied the model to other substances—primarily alcohol and marijuana. The major work in broadening the focus of the social influence approach has been carried out at RAND, the University of Southern California (USC), the University of Michigan, and the Cornell University Medical College.

RAND's Project ALERT, tested in 30 schools from eight school districts in California and Oregon, is one of the most rigorous drug prevention trials ever conducted. Designed to equip students with the motivation and skills to resist pro-drug pressures, the curriculum targets alcohol, cigarettes, and marijuana. It consists of eight lessons for seventh graders and three "booster" (reinforcement) lessons for eighth graders. The 30 participating schools were randomly assigned to three experimental conditions: teen leaders assisting adult teachers in classroom delivery, no teen leaders, and the control group. The schools represent a wide variety of communities and student populations, including urban, suburban, and rural environments, high- and low-minority schools, and neighborhoods that vary from lower to upper middle class.

Results after three, twelve, and fifteen months showed that Project ALERT reduced both marijuana and cigarette use. It was effective for both low- and high-risk students and with minorities as well as whites. The program delayed marijuana initiation among nonusers of marijuana and cigarettes (a reduction of about one-third) and held down regular (weekly) marijuana use among prior users. It also curbed frequent heavy smoking among students who had previously experimented with cigarettes (reductions of 50 to 60 percent) and induced a significant number to quit. However, it was less successful against alcohol—early effects disappeared by eighth grade—and it had a negative effect on students who were confirmed smokers before the seventh-grade program began. [23]

USC's Midwestern Prevention Project (Project STAR) differs from Project ALERT in that it adds several community components to a school-based program. The program was implemented in 50 schools in Kansas City (Kansas and Missouri) beginning in 1984–1985, and in 57 schools in Indianapolis, Indiana, three years later. Elements of the intervention include a 10-session school curriculum; parent programs (involving, e.g., homework assignments with their children); training for community leaders; changing community health policies; and media campaigns.

The Project STAR data have been analyzed several times, using different groups of schools and statistical approaches and yielding different results. One study (of eight schools) reported no effects on alcohol and ambiguous results for marijuana after one year; [24] another (of 42 schools) found reduced use of all three gateway drugs—alcohol, cigarettes, and marijuana—over the same period. [25] The most recent analysis covered three years and individuals from eight schools; it reported modest reductions in recent cigarette and marijuana use, but not in recent alcohol use. [26]

Michigan's Alcohol Misuse Prevention Study (49 schools) has taken a slightly different approach, testing the model's effectiveness at preventing alcohol misuse—overindulgence (getting drunk, getting sick), trouble with friends (of the same or the opposite sex), or trouble with adults (parents, teachers, or police). After two years, the program had reduced the rate of increase in alcohol-related problems among eighth graders who had received it in grade six *and* had already used alcohol in both supervised and unsupervised settings. However, it did not reduce the amount or frequency of their drinking. Nor were there effects for children who received the program in the fifth grade or for children who either had no previous alcohol experience or had used alcohol only in supervised settings. [27]

Cornell's Life Skills Training program, which teaches both drug resistance and personal competence skills, was offered to seventh graders from 10 schools in greater New York. The test included five conditions, with two schools per variation: (1) teacher-led; (2) teen-led; (3) teen-led plus grade eight and nine boosters; (4) teacher-led plus grade eight and nine boosters; and (5) controls. All students in the program received 20 lessons during grade seven. In the booster schools, students received 10 booster lessons during grade eight and five more during grade nine.

The Cornell results were strongest after one year, when students had received 20 seventh-grade lessons and 10 booster lessons. By the eighth grade, students in the two teen-plus-booster schools smoked significantly less compared with those in the control schools, used less marijuana, and consumed smaller amounts of alcohol. After two years, some smoking reductions persisted in the teen-plus-booster schools, but the effects on marijuana were no longer significant, and a boomerang effect showed up for alcohol. The comparable teacher-led program with boosters produced boomerang results for both cigarette and alcohol use in eighth grade and for all three substances in grade ten. [28]

Several other studies have yielded mixed results as well: (1) delays in tobacco and marijuana use, but not alcohol use, for at least a year; [29] (2) erosion of early gains within two years; [29] and (3) short-term reduction in alcohol use with a peer-led program but boomerang effects with an adult-led program. [30] Analysis of Project DARE, the police-led program that originated in Los Angeles, has shown little effect on behavior. [31]

Sparse evidence on success of sex education programs. Using this approach to reduce teenage sexual activity has shown promising results, but the evidence is sparse and largely limited to quasi-experimental studies. One test of Life Skills Training for high school students showed increased use of birth control but no overall change in rates of sexual activity or pregnancy. [32] A program for (mostly) black eighth graders in low-income Atlanta public schools yielded lower rates of sexual activity a year later among females who were not sexually active previously but had less success with males and none with those who were already sexually active before the program began. [33] In contrast, a program for 13- to 19-year olds in various settings (schools, summer programs, etc.) reported that male program participants were more likely to maintain abstinence than comparison males. In addition, sexually active males were more likely to use effective contraceptives consistently if they had been active *before* the program; that was also true for females who became sexually active *after* the program. [34]

Summary Assessment of the Research

The research described above clearly shows that school-based programs aimed at preventing or delaying high-risk behavior can work. As numerous studies have documented, programs designed to reduce drug use have shown results. They are more likely to be effective with cigarettes and marijuana than with alcohol. And they are more likely to be effective with noninitiates and experimenters than with committed users. When the goal is limiting sexual involvement (as opposed to promoting safer sexual practices), success rates are also likely to be better among the experimenters or previously uninitiated than among the sexually active.

Although critics have suggested that the social influence model works only for middle class white kids from fairly homogeneous communities, growing evidence suggests otherwise. Project ALERT was successful across a wide variety of settings—in urban, suburban, and rural environments and in middle- and low-income communities with homogeneous or diverse populations. Moreover, it worked equally well in high-minority and low-minority schools, actually favoring the former when comparisons showed significant differences between the two groups. Similarly, the Life Skills Training approach has shown promise with both Hispanic and black kids, and the Atlanta program for postponing sexual involvement was tested in low-income schools with predominantly black students.

Although the social influence approach is most effective with kids who have not committed themselves to a risky or deviant lifestyle, it has been shown to help both high- and low-risk kids. Project ALERT was actually more successful with cigarette experimenters than with nonsmokers, despite the fact that the former were four times more likely to become monthly smokers within a year. It also curbed regular marijuana use among the high-risk kids who had already tried it. Programs targeted at the gateway drugs as well as those aimed solely at smoking have helped high-risk teens whose friends and family members use cigarettes or other substances. [35,26]

Some authors have suggested that programs in which older teens or same-age peer leaders help teach the lessons are more effective than those taught solely by adults. We think that verdict is premature. Although the Life Skills Training study showed better results with older teens, the Project ALERT test did not yield conclusive evidence favoring one mode of delivery over the other. Moreover, same-age peers play a different role in the classroom. The greater maturity and experience of older teens qualify them as experts in resisting pro-drug pressures, whereas same-age peers function largely as teachers' helpers. Hence programs with same-age peers represent a separate mode of program delivery.

Essential Ingredients of School-Based Programs

We can use the outcomes of these program tests to derive guidelines about specific program features that enhance the probability of success.

1. *The prevention process should begin early—before or shortly after the onset of high-risk behavior.* For example, it is easier to prevent smoking among kids who have not yet tried it and thus have not become addicted to nicotine or publicly defined themselves as being smokers. It is much harder to change kids who have already committed themselves to problematic behavior.

Because the age at which kids begin a risky behavior varies across different groups, the appropriate age for prevention may vary from one community to another. If many children have already started smoking or drinking by the end of elementary school, it would be better to target sixth graders rather than junior high students. If very few have done so, it is better to start social influence programs in junior high, when teens are particularly vulnerable to peer pressure. Similar considerations should guide the implementation of programs that focus on sexual behavior. Programs designed to delay sexual intercourse are usually more appropriate for eighth or ninth graders. School officials in each community need to carefully consider the experience and maturity of their student population when choosing specific prevention programs.

2. *Prevention programs should plan for the possibility that some adolescents may rebel against the message.* Programs based on the social influence model typically point out that high-risk behaviors can have negative effects on social relationships (get you in trouble, make you act silly, give you ashtray breath, etc.). They also suggest that good friends would not ask you to do harm to yourself. Messages of this type help bolster the resolve of the uncommitted, but they may have a boomerang effect on those already committed to risky behavior.

Project ALERT's negative effect on committed smokers is particularly instructive here. These kids were defined as having smoked three or more times in the last year or once or more in the last month. While this level of smoking would be considered minor for adults, it signals multiple troubles in a seventh grader's life. The early smokers were much more likely than the nonsmokers and experimenters to have stolen something from a store; to be doing poorly in school; to have a network of peers who smoked, drank, and used pot; and to plan on using drugs in the future. [22]

Going from trying cigarettes once or twice to trying them three times or more appears to mark an important shift from casual experimenting to rebellious self-declaration. The fact that cigarette smoking tends to be public, whereas early marijuana use does not, makes it all the more difficult to back away from it. Indeed, getting people to make their positions or actions public is one way of locking them in place. Hence it is not surprising that the more "visible" early smokers reacted negatively to the Project ALERT curriculum, while the less obvious marijuana users did not.

Although prevention programs cannot be all things to all people, their designers need to recognize that some kids may be inappropriate targets for a prevention message. To minimize rebellious reactions, program developers should explicitly acknowledge that some teens may already be involved with drugs (or sex or other high-risk activities) and explain that the program can help them change if they should choose to do so. They might also provide tips on how to quit. The goal should be to keep the kids who have already adopted a deviant lifestyle "in the classroom" psychologically. Doing so should help ward off boomerang effects and may provide a basis for turning them around in the future.

3. *Prevention programs should stress both motivation and skill building.* If children really want to use drugs (be sexually active, act deviant in general), acquiring a repertoire of resistance skills without the motivation to use them is unlikely to stop them. On the other hand, kids who do not want to use drugs but lack the means to identify and resist pro-drug pressures are unlikely to be able to resist temptation. Hence both components are needed for success.

When the focus is on alcohol, insufficient motivation to resist appears to be the principal stumbling block. Several studies have shown that social influence programs have little or no effect on drinking behavior—or modest effects that quickly wear away. At the same time, similar programs have produced significant and longer-lasting effects on cigarette smoking or marijuana use. Although the skills used to resist those substances are easily generalized to alcohol [36], young teens seem not to have used them. We think the difference lies in how society views the three substances. Most adults do not smoke or use pot, but most of them do drink. In the light of that powerful message, convincing teenagers that they should not drink becomes a daunting task.

4. *The most successful programs build on societal norms that foster program objectives.* Evidence that antismoking programs work came on the heels of a radical decline in the popularity of cigarette smoking. After the 1964 Surgeon General's report and the antismoking campaigns of the late 1960s, cigarette consumption in the United States dropped dramatically. [37] Similarly, substantial declines in marijuana use preceded evidence that prevention programs could deter initiation. These shifts have created a societal climate in which the majority of U.S. citizens consider both cigarette and marijuana use undesirable.

Such a climate may be a prerequisite for successful prevention, but it does not exist for alcohol. Without a substantial change in the societal norms and practices that promote drinking, including how alcohol use is portrayed in the media, prevention programs are unlikely to have much influence on whether and when teenagers start drinking. However, because there is considerably more consensus about the inappropriateness of drinking and driving and other high-risk uses of alcohol, such programs may be able to reduce alcohol misuse. Not surprisingly, the study with the best effects for alcohol found them for alcohol-related problems. Although that program targeted young adolescents, its results suggest that efforts to curb high-risk drinking among older teens should receive our attention as well.

5. *One intervention experience is not enough; sustaining early gains requires multiple experiences staggered over time.* Programs that offered booster lessons after the initial inoculation generally yielded longer-lasting effects than those that did not. Nevertheless, most programs fail to continue that reinforcement during high school, and a consequent erosion of effects is seen throughout the high school years. Adolescents do not experience less pressure to engage in risky behaviors as they move from junior high to high school; if anything, they experience more because of the expanded peer network and independence of the older teenager. Hence programs that continue to offer booster lessons during high school have a better chance to maintain results.

Limitations of Child-Focused Programs

Each of these characteristics increases the probability of a program's success. However, a sober macro-lesson also emerges from our research: even the best-designed and -implemented program will have only modest success if it aims at the child alone. After reviewing results from multiple trials, one analysis concluded that antismoking programs yield the intended effects for only about 5 to 8 percent of the targeted population. [19] Our assessment of more recent drug prevention and sexual education programs yields a similar conclusion: trying to "fix the kid" without altering the environmental factors that help shape adolescent behavior works for only a small proportion of teenagers—perhaps 5 to 10 percent. To make more substantial inroads against high-risk behavior, we need to deal with the multiple forces that impinge on children—their families, schools, neighborhoods, and the broader society in which they live.

How do those forces contribute to problem behavior? Although peers play a key role in introducing kids to drugs, sex, and delinquency, family and school experiences can increase the child's vulnerability to peers who engage in problem behavior. If the family situation is stressful and school is problematic, children are more likely to be exposed to deviant peers (and adults) and more likely to emulate their behavior. [38] Conversely, a caring adult and successful experiences at school help protect kids from trouble. [39,40] Similarly, community and societal norms that promote drinking, smoking, and violence and that glamorize sexual activity foster the same behavior in kids. Societal norms that downplay or discourage these behaviors dampen early initiation.

At the family level, parental support and discipline and parent/child connectedness are particularly important. [41] Disrupted families, per se, are not the problem. However, the stress that too often comes with divorce—loss of income, constraints on time for the child, limited access to child care and health services, hostility between the former husband and wife—can strain parent/child relationships and erode the parent's capacity to maintain consistent discipline. These stresses have risen dramatically with (1) the increase in single-parent families, (2) the worsened economic status of the bottom fifth of American households, and (3) the consequent increase in the number of children who are poor.

At the school level, two factors operate: expectations of future academic achievement and actual performance. Children who are doing well in school and who have career or college aspirations are much less likely to get involved with drugs, to become teenage parents, or to be serious delinquents. [42,43,38] Because the influence of family and school *precedes* peers in the socialization process, efforts to help families cope with stress and to make schools more positive environments for success should begin in elementary school or before. These efforts should also provide targeted assistance for kids who already show signs of problem behavior, such as conduct disorder, poor attendance, or failing grades, all of which are important predictors of later problems. Because we have very limited information about their long-term effect on high-risk behavior, programs directed at families and schools should be carefully evaluated over time.

POLICY IMPLICATIONS

The problems that urban kids face are complex and linked; no single program or policy will fix them. We need to recognize that efforts aimed solely at the child will delay or deter problem behavior for, at most, 5 to 10 percent of teenagers. If that group falls within the 20 percent or so most in need of help, prevention programs may be reaching between one-quarter and one-half of high-risk kids. But it is difficult to know whether the deterrence effect has worked for those most or least likely to get in trouble later on.

Most experts would agree, however, that protecting kids from high-risk behavior during adolescence has big payoffs. The earlier they start high-risk activities, the more likely they are to continue and to escalate their involvement, [44,45] thereby increasing the likelihood of serious consequences. Thus delaying the onset of high-risk behaviors may deflect harms associated with early initiation.

It is a judgment call whether the benefits of programs that help a small proportion of the overall adolescent population are worth the resources needed to effect the change. The argument is strongest where the cost of failure is extremely high—for example, programs aimed at AIDS and teenage parenthood. There is also a good case for programs that have low costs per child, as is the case with most social influence programs, and that have moderate benefits per child "saved"—for example, programs aimed at delaying, though not necessarily preventing altogether, the onset of smoking. However, we still lack careful assessments of the costs and benefits of prevention programs.

In principle, targeting programs at the most vulnerable kids appears to be the most cost-effective approach. But we know very little about how to identify the high-risk child before serious problems occur. While research has discovered multiple antecedents of problem behavior, our ability to predict which kids will get in trouble is still quite primitive: we miss many who become problem kids later on and identify others who do not. Furthermore, we know that programs designed for kids who are already in trouble can actually make them worse by lumping them together with other misfits, labeling them as problems, etc. Developing targeted interventions for kids who *might* get in trouble sometime in the future runs the added risk of labeling them before the fact and thereby fostering the behavior we want to avoid.

Thus we need a long-term commitment to deal with the social and economic forces that foster high-risk behavior and make our children vulnerable to harm as adolescents and adults. Some ideas that might work include the following:

1. *Develop and test sequential programs for curbing high-risk behavior during middle, junior, and high school.* This would involve (1) using what we have learned about the social influence approach to improve our results for smoking, drinking, and other drugs; (2) integrating these programs with appropriate efforts to delay sexual activity and promote condom use; and (3) providing booster lessons that recognize the need for continued reinforcement as adolescents mature and that take into account changes in their cognitive, social, and emotional maturity.

2. *Implement and evaluate new policies and programs for younger children that help families and schools provide environments in which children can flourish.* To date, the best evidence that early intervention can have long-term effects comes from the Perry Preschool Project, one of the prototypes for Head Start. But that study involved highly intensive teacher involvement and followed only one group of children from a single community over time. [46] To get a better understanding of its effectiveness in a variety of environments, current and future Head Start programs should also receive careful—and long-term—evaluations. At the elementary school level, a promising effort to restructure elementary schools involves bringing parents and teachers into school governance, providing mental health services to parents and children, and developing educational programs tailored to individual high-risk children. Developed at Yale, this approach appears to have improved attendance and academic performance among low-income minority children. [47] However, the evidence demonstrating its efficacy is sparse and lacks scientific rigor. Although a large-scale test of this approach is currently underway at the middle school level, it should also receive rigorous experimental tests at the elementary school level.

3. *Recognize that some government policies make the problem worse and fix them.* By now it should be painfully clear that our nation's

youth need to know what puts them at risk for AIDS and teenage pregnancy and how to avoid those risks. A substantial proportion of AIDS victims contracted HIV infection as adolescents, and the numbers are likely to rise as heterosexual sex becomes a more dominant mode of transmission. Moreover, recent evidence demonstrates that females are particularly at risk for becoming infected through heterosexual sex. In addition, statistics show that teenage pregnancy rates are lower in many European countries than in the United States, despite the fact that rates of sexual activity are similar. [48] This suggests that European teens make much more effective use of contraception than do American youth.

We need to replace silence, moralizing, and withholding of information with a national program aimed at reducing the risks of AIDS and pregnancy among adolescents. Building on knowledge gained from antismoking campaigns, one component of such a program should involve the national media in promoting societal norms favoring responsible sexual behavior—practicing safe sex, avoiding multiple partners, etc. That effort should be backed up with school-based programs for helping teens learn why and how to avoid high-risk sexual activity. Such programs should be targeted to every teen of high school age and some in junior high, depending on how sexually active the younger kids are. The programs should also target school dropouts—a difficult population to reach but one whose risk profile is high.

America can no longer afford to stand by while millions of teenagers jeopardize their futures. We must invest in our children: build the foundation for them to become successful and productive adults *and* help them avoid risky choices that threaten their well-being. This investment should begin in childhood and be sustained through adolescence. It also requires evaluating our efforts so we can improve the prognosis for future generations.

NOTES

*The following example shows the difference between the two measures. Post-program results for treatment x, which show that current smokers account for 15 percent of control school students and 10 percent of treatment students, led to the conclusion that the treatment reduced current smoking by one-third (5 percent divided by 15 percent). However, the proportion of all students affected by that reduction is only 5 percent: without the program, 15 percent would have been current smokers; with it, only 10 percent smoke. Thus, 5 percent of the total have been deterred from cigarette use.

REFERENCES

1. Office on Smoking and Health, Executive Summary, *Smoking and Health: A National Status Report. A Report to Congress*, 2d ed., U.S. Department of Health and Human Services, Public Health Service, DHHS Publication No. (CDC)87-8396, 1990.

2. NIDA, "A Comparison of Drug Use Among 8th, 10th and 12th Graders from NIDA's High School Senior Survey," *NIDA Notes*, May/June 1992, p. 19.

3. U.S. Department of Transportation, National Highway Traffic Safety Administration, National Center for Statistics and Analysis, *Drunk Driving Facts*, Washington, D.C.: July 1989.

4. Centers for Disease Control, "Weapon-Carrying Among High School Students—United States, 1990," *Morbidity and Mortality Weekly Report*, Vol. 40, 1991, pp. 681–684.

5. Office of Technology Assessment, *Adolescent Health, Volume II: Background and the Effectiveness of Selected Prevention and Treatment Services*, Washington, D.C.: Government Printing Office, May 1991.

6. Fingerhut, L. A., D. D. Ingram, and J. J. Feldman, "Firearm and Nonfirearm Homicide Among Persons 15 through 19 Years of

Age," *Journal of the American Medical Association,* Vol. 267, No. 22, 1992, pp. 3048–3053.

7. Centers for Disease Control, "Sexual Behavior Among High School Students—United States, 1990," *Morbidity and Mortality Weekly Report,* Vol. 40, Nos. 51–52, 1992, pp. 885–888.

8. U.S. Congress, House of Representatives, Select Committee on Children, Youth, and Families, *U.S. Children and Their Families: Current Conditions and Recent Trends,* Washington, D.C.: U.S. Government Printing Office, 1989.

9. Hingson, R. W., L. Strunin, B. M. Berline et al., "Beliefs About AIDS, Use of Alcohol and Drugs, and Unprotected Sex Among Massachusetts Adolescents," *American Journal of Public Health,* Vol. 80, No. 3, 1990, pp. 295–299.

10. Vanderpool, N. A., and J. B. Richmond, "Child Health in the United States: Prospects for the 1990s," *Annual Review of Public Health,* Vol. 11, 1990, pp. 185–205.

11. Ellickson, P. L., and A. Robyn, "Goal: Effective Drug Prevention Programs," *California School Boards,* Vol. 45, No. 4, 1987, pp. 24–27.

12. Goodstadt, M., "School-based Drug Education in North America: What Is Wrong? What Can Be Done," *Journal of School Health,* Vol. 56, No. 7, 1986, pp. 278–280.

13. Botvin, G. J., and L. Dusenbury, "Substance Abuse Prevention: Implications for Reducing Risk of HIV Infection," *Psychology of Addictive Behaviors,* Vol. 6, No. 2, 1992, pp. 70–80.

14. Evans, R. I., R. M. Rozelle, M. Mittelmark, W. B. Hansen, A. Bane, and J. Havis, "Deterring the Onset of Smoking in Children: Knowledge of Immediate Psychological Effects and Coping with Peer Pressure, Media Pressure, and Parent Modeling," *Journal of Applied Social Psychology,* Vol. 8, 1978, pp. 126–135.

15. Ellickson, P. L., *Project ALERT: A Smoking and Drug Prevention Experiment, First-Year Progress Report,* Santa Monica, Calif.: RAND, N-2184-CHF, 1984.

16. Best, J., S. Thomson, S. Santi, E. Smith, and K. Brown, "Preventing Cigarette Smoking Among School Children," *Annual Review of Public Health*, Vol. 9, 1988, pp. 161–201.

17. Flay, B., D. Koepke, S. J. Thomson, S. Santi, J. A. Best, and K. S. Brown, "Six-Year Follow-up of the First Waterloo School Smoking Prevention Trial," *American Journal of Public Health*, Vol. 79, 1989, pp. 1371–1376.

18. Murray, D. M., P. Pirie, R. V. Luepker, and U. Pallonen, "Five- and Six-Year Follow-up Results from Four Seventh-Grade Smoking Prevention Strategies," *Journal of Behavioral Medicine*, Vol. 12, 1989, pp. 207–218.

19. Cleary, P. D., J. L. Hitchcock, N. Semmer, L. J. Flinchbaugh, and J. M. Pinney, "Adolescent Smoking: Research and Health Policy," *Milbank Quarterly*, Vol. 66, No. 1, 1988, pp. 137–171.

20. Glynn, T. J., "Essential Elements of School-based Smoking Prevention Programs," *Journal of School Health*, Vol. 59, No. 5, 1989, pp. 181–188.

21. Botvin, G. J., J. W. Batson, S. Witts-Vitale, V. Bess, E. Baker, and L. Dusenbury, "A Psychosocial Approach to Smoking Prevention for Urban Black Youth," *Public Health Reports*, Vol. 104, 1989a, pp. 573–582.

22. Botvin, G. J., L. Dusenbury, E. Baker, S. James-Ortiz, and J. Kerner, "A Skills Training Approach to Smoking Prevention Among Hispanic Youth," *Journal of Behavioral Medicine*, Vol. 12, 1989b, pp. 279-296.

23. Ellickson, P. L., and R. M. Bell, "Drug Prevention in Junior High: A Multi-Site Longitudinal Test," *Science*, Vol. 247, 1990, pp. 1299–1305.

24. Dwyer, J. H., D. P. MacKinnon, M. A. Pentz, B. R. Flay, W. B. Hansen, E. Y. I. Wang, and C. A. Johnson, "Estimating Intervention Effects in Longitudinal Studies," *American Journal of Epidemiology*, Vol. 130, No. 4, 1989, pp. 781–795.

25. Pentz, M. A., J. Dwyer, D. MacKinnon, B. Flay, W. Hansen, E. Yang, and C. Johnson, "A Multi-Community Trial for Primary

Prevention of Adolescent Drug Abuse: Effects on Drug Use Prevalence," *Journal of the American Medical Association,* Vol. 261, 1989, pp. 3259–3266.

26. Johnson, C. A., M. A. Pentz, M. D. Weber, J. H. Dwyer, N. Baer, D. P. MacKinnon, and W. B. Hansen, "Relative Effectiveness of Comprehensive Community Programming for Drug Abuse Prevention with High-Risk and Low-Risk Adolescents," *Journal of Consulting and Clinical Psychology,* Vol. 58, No. 4, 1990, pp. 1–10.

27. Dielman, T. E., J. T. Shope, S. L. Leech, A. T. Butchart, "Differential Effectiveness of an Elementary School-based Alcohol Misuse Prevention Program," *Journal of School Health,* Vol. 59, 1989, pp. 255–263.

28. Botvin, G. J., *Factors Inhibiting Drug Use: Teacher and Peer Effects,* Rockville, Md.: National Institute on Drug Abuse, 1987.

29. Hansen, W. B., C. A. Johnson, B. R. Flay, J. W. Graham, and J. Sobel, "Affective and Social Influences Approaches to the Prevention of Multiple Substance Abuse Among Seventh Grade Students: Results from Project SMART," *Preventive Medicine,* Vol. 17, No. 2, 1988, pp. 93–114.

30. Perry, C. L., M. Grant, G. Ernberg, R. U. Florenzano, M. C. Langdon, A. D. Myeni, R. Waalhberg, S. Berg, K. Andersson, K. J. Fisher, D. Blaze-Temple, D. Cross, B. Saunders, D. R. Jacobs, Jr., and T. Schmid, "WHO Collaborative Study on Alcohol Education and Young People: Outcomes of a Four-Country Pilot Study," *International Journal of the Addictions,* Vol. 24, No. 12, 1989, pp. 1145–1172.

31. Ringwalt, C., S. T. Ennett, and K. D. Holt, "An Outcome Evaluation of Project DARE," *Drug Abuse Resistance Education: What Do We Know About School-based Prevention Strategies?* Papers from University of San Diego Extension Conference, October 1990, pp. 138–151.

32. Barth, R. P., J. V. Fetro and N. Leland et al., "Preventing Teenage Pregnancy with Social and Cognitive Skills," *Journal of Adolescent Research,* in press.

33. Howard, M., and McCabe, J. B., "Helping Teenagers Postpone Sexual Involvement," *Family Planning Perspectives*, Vol. 22, 1990, pp. 21–26.

34. Eisen, M., G. L. Zellman, and A. L. McAlister et al., "Evaluating the Impact of a Theory-based Sexuality and Contraceptive Education Program," *Family Planning Perspectives*, Vol. 22, No. 6, 1990, pp. 261–271.

35. Flay, B., et al., "Are Social Psychological Smoking Prevention Programs Effective?: The Waterloo Study," *Journal of Behavioral Medicine*, Vol. 8, No. 5, 1989, pp. 37–59.

36. Hays, R. D., and P. L. Ellickson, "How Generalizable Are Adolescents' Beliefs About Pro-Drug Pressures and Resistance Self-Efficacy?" *Journal of Applied Social Psychology*, Vol. 20, No. 4, 1990, pp. 321–340.

37. Warner, K., "The Effects of the Antismoking Campaign on Cigarette Consumption," *American Journal of Public Health*, Vol. 67, 1977, pp. 645–650.

38. Ellickson, P. L., and R. D. Hays, "On Becoming Involved with Drugs: Modeling Adolescent Drug Use Over Time," *Health Psychology*, in press.

39. Werner, E. E., and R. S. Smith, *Vulnerable but Invincible: A Longitudinal Study of Resilient Children and Youth*, New York: McGraw–Hill, 1982.

40. Rutter, M., "Resilience in the Face of Adversity: Protective Factors and Resistance to Psychiatric Disorder," *British Journal of Psychiatry*, Vol. 147, 1985, pp. 598–611.

41. Baumrind, D., "Child Care Practices Anteceding Three Patterns of Preschool Behavior," *Genetic Psychology Monographs*, Vol. 75, 1965, pp. 43–88.

42. Elliot, D., D. Huizinga, and S. Ageton, *Explaining Delinquency and Drug Use*, Beverly Hills, Calif.: Sage Publications, 1985.

43. Ellickson, P. L., and R. D. Hays, "Antecedents of Drinking Among Young Adolescents with Different Alcohol Use

Histories," *Journal of Studies on Alcohol,* Vol. 52, No. 5, 1991, pp. 398–408.

44.   Robins, L. N., and T. Pryzbeck, "Age of Onset of Drug Use as a Factor in Drug and Other Disorders," in *Etiology of Drug Abuse: Implications for Prevention,* National Institute on Drug Abuse, DHHS Publication No. (ADM)85-1335:178–192, 1985.

45.   National Academy of Sciences, National Research Council, Commission on Behavioral and Social Sciences and Education, Committee on Child Development Research and Public Policy, Panel on Adolescent Pregnancy and Childbearing, *Risking the Future: Adolescent Sexuality, Pregnancy, and Childbearing, Volume I,* C. D. Hayes (ed.), Washington, D.C.: National Academy Press, 1985.

46.   Berrueta-Clement, J. R., L. J. Schweinhart, W. S. Barnett, A. S. Epstein, and D. P. Weikart, *Changed Lives: The Effects of the Perry Preschool Program on Youths Through Age 19,* Ypsilanti, Mich.: High Scope Press, 1984.

47.   Comer, James P., "The Yale-New Haven Primary Prevention Project: A Follow-up Study," *Journal of the American Academy of Child Psychiatry,* Vol. 24, 1985, pp. 154–160.

48.   Alan Guttmacher Institute, *Teenage Pregnancy in the United States: The Scope of the Problem and State Responses,* New York, 1989.

Chapter Five

Urban Education
Paul T. Hill

The decline of big American cities can be measured by the collapse of their public schools. Before the immigration wave of the late 1980s, the public school systems of the most important U.S. metropolises, including New York, Chicago, Los Angeles, Boston, and Houston, had suffered enrollment declines averaging 30 percent, and their student populations had become increasingly poor and welfare dependent. Working and middle class students of all racial and ethnic groups have deserted the big city public schools for suburban and private schools.

Until the 1950s, many big city school systems were among the best in the country. The New York, Chicago, and Boston public school systems, among others, were America's greatest sources of successful and outstanding business leaders, public officials, and scholars. Small town and rural schools were generally considered inferior in teacher quality, classrooms and other instructional resources, and community support. Since that time, however, urban schools have declined dramatically; half the students in big city school systems drop out before high school graduation, four times the national average rate. The majority of students in big city public schools drop behind the national average in reading after the fourth grade and never catch up. Only one-third of the graduates of some big city public high schools can score well enough on the military qualifying tests to enlist in the armed forces.

Since the days of their early success, the big city schools have changed in many ways. Schools built near the end of the 19th century are still in use, and many are suffering from decades of neglect. Spending in city schools, once the highest in the country, is now lower than the statewide average in many states. [1,2] School boards, once staid collections of educated citizens, are now arenas for conflict among the politically ambitious. Most schools are burdened by layer after layer of regulations emanating from board politics, federal and state funding programs, and court orders. Teachers are unionized, and their contracts, after decades of bargaining in which school boards made concessions on work rules rather than grant wage demands, constrain any attempt to adapt school programs to new needs.

The combined effect of all these trends is to make big city public school systems weak and inflexible—exactly the wrong characteristics for organizations that must master an exceptionally turbulent situation. City student populations are changing faster than at any time since the turn of the century, and city school budgets are declining even as their student populations increase. Since the 1960s, the student populations of most big cities have changed from majority white to majority Hispanic or black. After a period of enrollment decline caused by "white flight," many city school populations have grown dramatically due to immigration. Since the late-1980s, New York, Los Angeles, Chicago, and Miami have collectively enrolled nearly 100,000 new students each year who are either foreign born or children of immigrants. City school budgets are falling as dramatically as their populations are rising. New York, Chicago, and Los Angeles have had to make crippling midyear cuts in their school budgets in each of the last three years. No one knows how much Los Angeles must cut during the 1992–1993 school year, which is about to begin, but a good estimate is $240 million from a general fund budget of $2.9 billion plus smaller cuts in state categorical programs and capital funds. [3] Chicago must cut over $200 million from a budget of $2.3 billion; according to best estimates, Chicago must continue cutting and will still face a deficit of over $500 million in the 1997–1998 school year. [4]

It is hard to imagine how any organization could provide consistently good services in such a turbulent environment. Schools must have consistent and predictable funding, and the cuts of the last five years must be restored. But funding is not enough. If funding is used only to restore existing programs, schools will still not be effective for immigrants, for whom existing programs and materials are not appropriate, or for native-born minority students, whom the schools were failing long before the present fiscal crisis began. [3]

Big city schools are also embedded in communities that lack sound economic bases and are burdened by crime, unemployment, teenage parenthood, child abandonment, drug use, and disease. These problems, too, must be solved if children born in the inner city are to have the educational and career opportunities available to other Americans. The growth and persistence of these problems demonstrate a lack of public and private capacity to give inner-city children a fair shot at life.

In several RAND studies conducted in the past few years, we have interviewed many educators who claim that the schools are helpless in the face of these problems. Nothing can be done, they claim, until the schools get more money and children get better prenatal and health care, better home environments, and more conventional adult role models. Other educators draw a quite different conclusion: that the schools must become comprehensive social service agencies, delivering health, family planning, counseling, and income support services. These respondents may disagree about whether schools should wait for other services or aggressively seek to provide them, but they agree that the real problems are not in the schools but elsewhere and that schools would work if only children were properly cared for by their parents and the broader community.

This chapter makes the contrary argument: that public schools contribute to the problems of today's urban youth and that schools must do a better job of educating students. It admits that schools are burdened by the urban environment but contends that we cannot wait to change schools until other problems are solved. It grants that someone must address problems, such as poor student health and family instability, but argues that educators have enough to worry about in their own backyards. Better schools will not solve all the problems of American cities, but they are definitely part of the solution. The remainder of this chapter argues four points:

- Bad public schools are making their own distinct contributions to the problems of cities.

- There is a substantial consensus among educators and parents about how schools can be made to work for disadvantaged and minority students in the big cities.

- Better inner-city schools are unlikely given today's methods of financing and governance.

- Better schools are possible in the inner city but only if we make a major change in what is meant by a public school.

SCHOOLS MAKE THEIR OWN CONTRIBUTION TO URBAN ILLS

The Rodney King verdict was the spark that ignited the tinder of poor urban neighborhoods in Los Angeles. Those arrested in the ensuing violence were largely young adult males, unemployed and embittered. These conditions are established during the years of children's supposed compulsory attendance in school. Starting in the seventh grade, low-income urban students develop poor school attendance habits; most rapidly fall behind in their classes and eventually fail many. Those students who do attend school regularly learn to standards far lower than those expected by employers and postsecondary training institutions.

RAND studies of inner-city schools in Los Angeles and elsewhere have repeatedly encountered high school juniors and seniors who have never read local newspapers, have no knowledge about the local economic base or the names of major local employers, and do not know the location or significance of local landmarks. [3,5] These children have grown up isolated from the broader community in ghettos that provide few avenues of access to mainstream economic, cultural, and political life. Like the poor minority children whom Coles studied in Northern Ireland and South Africa, the children of our inner cities see government and its political processes as closed and indifferent, likely to do things to them, not for them. [6] They may serve as spectators through radio, television, and movies, but they do not prepare themselves and do not expect to take part in life in environments unlike their own. Aside from the media, such children's contact with the broader society is mainly through the police, whom they regard as a hostile and punitive force, not a source of help or protection. Even those who enter the legitimate economy through jobs in fast-food establishments or small retail stores usually stay in their own neighborhoods and deal mainly with people of similar background.

The school programs that most inner-city minority students encounter do little to remedy their isolation from the broader community. As several RAND studies by Oakes have shown, public high schools, especially in urban areas, "track" students on the basis of the motivation and performance levels they display on entering the ninth grade. [7,8] Students with poor attendance records or deficient mastery of basic skills (as is the case with a majority of students in most urban high schools) are typically assigned to remedial drill and practice on reading and arithmetic. Remedial instruction is boring; poorly motivated students seldom learn much from it or persist in it long. Even those students who stick with full-time remedial instruction seldom progress quickly enough to join the regular high school curriculum. Only a few ever take the normal "gatekeeper" courses that prepare students for college and good jobs (e.g., algebra, geometry, English literature, world history, or laboratory science).

Even when remedial instruction does teach students how to read, write, and figure, it does not teach them how those skills are used in adult life. Remedial classes teach skills subjects in isolation from one another and leave it up to the student to see and exploit the connections. Students in such classes do not take part in writing and research projects that give others at least some experience of using skills in combination. [8,9,10,11] Schools in general may do too little to help students learn how to integrate and use what they know, but remedial instruction does nothing to that end.

Urban public schools are also poor places to learn about how adults work in the real world. The only adults whom students observe working on a daily basis are teachers. Yet public schools are a poor model because they are not organized to be productive. They exemplify the kinds of businesses more typical of the United States in the 1960s and 1970s that were either restructured or failed in the 1980s and 1990s. Work is routinized and most workers (teachers) understand only their own duties, not the whole productive process. A few individuals work desperately hard and take responsibility for the results, but they are as likely to be regarded as zealots and nuisances as to be imitated and rewarded. Workers are accountable for following rules, not for contributing to overall success. Top management acts without consulting with workers to use their expertise or gain their support. [5]

Few teachers are concerned with their school's general appearance or climate; even those who are effective in controlling their own classrooms seldom act in response to disruptions outside their classrooms or obvious student truancy or class cutting. A norm of mutual noninterference also discourages teachers from identifying colleagues who are poorly prepared or who consistently turn out below-par students. [12]

Many teachers think they have no warrant for action beyond their instructional duties and fear (sometimes correctly) that students or other teachers might resent interference. Many urban teachers also exercise "leniency" in dealing with students, lowering standards for behavior and academic attainment. Lenient treatment of students is often well intentioned, motivated by teachers' reluctance to burden students who already have difficult lives. It is often reinforced by administrators' reluctance to back teachers who become controversial because of their demands on students. But the result is an impoverished education, producing students who are not even aware that their behavior and knowledge are insufficient for a successful life in the broader community.

Many teachers and principals think of themselves as administrators of a public agency. They feel responsible to deliver a prescribed curriculum and to respect students' rights as defined by law. As one principal told a RAND researcher, "My job is to make sure this school runs according to the policies and regulations of the _____ school system."

Albert Shanker of the American Federation of Teachers quotes a teacher's statement that encapsulates the problem: "I taught them but they did not learn it." The implication that the teacher is responsible to deliver material, but not to make sure that students master it, demonstrates teachers' bounded responsibility. Student respondents in a recent RAND survey demonstrated this attitude in another way. Several said, "I hate it when the teachers say, 'I get paid whether you learn this or not.'" Teachers may come to these attitudes through years of frustration, but students (and their parents as well as researchers and other outsiders) often see teachers as dutiful only within the letter of their job descriptions.

The nature of teachers' work has important consequences for what students learn about adult life. Students who see teachers executing narrow routines and avoiding collaboration or responsibility for the results of their work are unlikely to imagine that their own work as adults will require risk taking, solving of unfamiliar problems, shared responsibility, and concern for the ultimate success or failure of the enterprise in which they work. As this author has argued elsewhere, the kind of climate prevalent in urban public schools—high schools especially—teaches students that actions seldom have consequences and that "they," not "we," are responsible for making an organization work. [5]

Employers' complaints about young workers focus more on students' judgment and responsibility than on their mastery of basic skills. Employer surveys, such as those conducted by the Michigan State Employment Service, and national consultative bodies, such as the Labor Secretary's Commission on Necessary Skills (SCANS), focus on students' ability to solve problems, interpret general rules in light of particular circumstances, collaborate, and manage interpersonal relations. These skills may require the ability to read and do arithmetic, but they also require accepting responsibility, willingness to tackle the unknown, and adaptation. These actions are seldom taught or modeled in urban schools. The result is that many low-income urban students are unprepared to operate effectively in mainstream adult roles.

WHAT IS NEEEDED FROM SCHOOLS

A casual observer of school politics might think that Americans are deeply divided about what makes a good school. The debates about the need for a multicultural curriculum, instruction to maintain immigrant students' native languages, or teachers' right to use corporal punishment, represent serious differences of opinion on real issues. But by focusing attention on issues on which people disagree, these debates obscure a broad consensus about the essence of a good school. This consensus is evident from surveys of parent attitudes, from studies of teacher beliefs, and from the results of efforts to design better schools, which demonstrate agreement on a number of key elements of a good school.

- Teachers know their material and present it well.

- Each child is led to learn and accomplish as much as she can.

- Students who fall behind or encounter problems get help.

- The school works as a partner with parents, communicating clearly what their children will experience and why. Partnership means that the school respects parents' concerns and aspirations and that parents support the school's demands on students.

- Adults in the school form personal relationships with children and take responsibility for how well every child learns.

- Adults in the school set good examples of fairness, honesty, and generosity.

Despite the strong consensus on the importance of these factors, few schools provide them all. Two principles of effective schooling underlie this list: the first is concentrating effort on education, not delivery of social services or other noninstructional functions; the second is expecting that students, teachers, and parents will work long and hard and in as many different ways as are necessary to ensure that students learn.

Focus on Education

The first principle of effective schools is that they must educate. Many urban schools have lost their grip on that central fact. Schools must ensure that students have the opportunity to learn the bodies of knowledge that mark an adult in our society. They must also help students understand the world in which they will live and work. That cannot and does not happen in schools whose leaders have become preoccupied with social services. Out of concern for the stresses in students' lives, many urban public schools have become centers for social work and such ancillary services as health care, counseling, infant day care, and housing. Though teachers' time is seldom consumed by these activities, the attention of principals and administrators often is. Principals and senior administrators often spend major parts of their time coordinating the services of nurses and physicians, day care workers for students' babies, psychological counselors, and security officers. Once a school becomes committed to providing such services, administrators must also work constantly to obtain grant funds and maintain the cooperation of provider agencies.

Administrators find these activities rewarding because student benefits are often quick and obvious. School administrators also have more freedom and experience less conflict in dealing with social service agencies than with the school system's central office or the teachers' union. But the result of a preoccupation with social services is that school administrators often leave the instructional program to the teachers. And though many teachers work well without supervision, the result for the school as a whole is that there is no mechanism for setting priorities, establishing collaboration, and evaluating overall performance.

As one commentator recently said about American political parties, if one worries too much about the fringes, after a time the entire enterprise becomes fringe. Schools can easily become holding companies for diverse uncoordinated activities that do not add up. The results, in students' educational experience and in their learning about the nature of productive adult enterprise, have been described above.

Unflagging Commitment

The second principle of effective schooling is what Robert Slavin calls "relentlessness." [13] To beat the odds in dealing with disadvantaged students, schools must never let up. Teachers must keep trying, to the point of working individually with students who are not learning from regular classroom instruction. Parental support must be enlisted to ensure that students attend school every day and complete all their assignments. Students must be pressed to keep working, assured that they, their parents, and teachers can together overcome any obstacles to learning.

The example of urban Catholic schools, many of which now serve disadvantaged minority students drawn from the same population as public school students, is instructive. Catholic high schools, in particular, are built to put students under strong pressure to work and achieve and to ensure that all students encounter the same core of adult materials in English, science, mathematics, and history. They also expressly prepare students for adulthood, ensuring that they understand the local economy and political system well enough to become full participants. As the author has described elsewhere in *High Schools with Character,* the Catholic schools offer students a demanding bargain. [5] Students, including the many minority students who enter high school academically years behind and with poor junior high attendance records, are told that they must work hard and cooperate with the school's efforts to help them. In return they are assured that they can succeed academically and that the school will do everything in its power to make it so. The schools are accountable to parents, who can register displeasure by taking students out, but they are also aggressive in demanding that parents supervise students and reinforce the schools' demands. Catholic schools also prove their ability to deliver on the bargain by introducing new students to recent graduates who, like themselves, entered high school with grave academic problems.

The focus on instruction and dedication to leading disadvantaged students through a challenging curriculum is built into urban Catholic schools. Many of them were built in the early 20th century to give immigrants a start toward full participation in American life, and they are still staffed and managed expressly for that purpose. But these capabilities are not limited to private schools. Many public schools, including one or a few in almost every inner-city area, avoid the traps of bureaucracy and preoccupation with remedial instruction. Some are renegade schools run by principals who simply defy school boards and unions to disrupt an obviously successful school. Some were also built by school boards and superintendents to attract working white and black families who threatened to leave the public school system. These schools are driven by their missions and by the dedication of their staffs, not by rules. Like the inner-city Catholic schools, they now serve large numbers of students who are several years behind in basic skills. They teach a demanding curriculum, assuming that students faced with real mental challenges and interesting materials can learn basic skills rapidly. Though some students need an intensive first year, including weekend and summer classes from the end of the eighth grade until the beginning of the tenth, virtually all can learn standard high school materials by the beginning of the tenth grade.

Schools built expressly to educate disadvantaged students are distinctive in many ways. Unlike most public schools, they do not assume that students' values, motivations, and abilities are fixed by early adolescence. They set out deliberately to motivate and change students. They do so by setting specific goals for what students should be able to do when they leave the school and by organizing the whole school around a definite theory or approach to instruction.

They teach basic skills and standard academic subjects but integrate them with other experiences designed to prepare students to function as adults in jobs and professions. Students are introduced to the broader community, not isolated from it.

The promises such schools make about what students will encounter while in school and what they can do upon leaving are matched to demands about what the student must do to succeed. Teachers and administrators are not afraid to make demands on students. On the contrary, they assume that students need to work and that rigorous academic demands can put meaning and structure into students' lives. These schools demonstrate the rewards of hard work and build students' self-esteem by showing them that they can meet high standards.

Effective urban public schools are not all alike. Some are career oriented, preparing students for good jobs in particular industries, such as health care, government service, and finance. Some are college prep oriented, but their programs are based on well-defined and integrated approaches, such as Ted Sizer's "Essential Schools" approach or the International Baccalaureate. [14]

Like inner-city Catholic schools, effective public schools stand for something in particular. They are not work places for groups of autonomous teachers or holding companies for diverse social service providers. They are *schools* where adults and students work together to attain a definite outcome. These schools work. There is an unbroken chain of evidence from the early 1970s until the present that students attending public schools with these characteristics have better attendance records, gain credits more rapidly, take more demanding courses, have higher graduation rates, are more likely to graduate on time, get higher SAT scores, and are more likely to enter four-year colleges. [5,10,14,15]

In most central cities, parents clamor to get their children into such schools. Parents in some localities camp out overnight to be first in line to enroll their children in schools that offer specially focused programs. In New York City, which offers a small number of nonselective "magnet" schools (in addition to the selective magnets like the Bronx High School of Science), some such schools have 20 and 30 times as many applicants as they have available seats. The schools parents want are in short supply because they differ from the dominant model of regulated and bureaucratic schooling.

HOW THE SYSTEM IS STACKED AGAINST
BETTER PUBLIC SCHOOLS

Why did we get schools that are different from what everyone wants? The answer is complex and, because it lacks a single villain, unsatisfying. We, the adult Americans who vote, pay taxes, and badger or praise elected officials, made them that way. We made them through the gradual accretion of small decisions, not by design. Since the mid-1960s, when schools first became the focus of social policy, they have been subject to layer after layer of rules, regulations, court orders, teacher contract provisions, and other formal rules that bind and delimit what teachers and principals can do. Do schools have too few or too many minority students or does a desegregated school have too many segregated classes? The answer is a rule or court order. Are handicapped children neglected in some schools? The answer is a new legal principle and access to the courts for aggrieved parents. Do some students need extra help in school? The answer is a series of federal and state categorical programs, each with its own set of controls designed to ensure that the services bought with federal and state monies go to the intended beneficiaries and no one else.

Taken one by one, most of these policies and programs seem reasonable. So do the literally hundreds of other rules made by local school boards, state legislatures and state education agencies, Congress, the U.S. Department of Education, and federal and state courts. So do the many rules governing when schools open and close, how many minutes teachers may teach, and how a principal may supervise and evaluate a teacher, all agreed to one by one by school boards who chose to make work rule concessions rather than meet teachers' union salary demands. [16] In the aggregate, however, the accretion of rules has created schools that no one would have consciously designed and that do not work.

A highly regulated school system does not work because no one is personally responsible for whether children learn. The people inside the system, teachers, principals, and administrators, are responsible for performing tasks specified by regulations and contracts and for respecting the turf of others. Most teachers and their supervisors care about children, and many complain that their schools are hurt by a few "time servers" who do not work hard and will not cooperate with efforts to upgrade instruction. Poor performers are safe if they can demonstrate compliance and rectitude. Parents and community members who complain about poor results are often told that nothing can be done as long as no rules have been violated. School boards, caught in the web of their own rules, can do little about failing schools. Los Angeles and every other big city has dozens of schools that have abjectly failed students for years, producing several times more dropouts, truants, and semiliterate graduates than the local average. The board or superintendent may take marginal actions (e.g., replacing a principal or adding a new program to supplement the school's inadequate core program). A school is seldom changed fundamentally as long as it complies with all applicable regulations.

Public schools that focus on education and offer their students a specific approach to learning are rare because our system of public control naturally produces a different kind of school. On important matters where school boards are divided, policies are very carefully drawn to satisfy as many people as possible and to compensate pressure groups that lose on one issue with a win on another. The natural result is a system of schools in which all are constrained by the same thicket of requirements.

The foregoing is enough to explain much of the critique of public schools. It certainly accounts for the fact that public schools try to be all things to all people and are unable to develop coherent philosophies of education. Something else is needed, however, to explain why schools in poor areas are usually worse than schools in wealthy ones. District revenues are, of course, part of the picture. Differences in local property tax valuation and the general economic plight of big cities limit the funding available for city schools.

But some of the most striking differences in school quality are evident *within* city school districts. Even with their limited revenue bases, cities like Chicago and New York are able to create some of the best schools in the country that coexist in the same system with some of the worst. There are two keys to this striking inequality within cities. The first is politics: to hold on to middle class students and demonstrate their commitment to quality, city school systems often create "flagship schools." These schools may or may not get more public funds than others, but the staff members are free to develop instructional themes and adapt curriculum to students' needs. Many of these flagship schools also get support from national foundations and reform networks, which further enhance their independence and flexibility.

The second key to inequality within cities is teacher allocation. Teachers' union contracts with big city public school districts all give senior teachers first choice about jobs and school placements. Not surprisingly, senior teachers tend to congregate in schools located in safe and attractive neighborhoods with supportive parents and responsive students. Schools in less attractive neighborhoods have trouble attracting and keeping senior teachers. They have to accept newer, less-experienced teachers and, in many cases, teachers who lack complete training or who scored poorly on state teachers' exams.

The teacher allocation process leads to staff instability in low-income area schools. Many teachers with good qualifications leave such schools as soon as they have the seniority to do so. It also leads to lower *de facto* funding for poverty area schools. Schools are billed for teacher salaries as if all teachers cost the same amount. But senior teachers cost two and one-half times as much as beginning teachers in most cities. Since over 70 percent of all school costs go for teachers' salaries, schools with all senior teachers can cost nearly twice as much as schools with all junior teachers. The recent settlement of a lawsuit, *Rodriguez v. Los Angeles Unified School District,* may lead to the elimination of some of these funding inequities.

Job protections for senior teachers pose another problem for cities with rapidly changing populations like Los Angeles. As RAND's recent study of immigrant education showed, many schools serving immigrant populations are dominated by teachers who are left over from earlier times when all students were native born. [16] During times of budget crisis, school systems can neither create vacancies to hire new teachers with the appropriate language skills nor change school staffs rapidly as student needs change.

Not all inner-city schools are defeated by these factors. A few schools in every city attract and keep dedicated staff members and work aggressively to meet students' needs. But these schools work despite the system, not because of it. Like all systems, the public schools operate pretty much as they were designed most of the time. The result is that most inner-city public schools are bureaucratic, weak, unlikely to change on their own, and resistant to change from the outside.

In the past few years, superintendents and civic leaders in a number of cities have recognized that their schools were not working and have tried to create an instantaneous reform. They have declared "site-based management" an opportunity for principals and teachers in existing schools to use their own judgment in changing school programs to meet the needs of children. Site-based management plans in places like Miami, Chicago, Los Angeles, and New York gave teachers and parents greater influence over school-level decision making. But, as a recent RAND report shows, the roles of the superintendent, school board, and central office bureaucracy did not change. [9] School communities, though urged to change themselves, are still tied up by the same inequitable school budgets, limitations on the use of funds, teacher contract provisions, and central office regulations. Some parent councils in Chicago exercised their authority to fire their principals; others elsewhere found new ways to use the few thousand dollars of flexible equipment and supplies money available to each school. But very few were able to focus on a basic review of the school's performance and devise significant improvements. The existing system had kept its strings on them.

The big city system of governance and finance that produces weak public schools is robust and persistent. Though many teachers and administrators criticize the system, most find their individual jobs safe and tolerable. Civil service protections and union contracts ensure that schools deal fairly and consistently with adults, even if they do not work well for children. The system also deals very efficiently with challenges. Outstanding principals and community leaders can flout convention, but they are isolated and few; when they leave or retire, their schools usually regress toward the systemwide mean. Schools that receive special attention from outside funding sources and reform leaders are also allowed to distinguish themselves. But they too often become Potemkin villages, protecting the system from criticism by focusing attention on its few excellent schools.

Can a city like Los Angeles create a public school system that is less bound by its rules and adult protections and more able to promote school quality and adaptiveness? The final section in this chapter argues that the answer is yes.

AN ALTERNATIVE PUBLIC SCHOOL SYSTEM

A solution to the problems of today's schools must overcome tendencies that are inherent in the structure of large urban public school systems. An alternative school system must free the schools from micromanagement by the school board and other political bodies; it must remedy the inequities of funding and teacher allocation that exist within most urban districts; it must allow development of schools with specific approaches to education so that staff members can feel responsible for what they produce and parents can hold them accountable; it must force school boards and superintendents to act when they discover that a school is consistently failing its students.

A radical solution preferred by some is school choice based on consumer initiative. [17] The plan would give every child in a locality a voucher worth the current per pupil cost of public schooling. Parents could use the voucher to pay for tuition at any school, public or private. Parents would, presumably, seek out the better schools and avoid the weaker ones. Drawn by the possibility of lucrative tuition payments, entrepreneurs would offer alternatives to unpopular schools. In the long run, weak schools would be eliminated, strong ones would take their place, and all schools would feel the pressure of competition to maintain quality.

A choice plan including private schools raises the spectre of public funds being used to support Catholic and other sectarian schools. Some choice advocates have therefore proposed an all-public choice scheme, in which parents could choose any public school.*

The advantages of school choice are evident in light of the foregoing discussion of public school problems. School boards would not have to agree on what is the one best model of schooling for all students. Diverse tastes and demands could be satisfied by diverse schools. Schools would compete on quality, but like other sellers of complex services, they would also have to differentiate their product to appeal to purchasers' tastes and loyalty. Parents and students would therefore know what to expect from a school. Though schools could not discriminate in admissions, they could impose requirements related to student attendance and effort. As the research on magnet schools makes clear, students who choose a particular school knowing what it requires (even if they only consider it their least-bad alternative) have a greater incentive to meet its requirements than students who have no choice about where they will go. [5,15]

Schools would be forced to attract students and would therefore pay close attention to student needs and parent preferences. Funding would be explicitly based on attendance, not driven by the locational preferences of senior teachers or political negotiations. Schools would live and die on their reputations; teachers and principals would therefore have a strong incentive to collaborate, to press one another for good performance, to weed out weak staff members, and to work as hard as necessary to build their school's clientele. Like private schools, these schools would have to be concerned about their graduates, whether they could succeed in jobs and higher education and cope with adult life.

But choice plans, whether all-public or public-private, have a glaring problem. Vouchers may increase parents' capacity to demand better schools, but it is not clear where alternatives to the existing bad schools are to come from. Even in New York City, where Catholic schools educate over 100,000 students and constitute the twelfth largest school system in the country, there is no room for the 1,000,000 public school students. If choice is to provide new opportunities for all students, a much larger supply of good schools must be created.

For choice to have any appreciable effect on the quality of schooling in Los Angeles, a massive effort to create new schools or redevelop existing ones would be necessary. That is unlikely to happen purely through private investment. Some investors and community service organizations might venture to start one or two schools each, but only a few are likely to consider troubled central city areas the best place to start. The demand for better schools is high in inner suburbs and in minority working class areas, but prudent entrepreneurs will start in less challenging environments.

For the foreseeable future, a reform built solely on consumer choice will leave central cities with the problem they started with (i.e., how to create a large enough supply of good schools to serve all students). Choice does not eliminate the need for a strategy to improve public schools.

There are promising approaches to the supply problem. Several national organizations are creating new designs for schools and are building the capacity to help public school systems form new schools (or redevelop existing ones) around these designs. These design organizations are sponsored by foundations such as RJR Nabisco, Macy, and Exxon, and many work out of major universities. Professor Henry Levin runs such an organization at Stanford, and others exist at Harvard, Yale, and Brown. Other design organizations (e.g., Christopher Whittle's Edison Project) are privately sponsored and hope either to work under contract to local school districts or to run private schools with money from education vouchers.

These design organizations could provide the supply side of the market envisioned by choice advocates. They could develop school concepts, test and demonstrate their feasibility and appeal, and then offer them to parents in one or many localities. Like Montessori and the Catholic religious orders, they could ensure that the staff of a school were properly trained to run it and that a competent parent organization was available to monitor quality and help solve problems.

A national effort to create such design organizations is sponsored by the New American Schools Development Corporation (NASDC), a coalition of business leaders. Among the projects sponsored by NASDC is a Los Angeles–based effort to design an inner-city school that will use older students as tutors for younger ones and focus the efforts of all neighborhood adults on education. Other designs sponsored by NASDC include a school based on old-fashioned character building and study of the classics; schools in which students learn basic skills in the course of research projects; and schools using computers in all phases of instruction. Within three years, NASDC's design teams will be available to help communities all around the country use its designs to build new schools or redevelop existing ones.

Some public agencies are creating their own design and assistance organizations. The school systems of Philadelphia and New York City are both creating new "theme" schools that take over the buildings of failed neighborhood schools and offer students choices among simple, focused, goal-oriented schools. State governments in Ohio, Oregon, and Wyoming are also developing capacities to help school systems identify and redevelop their weakest schools.

All these organizations are creating alternatives to existing public schools. None seek to become the universal model for all the schools in a locality. They are creating a menu of alternative approaches that school systems can use as they try to improve or redevelop their worst schools. The designers sponsored by NASDC, in particular, intend within five years to offer their services to any school system that wants to adopt one or more of the new designs.

However, with the exception of the efforts sponsored by the New York and Philadelphia schools, new designs for individual schools do not change the ways that public school systems do business. One or two well-designed new schools in inner-city Los Angeles (or several hundred schools nationwide) do not amount to a solution to the problems of urban education. Today's urban public school systems are built to manage large numbers of schools via regulation and compliance enforcement. They are not built to create and nurture a variety of schools or to invest in the redevelopment of schools that have gone bad. Unless we find a new way to govern whole systems of urban schools, the new designs can only slightly increase the number of exemplary-but-not-imitated public schools.

Can we find a way to govern public schools that permits and encourages variety and that moves quickly to supply better schools in place of ones that have failed their students or that nobody wants? Can we build a public school system that nurtures the development of clear, coherent educational approaches in individual schools so that parents have real choices?

A rough blueprint for a public school system that offers the benefits of choice is suggested in David Osborne and Ted Gaebler's new book, *Reinventing Government.* [18] They argue that the key to improving schools and other public institutions is to separate governance from the delivery of services. Governance bodies like school boards naturally tend to create uniformity. Because they have formal authority over schools, they find it difficult to resist constituent pressure to settle every problem or complaint with a rule that prevents the offending circumstance from arising again. The result is that a problem that arises in one school leads to rules that constrain all schools—even those in which the problem had either been handled smoothly or had not arisen at all. Because many such problems concern the treatment of employees, public bodies like school boards gradually constrain the schools—and themselves—with elaborate civil service employment rules and union contracts.

Osborne and Gaebler argue that public bodies can be saved from their own tendency to overregulate. Their strategy for separating policy-making bodies from the day-to-day management of services is to have services delivered under contract. Public decision-making bodies can set basic goals and principles of operation (e.g., nondiscrimination in student admissions and teacher hiring), but services will not be delivered by public employees. Services will, instead, be delivered by contractors, operating under limited-term and fixed-cost agreements. Public bodies could retain the right to terminate contracts for nonperformance, and contractors would have no automatic rights of renewal.

Under the contracting scheme, school boards could manage a number of different contracts—with a child development organization for some elementary schools and with a university school of education for others; with an organization like Ted Sizer's Coalition for Essential Schools for some high schools and with a college of arts and sciences or career training academy for others. Nothing would prevent a group of teachers in existing schools from organizing themselves as a contractor. Teachers' unions might offer to run a few schools in one locality; a successful local union might land contracts to provide schools in another school district or even another state.

Public school systems would still need superintendents and some form of a central office, but their roles and powers should be modest. The superintendent's job would be to advise the board on contracting—how to attract good offers; when to warn a failing contractor or reassign some or all of its schools to other contractors. The school system's central office would support the superintendent in this basic monitoring function, but it would not directly supervise principals or teachers or provide in-service training. Contractor organizations would be responsible for those functions. The school board could set general requirements for teacher qualifications and might even negotiate with contractors and the teachers' union about general wage scales. Contractors could be required to hire teachers from the existing city teaching staff, but they would be able to pick those who best fit their schools' approaches to education. The teachers' union might operate as a guild, helping teachers find placements and trying to upgrade the skills of teachers who could not readily find work.

Contracting may be the framework for the solution of many problems of urban schools. It could, if properly implemented, allow school boards to focus on the core issues of what children need to learn and how to save children from schools that are failing them. It could also relieve school boards of the obligation to resolve every complaint about any aspect of school operations. Contracting with statewide or national design organizations such as those discussed above would force school boards to make an explicit allocation of funds to each school, thus eliminating the current within-district inequities in school funding. Many of the teachers and administrators would come from the current teaching force, but they would work in organizations that must maintain quality and will therefore reward good teachers and retrain or replace ineffective ones.

Schools would remain public: they would be funded from tax dollars and would operate under contracts that guaranteed fair admissions, nondiscrimination, and the rights of the disadvantaged. The state could still establish requirements for teacher certification. Local school boards would be, in effect, public investment managers, deciding which contractor's approach best fits a neighborhood's need. Parental choice would force school boards and superintendents to pay special attention to their shakiest investments. Schools that had become unpopular would lose students and force a reallocation of district funds. When troubled schools became too small to run economically, contractors would be forced either to negotiate for higher per pupil payments or default on their contracts. In either case, the board and superintendent would face an action-forcing event. Even if the board shirked its duty during the life of a contract, the end of a contractor's term would force a new decision.

A board that could not get contractors to bid on a particular set of schools would know quickly that it needed to offer more money or more realistic terms. This might be a warrant for selectively allocating federal or state categorical program funds. If a school district consistently had trouble attracting contractors for its schools, the state government would have a clear signal that something must be done—a review of the district's contracting methods and specifications, special incentive funding for contractors, or reconstitution of the local school district. Failures would be evident and the remedies would be readily available. There would no longer be any justification for tolerating school failure or for leaving generations of children from inner-city neighborhoods in the same ineffective hands.

Contracting with school design organizations, such as those sponsored by the NASDC, can provide a supply of schools that make parental choice meaningful. It also provides a way out for communities like Los Angeles whose schools have collapsed under the old system. No such dramatic change can be instantaneous, but effective steps can be taken now if community leaders and the school board focus on the worst inner-city schools and commit to redeveloping them via contracts with universities and design organizations that will provide a range of focused alternatives for students.

Contracting for schools will not solve all problems. Some contractors may be inadequate and will have to be assisted by others or fired. Some parents may not exercise their rights of choice aggressively and may unwittingly help deficient schools survive. School boards will have to overcome their tendency to "solve" a problem by enacting a new policy (e.g., a new specification for contractors to meet) rather than by looking into the causes and providing needed resources. But contracting will entirely eliminate two sources of problems for today's public schools. First, it will eliminate the central office bureaucracy that is built to control and regulate schools from the outside, replacing it with a much simpler organization built to assist the board in the selection and audit of contractors. Second, it will eliminate the need for the school board to resolve disputes by making rules that apply to all schools. Parents or interest groups with particular tastes in schooling can be encouraged to find a school that suits them rather than petitioning for general policy changes.

CONCLUSION

Many things must change before the immigrant and black students of South Central have the same life prospects as the students of Pacific Palisades and Woodland Hills. Schools cannot overcome all the problems of poverty, unemployment, crime, and community disintegration. They also need stable funding, something that only a more responsible state government can provide. But schools can do much more than they are doing.

The public school system must change fundamentally. Enabling changes in state laws and state and federal funding programs are necessary. But the greatest change must be local. School systems must allocate money to schools fairly. School boards, superintendents, and teachers' unions must all change their modes of operation to work with contractors who operate schools. School system central offices would change most dramatically, from regulators of a monopoly enterprise to evaluators and managers of a set of contracts.

None of these changes is likely to come about solely through the initiative of superintendents, school boards, or teachers' unions—the changes they face are too uncomfortable. Broader community initiative, led by the heads of neighborhood and civil rights organizations, local general purpose governments, and key businesses, is necessary. It is obvious that regulation, exhortation, and pressure on the existing school system cannot do the job. Only a concerted community effort to change the way that the community governs education can save the public schools.

NOTES

*In any case, as Elmore has shown, parent choice of schools would require some degree of government administration. Disputes over the fairness of admissions policies and accuracy of schools' claims would inevitably lead to legal action and mandates for government oversight for publicly funded schools. [19]

REFERENCES

1. U.S. Department of Education, *The Digest of Educational Statistics*, Washington, D.C., 1991.

2. U.S. Department of Education, *The Condition of Education*, Washington, D.C., 1991.

3. McDonnell, Lorraine M., and Paul T. Hill, *Schooling for Immigrant Youth*, Unpublished Research.

4. Booz, Allen and Hamilton, Inc., *Financial Outlook for the Chicago Public Schools*, Chicago, 1992.

5. Hill, Paul T., Gail E. Foster, and Tamar Gendler, *High Schools with Character*, Santa Monica, Calif.: RAND, R-3944-RC, 1990.

6. Coles, Robert, *The Political Lives of Children*, Boston: Houghton Mifflin Co, 1986.

7. Oakes, Jeannie, *Keeping Track*, New Haven: Yale University Press, 1985.

8. Oakes, Jeannie, *Multiplying Inequalities: The Effects of Race, Social Class, and Tracking on Opportunities to Learn Mathematics and Science*, Santa Monica, Calif.: RAND, R-3928-NSF, 1990.

9. Hill, Paul T., and Josephine J. Bonan, *Decentralization and Accountability in Public Education*, Santa Monica, Calif.: RAND, R-4066-MCF/IET, 1991.

10. Lipsitz, Joan, *Successful Schools for Young Adolescents*, New Brunswick, N.J.: Transaction Books, 1983.

11. Perry, Iwani, "A Black Student's Reflection on Public and Private Schools," *Harvard Educational Review*, Vol. 58, No. 3, August 1988, pp. 332–336.

12. Rosenholtz, Susan J., *Teachers' Workplace: The Social Organization of Schools*, New York: Longman, 1989.

13. Slavin, Robert, et al., *Success for All: A Relentless Approach to Prevention and Early Intervention in Elementary Schools*, Arlington, Va.: Education Research Service, 1992.

14. Sizer, Theodore R., *Horace's School: Redesigning the American High School*, New York: Houghton Mifflin Co., 1992.

15. Crain, Robert, et al., *The Effectiveness of New York City's Career Magnets*, Berkeley, Calif.: The National Center for Research on Vocational Education, 1992.

16. McDonnell, Lorraine M., and Anthony H. Pascal, *Teacher Unions and Educational Reform*, Santa Monica, Calif.: RAND, JRE-02, 1988.

17. Chubb, John E., and Terry Moe, *Politics, Markets, and America's Schools*, Washington, D.C.: The Brookings Institution, 1990.

18. Osborne, David, and Ted Gaebler, *Reinventing Government*, Menlo Park, Calif.: Addison-Wesley, 1992.

19. Elmore, Richard, *Choice in Public Education*, New Brunswick, N.J.: Center for Policy Research in Education, 1986.

Chapter Six

Military Service
A Closing Door of Opportunity for Youth

James R. Hosek and Jacob Alex Klerman

Since President Truman desegregated the U.S. armed forces, many of the nation's poor and disadvantaged youth, especially minorities, have looked to military service as a path to opportunity and advancement. The armed forces themselves have promoted the idea that military service will lead to better civilian job opportunities.

As a result of the end of the Cold War, the U.S. military now plans to reduce its active duty enlisted force by 400,000 persons between 1990 and 1997, shrinking it from 1.7 million to 1.3 million personnel. Many people are concerned that this reduction will fall disproportionately on minorities.

The active duty military is the nation's largest employer of young men. From the mid-1970s to the end of the 1980s, about one in every six young men enlisted in the military.* The proportion of young blacks enlisting has been much higher than that of whites or Hispanics. We can capture the changes in enlistment over the last decade and a half by comparing the number of recruits to the total number of 18 year old males for each race/ethnic group (Figure 1). We will refer to this ratio as the percentage of youth enlisting.

Because the active duty force is shrinking, the percentage of youth—black, white, and Hispanic—enlisting has fallen since 1989, the last Cold War year. However, enlistment trends for the three groups are not identical.

Over the entire period, the trend in black enlistments is clearly down both absolutely and relative to whites. In the mid-1970s more than one in four blacks enlisted. In 1986 more than one in five blacks enlisted. In 1991 less than one in 10 blacks enlisted. As opportunities for enlistment in the military shrink, 10 to 15 percent of all young black youths are now looking for a different first job. Put differently,

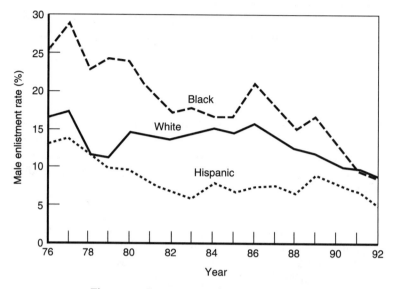

Figure 1—Percentage of Male Youth Enlisting

in 1979 blacks were twice as likely as whites to enlist. Today they are less likely to enlist.

Over the entire period, the pattern for Hispanic enlistments is similar. At its peak in 1977, about 14 percent of all Hispanic young men enlisted. In 1991 a young Hispanic man was only half as likely to enlist (7 percent). In 1978 Hispanics were about as likely to enlist as whites. Today they are only about three-quarters as likely.

This chapter explores the forces underlying these changes, speculates about their possible future paths, and discusses the likely effects of lower enlistment on minority youth. We conclude that the dramatic decrease in the percentage of young black men entering the military derives from the intersection of several forces. The military is shrinking and fewer young men are needed. In addition, the military has become more selective about whom it accepts. Since blacks and Hispanics have lower average scores on the military's "quality" standards, more selective recruiting means fewer blacks and Hispanics are eligible to enlist. Taken together, these factors lead to fewer minorities in the military.[†] This effect may seem somewhat mitigated because a high percentage of eligible minorities actually join the military, in part because the military appears to be a relatively more attractive opportunity for minorities, especially blacks, than whites. But particularly for eligible blacks, the enlistment percentage has fallen rapidly in recent years.

This chapter proceeds as follows. We begin by considering the size of the military and its implications for the number of new enlistments. We then discuss what types of people the military wants and its success in getting them. The third section examines the implications of these recruiting policies for minorities. The paper concludes with a discussion of the implications of these changes for young minority men.

HOW MANY RECRUITS?

Two key factors determine the number of recruits required: the size of the force that needs to be staffed and the rate of personnel turnover. With growing U.S. involvement in the Vietnam War (1965–1968), the armed forces grew by nearly a million men (Figure 2). As U.S. involvement wound down, culminating with the end of the draft and the birth of the all volunteer force (AVF) in 1973, the male enlisted force dropped below the pre-Vietnam level. The force continued to shrink through the early years of the AVF so that the 1980 force level of 1.7 million males was about half a million below the pre-Vietnam level. Much of the decline in the male enlisted force after 1973 was offset by a growing number of women in the military, leaving the size of the total active duty enlisted force fairly constant. From 1980 to 1989 the male enlisted force changed little.[‡] Since 1989, in response to the geopolitical changes in the former Soviet Union and Eastern Europe, the military has begun to reduce its enlisted force by a planned 25 percent.

As the size of the force declined, so too did the rate of turnover (Figure 3). Turnover has declined almost continuously for 25 years; reasons for the decline include the end of the Vietnam War; the shift to an AVF; and timely improvements in military pay, benefits, and bonuses.[§] The combination of a smaller military and lower turnover has considerably reduced the number of recruits, whether

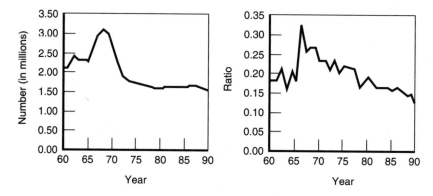

Figure 2—Male Enlisted Force **Figure 3—Ratio of Accessions to Enlisted Force**

measured from the Vietnam peak or even from the beginning of the AVF (Figure 4).

The military recruits from a youth pool that has varied considerably in size over the last three decades (Figure 5). Until 1980, as the baby boomers of the 1950s matured, there were more 18-year-old males in each year than in the previous year. By 1980 the military drew from a pool of young people nearly twice as large as it had been in 1960 (2.2 million 18-year-old men in 1980 vs. 1.2 million in 1960). The succeeding baby bust led to a 20 percent decline in 18-year-old males from 1980 to 1992 (for an early discussion of the role of cohort size, see [1]; for a post–Cold War perspective on these cohort size issues, see [2]). However, the size of the pool of 18 year olds has reached its trough and will rise slowly through the end of the decade.

The stable (and soon growing) youth population, coupled with the rapidly shrinking force size and reduced turnover, accounts for the sharp drop in the percentage of youth enlisting for each race/ethnic group over the period from 1989–1992 (shown in Figure 1).

WHO JOINS THE MILITARY?

Military recruiting commanders are fond of pointing out that the AVF is in reality an "all recruited force." Although under the AVF concept

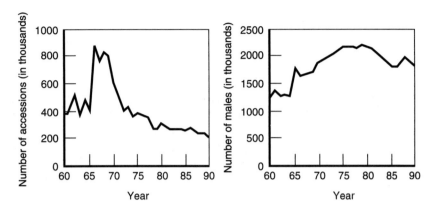

Figure 4—Accessions Have
Fallen Steadily Since Vietnam

Figure 5—18-Year-Old Males
Peaked at the End of the 1970s

only volunteers enlist, the services will not accept everyone who volunteers. Rather, each year the services develop their goals for the quantity and quality of new service members and then actively recruit to meet those goals. The quantity goals depend on the authorized size of the active duty force and the level of retention. Within these quantity goals, the services strive to attract the highest-quality recruits possible, given recruiting budgets (advertising, bonuses, recruiting staff). To determine quality, the military uses two measures: high school graduation status and scores on the Armed Forces Qualification Test (AFQT). Studies show that these measures are good predictors of whether a recruit is likely to complete military training, to complete the first term of service, and to be more proficient in operating and maintaining weapons and performing other military tasks. [3,4,5,6]

The military's success in attracting high-quality youth depends on its ability to offer competitive compensation compared with other available options, such as civilian jobs or college. The military package includes pay, benefits, bonuses, training opportunities, and postservice educational benefits. Prospective recruits compare this package against civilian labor market conditions (unemployment, wages, availability of on-the-job training) and academic opportunities (availability, acceptance, financial aid, ability to self-finance). When the military package is relatively more attractive, the military attracts more high-quality recruits; when it is less attractive, it must make do with lower-quality recruits (for more complete discussion of the compensation package and its effect on this history of the AVF, see [7]).

There is a striking correlation between the relative attractiveness of military versus civilian opportunities and the quality of recruits (for expanded documentation of this point, see [8]). Figures 6 and 7 display two measures of relative attractiveness: the ratio of military to civilian pay and civilian employment opportunities, measured by the unemployment rate.

Figure 6 depicts military pay relative to the average weekly wage of white male high school graduates aged 17 to 22 for the period 1976 to 1991, with 1982 = 100. Military pay fell compared to civilian pay in the late 1970s, worsening (indeed perhaps creating) a recruiting crisis in those years. Turnover and accessions both rose from 1978 to 1980. Recruit targets proved hard to reach, recruit quality fell, and the realization that the pool of 18 year olds would decline added to pessimism about the viability of the all volunteer concept. Steps taken during 1980–1982 counteracted the AVF's deterioration. Catch-up pay raises took effect at the beginning of fiscal years 1981 and 1982, restoring the ratio of military to civilian pay to approximately its original (1973) AVF level. At the same time, military budgets for recruiting (bonuses, advertising, staff) were increased, and the military improved the effectiveness of its recruiting efforts. From 1982 to date, the pay ratio for young high school graduates has held at or above its 1982 level.

Figure 7 shows what was happening to the employment rate during this period. In the late 1970s, when military pay looked relatively less attractive than civilian wages, youth unemployment was low, making recruiting difficult. However, as the 1980s began, the unemployment rate for 20 to 24 year olds rose, peaking in 1982. This trend aided recruiting, which was also stimulated by the 1981–1982 military pay increases. Unemployment then dipped again and remained low until the end of the decade. During the current recession, unemployment has remained high for over two years, again making recruiting easier.

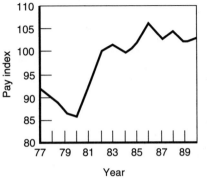

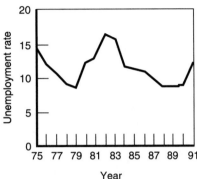

Figure 6—Military Pay Relative to
Civilian Pay for White Male
HS Grads

Figure 7—Unemployment Rate
for 20 to 24 Year Olds

Figures 8 and 9 show the recruiting quality problems of the late 1970s
and the increasing quality of recruits since that time. They plot the
percentages of recruits by schooling level and by AFQT category, respectively. AFQT scores are reported on a percentile basis (1–99) and
are grouped into six categories: CAT I (93–99), CAT II (65–92), CAT
IIIA (50–64), CAT IIIB (31–49), CAT IV (10–30), and CAT V (1–9).
Those in CAT V are by statute ineligible to enlist. CAT I–CAT IIIA
constitute the top half of all scores nationwide, and it is from this
pool of youth that the military prefers to draw its recruits.

In the late 1970s the share of recruits who were high school dropouts
or who scored in the lowest acceptable AFQT category (CAT IV)
increased by over 15 percentage points. In 1980 a quarter of the
recruits were dropouts and over a third were CAT IVs (Figure 8). With
the two pay raises taking effect in 1981 and 1982, recruit quality increased rapidly. The percentage of recruits who were high school
graduates rose from 66 percent in 1980 to 92 percent in 1984 and is
now well over 95 percent. The percentage of recruits who are CAT I–
CAT IIIA has climbed steadily, from below 40 percent in 1980, and is
now about 75 percent, its highest level since the inception of the AVF
(Figure 9).

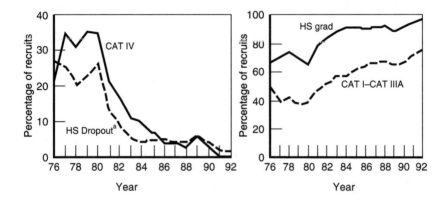

^aExcludes those with a GED (Graduate Equivalency Degree).

Figure 8—Percentage of Recruits
Who Are Low Quality

Figure 9—Percentage of Recruits
Who Are High Quality

MINORITY RECRUITMENT

The number of minorities in the military service is affected by the interaction of two often opposing considerations. On the one hand, in the civilian labor market minorities have considerably worse economic opportunities and outcomes than whites. Other things being equal, this makes the military more attractive to minorities than to whites. On the other hand, the military prefers recruits who are high school graduates and who score in the top half of the AFQT (i.e., CAT I–CAT IIIA); relatively fewer minorities meet these criteria. In addition, other factors, such as youth preferences in different ethnic/race groups, the proximity of recruiting stations, and recruiting incentives, may also influence minority recruiting.

Figures 10 and 11 show the difference in civilian job opportunities among whites, blacks, and Hispanics. They compare weekly earnings and unemployment rates by race/ethnic group over the past 15 years. Figure 10 shows that, relative to white wages, Hispanic and especially black weekly wages trended down in the first half of the 1980s and then regained ground. Clearly, in the mid-1980s many

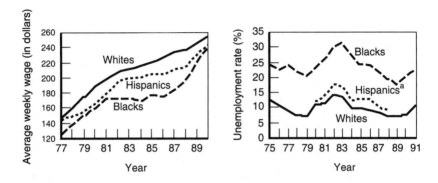

[a]Hispanic unemployment rates are only available for 1980–1988.

**Figure 10—Average Weekly
Wage, by Race/Ethnicity**

**Figure 11—Unemployment Rate
for 20 to 24 Year Olds, by
Race /Ethnicity**

minorities would have perceived the military as an excellent economic opportunity. In 1986, the point of maximum wage disparity, white weekly wages averaged $227 compared with $177 for blacks and $205 for Hispanics. By 1990 the gap had narrowed considerably: $255 for whites, $245 for Hispanics, and $240 for blacks.

Unemployment rates (Figure 11) for 20 to 24 year olds are twice as high for blacks as for either whites or Hispanics, whose rates are similar. Thus, on the unemployment dimension, blacks would also have a stronger motivation to enlist.

Because the military pay schedule is by law the same for all enlisted personnel, these comparisons imply that, relative to whites, blacks and Hispanics should find the military a more attractive environment. This is consistent with the fact that a higher percentage of black youth enlist (Figure 1) but is inconsistent with the lower percentage of Hispanics enlisting. The reasons for a lower enlistment ratio among Hispanics are not well understood. Among the plausible explanations are lower high school graduation rates; lower preference for military service; fewer returning Hispanic enlistees or recent recruits who are effective in attracting new recruits; poor English; and, finally, perhaps fewer resources and less effort devoted to recruiting Hispanics.

Although economic opportunity gives minorities an incentive to enlist in the military, the military's preference for upper AFQT high school graduates tends to exclude a relatively high proportion of minorities. In the youth population today, about 85 percent of 19- to 20-year-old whites have completed 12 or more years of schooling compared with 75 percent of blacks and about 60 percent of Hispanics (Figure 12). The white percentage has been stable for 15 years, the Hispanic percentage has remained at roughly the same average but has fluctuated more, probably because of immigration and second language–related effects. In sharp contrast, black high school graduation rates have climbed steadily from 66 percent in 1974 to 75 percent in 1989 (the most recent year for which data are available).

Simultaneously, the percentage of recruits with 12 or more years of school has risen markedly. Unlike civilian patterns and trends, where high school graduation rates differed by race/ethnicity, between 1976 and 1992 the trend in the percentage of recruits who were high school graduates was similar for whites, blacks, and Hispanics, rising from below 70 percent in the mid-1970s to around 90 percent by the mid-1980s, and to 95 percent and over in 1991-1992 (Figure 9).

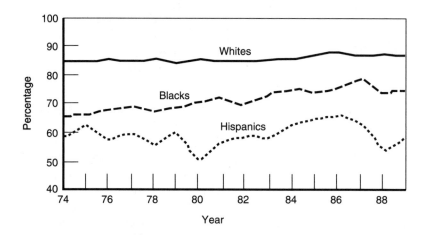

Figure 12—Percentage of 19 to 20 Year Olds with
12 or More Years of Schooling

This places the percentage of recruits who are high school graduates 10 points above that of white youth as a whole, 20 points greater than black youth today, and 35 points greater than Hispanic youth. Moreover, since today 19 out of 20 enlistments are high school graduates, the 25 percent of all blacks and 35 percent of all Hispanics who drop out of high school have quite low chances of enlisting.

The upward trend in recruit AFQT scores, while a success story in raising the quality of service personnel (Figure 9), has disproportionately affected minorities. Scores on the AFQT in the 1980 youth population reveal large differences by race/ethnicity (for more information see [9], Table C-1). The military prefers to recruit those scoring in the upper half of the distribution (CAT I–CAT IIIA) for the population overall. Figure 13 shows that 62 percent of the whites satisfied this preference, but only 17 percent of blacks and 28 percent of Hispanics did. AFQT CAT Vs, the lowest 9 percent of the distribution, are ineligible to serve. Five percent of whites but more than 23

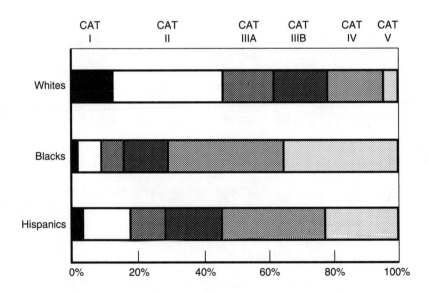

SOURCE: Authors' tabulations from National Longitudinal Survey of Youth/Profile of American Youth File (NLS-Y).

Figure 13—Distribution of AFQT Scores Among Men Aged 18 to 23 in 1980

percent of Hispanics and 35 percent of blacks were excluded by this rule.

Since 1980, when the national test was administered, high school completion rates of blacks have improved by perhaps 5 percentage points, which probably raised the percentage of CAT I–CAT IIIA blacks. Still, it seems unlikely that the percentage would be above, say, 25–30 percent today. The lack of change in Hispanic high school completion rates and the influx of new immigrants have probably worked to keep the percentage of Hispanics who would score CAT I–CAT IIIA in the 25–30 percent range.

The military has been particularly successful in increasing minority recruits from CAT I–CAT IIIA and in reducing the number from CAT IV. In 1992, 81 percent of white *recruits* were CAT I–CAT IIIA, 56 percent of black recruits, and 66 percent of Hispanic recruits. Again, the respective civilian *population* percentages were 62 percent for whites and 25–30 percent for blacks and Hispanics.

Since blacks and Hispanics have lower average scores according to the military's quality criteria, it follows that raising the quality screen can lower the share of minorities unless strong recruiting steps are taken to prevent this. Figure 14 shows the racial distribution of recruits through time. When recruit quality fell in the late 1970s, the percentage of blacks rose. Now during the drawdown and recession, when recruit quality has risen, the percentage of blacks has fallen.

MILITARY AS OUTLET FOR TALENTED MINORITIES

The armed services are clearly attracting well-educated, talented recruits from each race/ethnic group. In order to show the importance of the military as an outlet, or pathway, for such talented minorities, we next present information on the proportion of recruitable males who enter the services (Table 1).

Compared with whites, the percentage of blacks or Hispanics that can expect to complete 12 or more years of school and score well on the AFQT is low. Sixty-nine percent of white males aged 19 to 22 in 1980 had completed high school and scored CAT I–CAT IIIA (85 percent when we include IIIB) compared with 21 percent of blacks (38 percent including IIIB) and 40 percent of Hispanics (60 percent). We

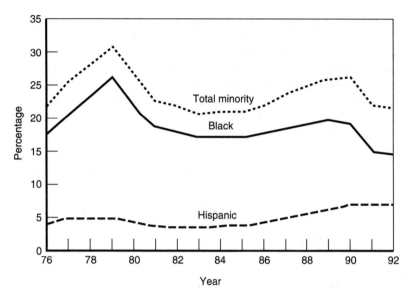

Figure 14—Black and Hispanic Recruits as a Percentage of
Total Minority Recruits

Table 1

Percent of 18-Year-Old Males Who Are High School Graduates and
CAT I–IIIA or CAT I–IIIB; and Percent of Those Enlisting in 1989 and 1992

	HSG and CAT I–IIIA (%)	Enlisting (%)		HSG and CAT I–IIIB (%)	Enlisting (%)	
		1989	1992		1989	1992
White	69	13	9	85	13	9
Black	26	25	16	43	32	17
Hispanic	40	9	9	60	11	9

use the white and Hispanic percentages outright, but we have chosen
to increase the black percentage to 26 percent (43 percent for I–IIIB)
in view of the increase in the high school completion rate among
blacks over the past 10 years.[#]

Although the number of blacks who met the military quality criteria
was relatively low, the percentage of those in that group who joined

was high in 1989. In that year, 25 percent of eligible blacks in CAT I–CAT IIIA and 32 percent in CAT I–CAT IIIB chose the military over the alternatives of the civilian labor market or postsecondary education. Thus the military represented a major career pathway for academically accomplished blacks. The percentage of white and Hispanic youth enlisting was also substantial, ranging from 9 percent to 13 percent of the relevant population (for similar calculations during the recruiting crisis in the late 1970s, see [10]).

But with the shrinking force, the percentage of these high-quality male youth entering the military has declined markedly. Among high school graduates scoring in the top half of the AFQT distribution, the share of blacks entering the military has dropped from 25 percent in 1989 to 16 percent in 1992. When we extend this comparison to include black high school graduates in the top 70 percent of the AFQT distribution, the decline is steeper—32 percent to 17 percent. This implies that recruiting opportunities declined even more rapidly among the group added to the comparison, CAT IIIB high school graduate blacks. Although whites and Hispanics experienced similar relative changes, their absolute percentage changes are smaller since their propensities to join the military have historically been lower.

CONCLUSION

The number of young men entering the military has fallen from 240,000 in 1989 to a projected 138,000 in 1992, a drop of 100,000. Because the military prefers to cut new accessions rather than current personnel, this reduction, driven by military downsizing, probably represents most of the reduction in demand for recruits that will occur. Moreover, the cut in recruiting comes on top of a decade-long trend toward higher quality that has been felt by all race/ethnic groups. Given the nearly constant force size of the 1980s and its increasing retention rates, the increase in the number of high-quality recruits was accompanied by an even larger decrease in the number of non-high-quality recruits. Thus, the 1980s can be seen as a time of downsizing the number of low-quality recruits. The number of non–CAT I–CAT IIIA high school graduate recruits fell from 222,000 in 1980 to 99,000 in 1989 and to a projected 35,000 in 1992. By contrast, the current reductions in effect cut back on higher-quality recruits. Although the number of CAT I–CAT IIIA high school graduate recruits rose from 98,000 to 141,000 between 1980 and 1989, our projection for 1992 is 104,000.

Moreover, the recent rise in the average quality of military recruits (e.g., CAT IV recruits have all but been eliminated and the percentage of CAT I–CAT IIIA high school graduate recruits, which grew from 31 percent in 1980 to 59 percent in 1989, spurted to 75 percent in 1992) has lowered the percentage of minority recruits, notably black recruits. The number of black recruits relative to black youth population has fallen faster than for whites or Hispanics. In the late 1970s and again in 1986 over 20 percent of all young black males entered the military; the 1991 figure was under 10 percent. Thus, over 10 percent of all black males must find a different first job. The decline for blacks is even more striking when we focus our attention on the high-scoring high school graduates whom the military prefers. In 1989 one in three CAT I–CAT IIIB high school graduate blacks enlisted; in 1992 one in six did.

Fifty years ago, Gunnar Myrdal commented on the role of the military in the lives of minorities:

> In terms of economic value they offer some of the best opportunities open to many young Negro men. Food and clothing are excellent; the pay is higher than that in many occupations available to Negroes. And those conditions of employment are equal for Negroes and whites. A great number of poor Negroes must have raised their level of living considerably by entering the armed forces. [11]

Given the relatively low earnings and high unemployment rates of blacks and Hispanics, it is plausible that life in the military is better than civilian life for enlistees; they choose it voluntarily. With the lower recruiting goals, this choice is available to many fewer young minority men. Furthermore, the magnitude of the decrease in enlistments—and thus the increased number of young minority men in the labor market—is large enough to depress civilian wages and to raise civilian unemployment.

From a community perspective, one could argue that over the past 10 years the military has creamed the most academically accomplished young minority men, at least temporarily removing them from their communities. Lower accessions will raise the number of such men staying in their communities. The effects of such changes on the young men and their communities deserve further attention.

For men who would have served in the military, the long-term effects on their careers are unclear. Most enlistees, white or minority, do not choose the military as a lifelong career. They serve for several years and then return to civilian life. Those men who would have served in a larger military will not benefit from the opportunities afforded by the Montgomery GI Bill and the educational incentives offered to enlistees. However, we do not know how valuable these opportunities are relative to those offered to nonveterans or whether their value differs by race/ethnic group. Existing evidence is inconclusive. Far from all eligible veterans use the educational benefits to which they are entitled, and we do not know how veterans' educational attainment compares with similarly situated nonveterans. [12,13] The patterns of educational benefit usage and educational attainment could differ by race/ethnicity. We also do not know whether displaced high-quality recruits will be able to find academic financial aid as generous as military benefits. If not, their ability to go to college will be lower. On the other hand, many may want to attend college, both because of a lack of jobs in the recessionary economy and in order to seek education or skills they otherwise would have acquired in the military.

The evidence on gains in civilian earnings resulting from short service in the military is also inconclusive. Generally speaking, greater training should lead to higher earnings. Post–Cold War youth who do not serve will miss the benefits of in-service occupational training. It is uncertain whether these displaced recruits will obtain comparable training in civilian jobs. The military has claimed in its advertising that this training is transferrable to civilian employment. The evidence for this claim is weak.

With respect to earnings per se, one study finds that Vietnam War–era veterans have lower earnings than comparable nonveterans, while another study indicates that the evidence for AVF veterans is mixed. [14,15]

We still have much to learn about how a smaller military will affect American youth in general and minority youth in particular. That knowledge could help us understand whether specific policy responses are needed to compensate for reduced military service opportunities.

NOTES

We would like to thank our reviewers, Beth Asch and Bruce Orvis, and editors, Jim Steinberg and Mary Vaiana. Nora Wolverton and Natasha Kostan helped prepare the manuscript, and Sally Carson, Carol Edwards, and Marian Oshiro provided computational assistance. Christine Peterson supplied information on weekly wages. This chapter is the responsibility of the authors alone and does not represent the positions of RAND or RAND research sponsors.

We use data from the RAND Census/CPS Data Archive, which was built using primary funding from Grant No. P-50-HD-12639 from the National Institute for Child Health and Human Development to RAND's Population Research Center. We also wish to thank the Defense Manpower Data Center for their cooperation in generating files for this chapter. The work reported in this paper was not done as part of RAND's Defense Manpower Research Center.

Data from the Defense Manpower Data Center form the basis of Figures 1, 8, 9, and 14.

Figure 6 presents the ratio of military to civilian pay computed for white male high school graduates (12 years of schooling), aged 17 to 22, working full time (35 hours of work or more per week) and full year (35 weeks of work or more per year). Military pay is based on Basic Pay, which is a large fraction of the pay (around 70 percent) received by any first termer. The other main components of first-term pay are Basic Allowance for Quarters and Basic Allowance for Subsistence. Over the past 15 years, these components have been adjusted at about the same rate as Basic Pay, so the movement in Basic Pay is a good indicator of the overall movement in military pay. Civilian pay is based on the annual average weekly wage (three-year moving average). The figure depicts the trend in military/civilian pay from 1976–1991 (1982 = 100).

In Figure 10 we compute nominal (undeflated) average weekly wages for young men aged 17 to 22 with high school education (12 years of schooling), working full time, full year. We take a three-year moving average of these wages.

In Table 1 we measure youth population by the number of 18-year-old males in 1990, based on 1990 Current Population Survey (CPS) data; data on school completion and AFQT come from the 1981 NLS-Y; recruit data come from the DMDC. The CPS youth population counts are 1,331,400 whites; 271,780 blacks; 177,180 Hispanics. Recruit data cover two-thirds of fiscal year 1992, and our projections for that year are based on three-halves of those counts. We make no adjustment for health conditions or criminal records that might disqualify a portion of the population for military service. If such adjustments were made, the ratio of recruits to the eligible youth population would be higher than reported.

For an earlier discussion of the role of minorities in the military and the military in the lives of minority youth, see [16] and [17]. These discussions were written shortly after the recruiting crisis of the late 1970s. That timing explains the difference in perspective from this chapter.

*These figures cover accessions into active duty service and include both nonprior service recruits and prior service recruits. Typically, over 90 percent are nonprior service.

†This statement implicitly holds other things constant. Increases in recruiting effort and resources or a decline in minority employment opportunities could mitigate the decline in black and Hispanic recruiting.

‡The only notable deviation was an increase of 50,000 in 1986 and its elimination in 1987–1988.

§Part of this effect is due to the fact that increases in military pay allowed the military to recruit more high school graduates. High school graduates are more likely to complete their first term of service than are nongraduates.

#This is consistent with the finding in [9] that scores rise with education. This relationship may not be causal. If so, then we underestimate the enlistment ratios in Table 1. Also, we note that the percentages in Table 1 for whites and Hispanics are higher than those in Figure 13 and its discussion. The differences stem from the fact that Table 1 is based on ages 19 to 22, whereas Figure 13 refers to ages 18 to 23.

‖For instance, there were 98,000 I–IIIA high school graduates in 1980 out of a total of 320,000 active duty recruits (31 percent). By 1989 the number of I–IIIA high school graduates had increased to 141,000, and the total number of recruits had dropped to 240,000. Thus, 59 percent of the recruits were high quality. Since 1989 both numbers have dropped. Our projections for 1992 indicate 104,000 I–IIIA high school graduates recruits out of a total of 138,000 recruits. This implies that 75 percent are high quality. Putting the numbers in the context of non-high-quality recruits, in 1980 there were 222,000 non-I–III A high school graduate recruits versus 35,000 in 1992.

REFERENCES

1. Cooper, Richard, Military Manpower in the All-Volunteer Force, Santa Monica, Calif.: RAND, R-1450-ARPA, September 1977.

2. Klerman, Jacob Alex, and Lynn Karoly, "Trends and Future Directions in Youth Labor Markets: Implications for Army Recruiting," *Marching Towards the Future*, Westport, Conn.: Greenwood Press, forthcoming.

3. Armor, David J., Richard L. Fernandez, Kathy Bers, Donna S. Schwarzbach, S. C. Moore, and L. Cutler, *Recruit Aptitudes and*

Army Job Performance: Setting Enlistment Standards for Infantrymen, Santa Monica, Calif.: RAND, R-2874–MRAL, 1982.

4. Scribner, Barry L., D. Alton Smith, Robert H. Baldwin, and Robert L. Phillips, "Are Smart Tankers Better Tankers: AFQT and Military Productivity," *Armed Forces and Society*, Vol. 12, No. 2, Winter 1986, pp. 193–206.

5. Nelson, Abraham, Edward Schmitz, David Promisel, *The Impact of Personnel Quality on STINGER Weapon System Performance*, Technical Report 640, Alexandria, Va.: U.S. Army Research Institute, 1984.

6. Orvis, Bruce R., Michael T. Childress, and J. Michael Polich, "Effect of Personnel Quality on the Performance of Patriot Air Defense System Operators," Santa Monica, Calif.: RAND, R-3901-A, 1992.

7. Gilroy, Curtis L., Robert L. Phillips, and John D. Blair, "The All-Volunteer Army: Fifteen Years Later," *Armed Forces and Society*, Vol. 16, No. 3, Spring 1990, pp. 329–350.

8. Hosek, James R., Christine E. Peterson, Jeannette VanWinkle, and Hui Wang, "A Civilian Wage Index for Defense Manpower," RAND, R-4190-FMP, 1992.

9. Office of the Assistant Secretary of Defense, Manpower, Reserve Affairs, and Logistics, *Profile of American Youth*, March 1982.

10. Eitelberg, M. J., J. H. Laurence, L. S. Perelman, and B. K. Walters, *Screening for Service*, Alexandria, Va.: HumRRO, September 1984, and special tabulations provided by the DMDC.

11. Myrdal, Gunnar, *An American Dilemma: The Negro Problem and Modern Democracy*, New York: Pantheon Books, 1972, Vol. 1, p. 419.

12. Asch, Beth, James N. Dertouzos, James R. Hosek, and Bernard Rostker, *Restructuring DoD's Accessions Programs in the Coming Decade*, Unpublished Research.

13. Tanner, Michael B., "Is the Army College Fund Meeting Its Objectives?" *Industrial and Labor Relations Review*, Vol. 41, No. 1, October 1987, pp. 50–62.

14.   Angrist, Joshua D., "Lifetime Earnings and the Vietnam Era Draft Lottery: Evidence from Social Security Administration Records," *American Economic Review*, Vol. 80, pp 313–336.

15.   Gilroy, Curtis, Thomas N. Daymont, Paul J. Andrisani, and Robert J. Phillips, *Economic Returns to Military Service: Race-Ethnic Differences*, Technical Report 91-1, OSD(FM&P), July 1991.

16.   Binkin, Martin, and Mark J. Eitelberg, "Women and Minorities in the All-Volunteer Force," in *The All-Volunteer Force After a Decade: Retrospect and Prospect*, Washington, D.C.: Pergamon-Brassey's, 1986.

17.   Binkin, Martin, and Mark J. Eitelberg with Alvin J. Schexnider and Marvin M. Smith, *Blacks and the Military*, Washington, D.C.: The Brookings Institution, 1982, p. 72.

3

Crime and Criminal Justice

Chapter Seven

Crime and Punishment in California
Full Cells, Empty Pockets, and Questionable Benefits

Joan Petersilia

The recent civil disturbances in Los Angeles have again focused the public's attention on crime and justice in California. Television news depicted stores ravaged by looters, gangs were said to be spreading the violence, and frightened citizens were afraid to leave their homes. Many believed that the police were unable to control crime in these neighborhoods. Data reported in the aftermath showed that those arrested were mostly young repeat criminals, 40 percent of whom were on probation or parole at the time of their arrest. [1] For residents and outsiders alike, Los Angeles seemed a place where crime was out of control, the justice system ineffective, and criminals able to take advantage of "revolving-door" justice.

Wide publicity surrounding criminal activity almost always fuels demands that the justice system "get tough with criminals," and the civil disturbances in Los Angeles have been no exception. Mayor Bradley called for hiring more police officers and building more jails. Los Angeles District Attorney Ira Reiner announced a hard-line policy, saying he would seek minimum one-year jail terms for anyone convicted of a disturbance-related crime. United States Attorney General William P. Barr, addressing the California District Attorneys' Association following the April events, emphasized greater imprisonment as the best means for reducing future crime. He stated: "The choice is clear: more prison space or more crime."

Tough-on-crime edicts are not new and have dominated national crime policy since the late 1970s. At that time, the nation shifted its focus away from addressing the "root causes" of crime and the rehabilitation of criminals toward making crime penalties more swift, certain, and severe. Proponents cited three basic arguments for their "get tough" approach. Some argued that if crime did not pay, if harsher penalties outweighed the gains from crime, then fewer crimes would be committed. Others suggested that if prisons could

175

not rehabilitate offenders, at least they could prevent them from preying on society by putting them behind bars (i.e., by incapacitating them). Finally, some contended that even if tough sentences did not affect crime rates, they reflected a clear social condemnation of the criminal's behavior.

California, once a leader in developing rehabilitation programs, quickly embraced the new crime-control model. The state passed the Determinate Sentence Law in 1977, which, among other things, embraced *punishment* (and, explicitly, *not* rehabilitation) as the purpose of prison, required mandatory prison sentences for many offenses formerly eligible for probation, and dramatically increased the rate at which probation and parole violators were returned to prison. As a result, California corrections populations skyrocketed:

- The prison population grew from 22,500 prisoners in 1980 to over 106,000 by 1992—an increase of nearly 300 percent, the largest such increase experienced by any state in the nation.

- The probation population more than doubled, from 151,000 persons under supervision at the start of 1980 to 310,000 today.

- The number of people in county jails tripled from 25,000 in 1980 to 76,000 today.

- The adult parole population increased from 10,450 in 1980 to more than 70,000 in 1992.

The upshot is that by 1992, about 562,000 adults—or 2.2 percent of all Californians 18 years of age or older—are either in jail or prison, or on probation or parole.

All of this has come at tremendous cost to the California taxpayer. In just the last five years, state spending for criminal justice grew by more than 70 percent—almost four times greater than total state spending. This increase was higher than that for any other state-funded service (spending for education grew by about 10 percent over the same time period). An increasing share of the state's general fund budget is now allocated to operating the state's prison system, from about 2 percent in fiscal year 1981–1982 to over 6 percent in fiscal year 1991–1992. If current trends continue, state corrections expenditures are predicted to require an amount equivalent to 10 percent of the general fund budget by the year 2000. And county justice revenues, which fund local police, jails, and probation, have increased significantly as well—growing at 14 percent per year while the county revenues to pay for them have been growing at 11 percent per year. [2]

As legislators and Governor Pete Wilson struggle with declining state revenues and increased demand for state-funded services, justice expenditures—long sacrosanct in the budget process—are being closely scrutinized. Policymakers are having to ask some very difficult and sometimes painful questions:

- Has the vast investment in criminal justice done any good?

- In particular, has it made local communities any safer?

- How do the costs and benefits associated with criminal justice compare with those of other social services, such as health care and education?

This chapter addresses these questions by reviewing California crime and victimization data, imprisonment rates, and criminal justice expenditures over the past two decades. The data suggest that the massive investment in crime control—and the doubling and redoubling of the prison population in recent years—may have had little effect on California's crime rate, particularly violent crime. Spending even more is unlikely to reduce crime significantly: while there may be moral justifications for locking up offenders, imprisonment appears to have little impact on the amount of crime experienced in local communities. This chapter begins by describing the impact and reasons for California's current crime policy, then it discusses why expanded imprisonment has not reduced crime, why it is unlikely to do so in the future, and what policy options hold promise for addressing the crime rate more directly.

As shown in Figure 1, California prisons now house over 106,000 adults, an all-time high. During the past two decades, the prison population increased at an average annual rate of about 10 percent, or about 6,000 persons per year. [3] California currently ranks first in the U.S. prison population, with 34,000 more prisoners than New York, the second largest prison system in the nation. Unless the

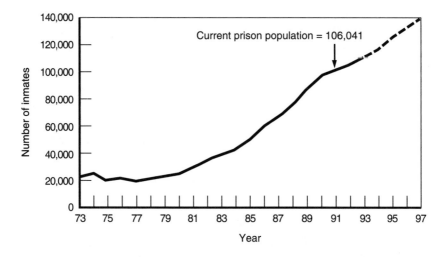

SOURCE: California Department of Corrections, Offender Information Services Branch, *California Prisoners and Parolees, 1990,* Sacramento, 1991. California population projections are from California Department of Finance, *Interim Population Projections for California, State and Counties, 1900–2005,* Report 91-P-1, 1991.

Figure 1—California Prison Population, 1973–1992 (projections to 1991)

growth rate abates, the California Department of Corrections (CDC) projects that, by 1997, the number of adults in prison will reach 140,000.

While California has the largest overall prison population, it does not have the highest incarceration *rate* (as shown in Table 1). Florida imprisons 335 per 100,000 resident population, as compared with California's 311.

While the overall numbers have grown, the characteristics of Californians incarcerated has not changed much since 1985. The majority of prisoners are still male (94 percent in 1990; 92 percent in 1985) and minority (35 percent black and 30 percent Hispanic in 1990; 31 percent black and 29 percent Hispanic in 1985). The average inmate age in both 1985 and 1990 was 30 years old. In terms of commitment offenses, 41 percent are violent offenders (vs. 42 per-

Table 1

Prison Populations in the Seven Most Populous U.S. States, 1990

	Total No. of Prisoners	Incarceration Rate[a]	1980–1990 Change in Prison Population (%)
California	**97,309**	**311**	**245**
New York	54,894	304	125
Pennsylvania	22,290	183	140
Illinois	27,516	234	110
Ohio	31,855	289	110
Florida	44,387	336	90
Texas	50,042	290	40
U.S. total	771,243	293	120

[a]The number of prisoners with sentences of more than one year per 100,000 resident population.

SOURCE: Bureau of Justice Statistics, U.S. Department of Justice, *Prisons and Prisoners in the United States,* Washington, D.C., 1992.

cent in 1985), 27 percent are property offenders (vs. 39 percent in 1985), 26 percent are drug offenders (vs. 11 percent in 1985), and 6 percent are "other" (8 percent in 1985). The average length of time California prisoners spend incarcerated (including local jail time) across all offense types is 1.7 years. There have been two principal changes since 1985: drug offenders are now a much larger proportion of the total inmate population (up from 11 percent in 1985) and the average length of term has decreased slightly (down from two years in 1985).

The sudden rise in prison populations caught most states unprepared. They had to either build new facilities or face expensive lawsuits regarding crowded prison conditions. California, to a greater extent than any other state, attempted to build its way out of the crowding crisis and undertook the largest prison construction program in the history of the country. California's prison system grew from 12 facilities in 1982 to 25 in 1992. In addition to constructing 13 new prisons, California greatly expanded seven existing facilities, and six more prisons are now in either the construction or planning stage. The price tag for the construction program is $3.8 billion so far, and corrections officials envision the building of another six prisons, which have not yet been fully funded, by the end of the decade. [4]

The CDC reports that the cost of operating the prisons once they are built amounts to about $20,000 per inmate per year.

As shown in Figure 2, criminal justice expenditures have increased rapidly, even after adjusting for inflation. From 1981 to 1991, California nearly doubled spending on criminal justice agencies to about $11 billion annually. [3]

Justice expenditures also increased more rapidly than general government spending and relative to other social areas, for example, education (Figure 3).

WHAT ACCOUNTS FOR THE GROWTH OF CRIMINAL JUSTICE SPENDING AND PRISON POPULATIONS?

One would expect an increase in the number of sentenced prisoners as the state population goes up—the more residents, the more crime,

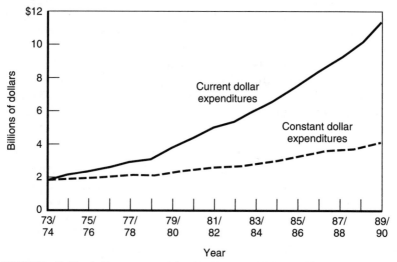

SOURCE: California Department of Justice, Bureau of Criminal Statistics and Special Services, *Crime and Delinquency in California, 1990,* Sacramento, 1991.

Figure 2—California Criminal Justice Expenditures Indexed to Fiscal Year 1973–1974 Dollars (data shown in billions of dollars)

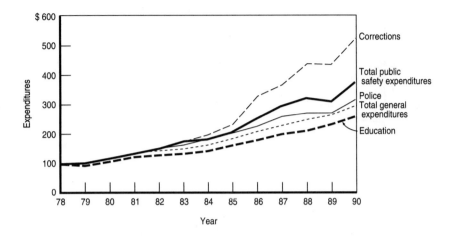

SOURCE: Bureau of the Census, *Government Finances,* various years.

Figure 3—California State and Local Spending for Various Functions
(1978 = 100)

arrests, convictions, and prison sentences. But the number of prisoners has increased much faster than California's resident population. The rate of prison incarceration rose from a low of 107 per 100,000 California residents in 1973 to a steeply increased 311 per 100,000 in 1990.

The higher per capita imprisonment rate could be due to a shifting age distribution. People in their late teens and early 20s are more likely than older or younger people to be charged with crimes and sentenced to prison. But there has been almost no increase in the percentage of California residents in these age groups. Therefore age distribution does not explain the prison population increase.

Our confidence in the effects of increased incarceration might be bolstered by a steady decrease in crime rates. But as shown in Figure 4, the overall crime rate in California has remained relatively constant since the early 1980s. [5] Figure 4 shows the California crime index (CCI), which measures crime rate trends for violent (i.e., homicide, rape, assault, robbery) and property crimes (i.e., larceny,

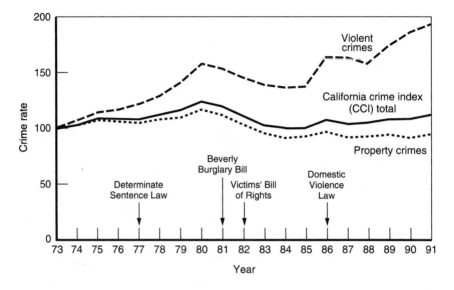

SOURCE: California Bureau of Criminal Statistics.

Figure 4—California Crime Index
(rate per 100,000 population indexed to 1973)

auto theft, burglary) from 1973 through 1991. The CCI is the official state system maintained by the California Bureau of Criminal Statistics (BCS). BCS (like its counterpart FBI) provides data on crime *as reported by police agencies.* From 1973 through 1980, the overall crime rate increased gradually, reaching its peak in 1980; then it declined gradually between 1980 and 1985. From 1986 to 1991, the overall CCI per capita crime rate has remained relatively stable, increasing 3.7 percent. Figure 4 also marks the four major legal changes that are presumed to have affected the processing of reported crimes and arrests in California during this time period.*

Reported property crime was actually lower in 1991 than it was in 1973. Property crimes reached their peak in 1980, declined until 1983 and have since remained stable. Data just released by the BCS report that, from 1986 to 1991, the property crime rate actually decreased 1.4 percent.

In contrast, violent crime took a dramatic upward turn between 1985 and 1986, leveling off in 1988. However, BCS indicates that this one-year shift was entirely attributable to the 1986 Domestic Violence Law, which reclassified domestic violence as aggravated assault, a felony punishable by prison (see Figure 5). If aggravated assaults are removed from the violent crime category, violent crime remained virtually constant from 1983 to 1988. Beginning in 1988, however, two types of violent crime—robbery and homicide—began to increase. The rate of reported rapes in California has declined steadily since 1980—the only violent crime with a reported decrease.

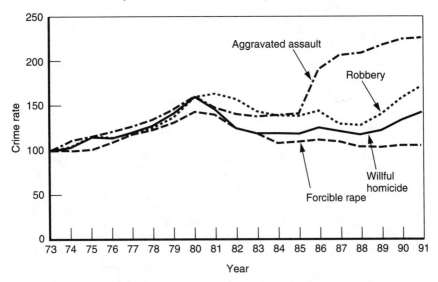

SOURCE: California Bureau of Criminal Statistics.

**Figure 5—California Crime Index, by Type of Crime
(rate per 100,000 population indexed to 1973)**

In sum, the CCI figures reveal a mixture of results suggesting that overall crime rates in California have remained relatively stable since reaching a high point in 1980, that property crime has actually declined, but that violent crime (with the exception of rape) shows recent increases. California crime trends closely match national ones, with the exception of rape and auto theft. [6] California's rape rate has declined faster than the national average, and its auto theft rate has risen faster. [7][†] But we do not see the decline in the state's crime rates we would have hoped for by vastly increasing incarceration rates.

However, since official crime measures like the CCI only measure seven specific crimes "known to the police," they may not reflect a real rise in crime that would be felt by the public, triggering a demand for new policies. Trends in official crime statistics may reflect more about changes in reporting and recording practices than the actual level of crime experienced in the community. Studies show that only about 40 percent of all crime victimizations are reported to the police.

The National Crime Victimization Survey (NCVS), administered by the Bureau of the Census, is designed to measure more accurately the amount of crime, unbiased by whether the victim reported it to the police or not. The NCVS interviews a representative national cross section of persons 12 years of age and older.

The NCVS indicates that the level of violent crime experienced by individuals and households has not increased since the early 1970s (Figure 6). [8] In fact, the NCVS shows an even greater decline in overall crime than suggested by official statistics and does not show violent crime increasing. According to NCVS data, between 1973 and 1990 the national rate of violent crime—assault and rape—declined slightly, and in 1990 it was slightly lower than it had been in 1973. Household crimes (e.g., burglary) and personal theft (e.g., robbery) also declined. During this period, only one rate of criminal victimization—auto theft—did not decline. Although the NCVS does not provide California-specific data, when coupled with official police statistics, it tends to confirm that crime has not surged.

This suggests that rising criminal justice expenditures and growing prison populations are attributable to a deliberate change in policy rather than a consequence of demographic and social change or rising crime rates. One element of this changed policy is the Reagan and Bush administrations' "War on Drugs," a major focus of which was identifying and incarcerating drug sellers. Table 2 shows the growth in arrests, convictions, and incarcerations for felony drug

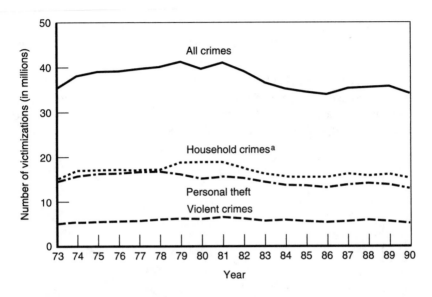

^aHousehold crimes are burglary, household larceny, and motor vehicle theft. Violent crimes are rape, robbery, and assault.

SOURCE: Bureau of Justice Statistics, U.S. Department of Justice, *Criminal Victimization in the United States, 1990.* Washington, D.C., October 1991.

Figure 6—U.S. Crime Victimization Rates, 1973–1990

Table 2

Disposition of California Felony Drug Arrests 1980, 1985, 1990

	1980	1985	1990
Felony arrests disposed of	40,451	63,766	84,538
Number convicted	18,800	30,100	53,200
(% of arrests)	(45)	(48)	(63)
Number to jail	9,700	22,500	33,800
(% of convicted)	(52)	(75)	(64)
Number to state prisons	921	3,366	10,494
(% of convicted)	(5)	(11)	(20)

SOURCE: California Bureau of Criminal Statistics, unpublished tabulations.

crimes in California since 1980. The annual number of felony drug arrests disposed of doubled from 1980 to 1990. Moreover, a greater number of those arrested were convicted, and more of those convicted went to prison. Over the entire decade, the total number of persons sent to prison annually for drug offenses rose from less than 1,000 to over 10,000.

But arrests and imprisonments for drug crimes do not explain the entire increase in prison populations. Figure 7 shows that incarceration rates began rising well *before* the increase in drug arrests and that prison populations increased at a faster rate than drug arrests.[‡]

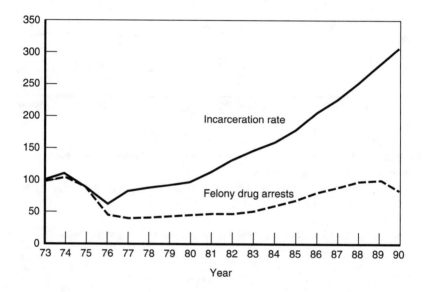

SOURCES: California Department of Corrections, Offender Information Services Branch, *California Prisoners and Parolees, 1990,* Sacramento, 1991; California Department of Corrections, *Population Projections,* 1991–1997, Sacramento, Spring 1992; California Department of Justice, Bureau of Criminal Statistics and Special Services, *Crime and Delinquency in California, 1990,* Sacramento, 1991. California population projections are from California Department of Finance, California, *Interim Population Projections for California, State and Counties,* 1990–2005, Report 91-P-1, 1991.

Figure 7—California Imprisonment Rates Versus Drug Arrests per 100,000 California Population, 1973–1990 (indexed to 1973)

A comprehensive analysis conducted by Patrick Langan, U.S. Bureau of Justice Statistics, and published in *Science* concluded that "changes in drug arrest and imprisonment rates only explain about 8 percent of the growth in prison populations since 1974." [9]

So what did account for the massive prison increases? Criminologists debate various theories, but most agree that the politicization of sentencing policy played a prominent role. Once the public lost confidence in rehabilitation, politicians were less willing to defer to criminal justice professionals' judgments on how to reduce crime and, in response to perceived public demands for a tougher approach, began enacting mandatory minimum prison sentences and increasing sentence lengths for many offenses.

This tendency was particularly pronounced in California, where the legislature enacted more than 1,000 bills changing felony and misdemeanor statutes between 1984 and 1991. [2] Most measures either increased the length of prison sentences or upgraded misdemeanors to felonies punishable by prison. For instance, Senate Bill 200 (Rains), which became effective on January 1, 1983, required that *all* residential burglaries be punished as first-degree burglary. In the past, offenders without a prior criminal record would have probably been sentenced to jail or probation. The legislature also increased penalties for domestic violence, drunk driving, rape, and using a gun during a crime. As shown in Figure 8, persons convicted of many types of felonies are now more likely to be imprisoned.

These legislative changes significantly increased the overall use of imprisonment: in 1975 sentences to state prison represented about 18 percent of all Superior Court sentences in California; by 1991 they had increased to 35 percent. Ninety percent of those granted any form of probation by the court had to serve a jail term first, up from 56 percent in 1975. For the same time period, grants of probation without jail decreased from about 22 percent to about 6 percent (Figure 9).

Another major factor contributing to rising prison populations is the higher rate of probation and parole revocations and the growing number of revocations that result in imprisonment. Parole violators are those who violate their parole conditions or who commit other criminal violations that parole authorities believe occurred, based on

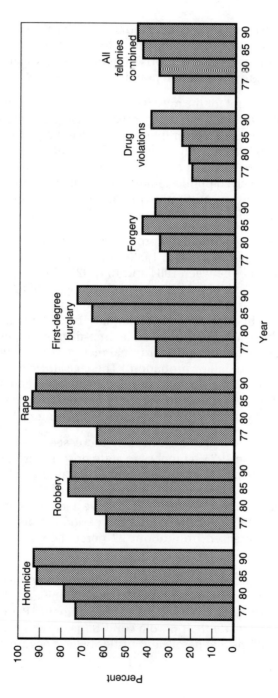

SOURCE: Judicial Council of California, Administrative Office of the Courts, *Sentencing Practices Quarterly*, No. 58, quarter ending March 31, 1992.

Figure 8—Convictions Resulting in Imprisonment (selected crimes)

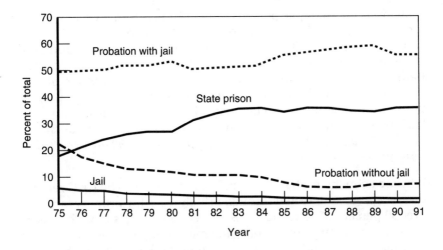

SOURCE: Bureau of Criminal Statistics.

Figure 9—California Superior Court Sentences, 1975–1991

administrative review and a "preponderance of evidence" finding (a weaker standard than the "beyond a reasonable doubt" standard needed to convict initially on a criminal offense).

Sending probation and parole violators to prison has been a major shift in California's corrections policy. Such offenders used to spend their two-to-six-month revocation periods in local jails, but as jails became crowded, violators have been increasingly returned directly to prison. [2] In 1978 there were 1,011 adult parole violators returned to prison; by 1991 that number had increased to 41,573. [5] In the 10-year period from 1978 to 1988, parole violators as a percent of total admissions to prison increased from approximately 8 percent to 47 percent. Additionally, it is estimated that, in 1991, probation violators comprised about 16 percent of new felony admissions to state prison.

The growing number of imprisoned parole or probation revokees helps explain why the average prison sentence has declined slightly from two years (1985) to 1.7 years (1991). It is not because average sentences for a given crime have decreased. In fact, offenders convicted of certain crimes now receive longer court-imposed prison sentences. For example, persons sentenced to prison for manslaughter now receive 9.5 years, as compared to 6.5 years in 1984. (Of course, with full credit for prison work and good behavior, inmates are required to serve just 50 percent of their court-imposed term.) Rather, it is largely attributable to the growing number of parole/probation violators in prison. Eighty percent of all probation/parole violators spend less than six months in prison, and over half spend less than three months (CDC, 1990). *The upshot is that more than half of all offenders entering prison in 1992 are expected to serve six months or less.*

Why are so many probationers/parolees revoked? The CDC reports that drug use, as detected through urinalysis, is the primary factor in over 50 percent of all revocations. [4] Drug testing is now commonplace in community corrections, and many offenders test positive for drug use. Courts and parole boards often revoke to custody because they see few local options—treatment programs are nonexistent or full, and local probation and parole caseloads are too large to provide much surveillance or treatment.

In sum, three reasons seem to explain increases in California prison populations: the harsher treatment of drug offenders; the implementation of mandatory prison sentencing for many offenses formerly granted probation; and the rise in probation and parole revocations that result in a new prison stay.

HAS THE INVESTMENT IN PRISONS MADE US ANY SAFER?

The critical question is whether the massive increases in imprisonment have had any appreciable effect on crime in the community. The question is impossible to answer with certainty because we don't know what crime levels would have been in *absence* of greater imprisonment rates. Figure 10 shows that, adjusted for population growth, California's incarceration rate increased sharply while the crime rate stayed roughly constant. This data can be used by those like U.S. Attorney General William Barr who favor further prison expansion, arguing that crime would have risen sharply if incarceration rates had not increased. Those opposed to new prisons point to the fact that crime rates held steady even with ever-increasing imprisonment.

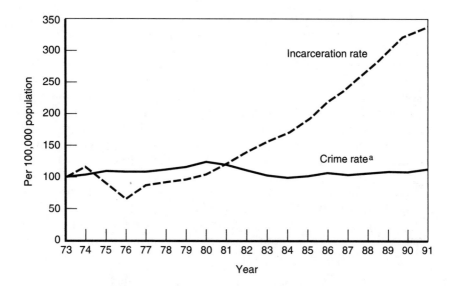

aCrime rate is the California crime index (CCI); imprisonment rate is
the rate per 100,000 California population at risk (ages 10–64).

SOURCE: California Bureau of Criminal Statistics.

**Figure 10—California's Crime Rate Versus Imprisonment Rate
(indexed to 1973)**

The presumed relationship between stiffer sentences and lower
crime is based on two distinct theories. Some argue that stiffer sentences alter a potential criminal's cost-benefit calculation, thus deterring crime. A second theory contends that if offenders are put in
prison, they are prevented, for the time of their incarceration, from
committing further crimes in the community.

UCLA's James Q. Wilson, a leading advocate of this second theory,
wrote an influential book in the mid-1970s to advocate determinate
sentencing policies. He argued that "gains from merely incapacitating convicted criminals may be very large . . . and if the policy of
prison sentences were consistently followed, even with relatively
short (one year or two years) sentences, the gains would be endur-
ing." [10]

Despite the theoretical appeal of these arguments, the data discussed earlier in this chapter suggest that the impact of tougher sentences (particularly prison sentences) on crime rates is weak at best. *Figure 10 shows that, although prison populations quadrupled in size, the overall per capita crime rate remained essentially unchanged.* Looking at some of the categories of crime, property crime held steady and violent crime actually increased during this period (Figure 4), despite the higher overall incarceration rate; and since 1988, two types of violent crime, robbery and homicide, began to rise significantly. Only in the case of forcible rape, which has declined in the last decade, is there some apparent correlation with overall incarceration rates, a conclusion supported by Candace Cross-Drew's recent study, which attributed the decline in rape to harsher sentencing of rapists and California's changing demographics (groups that are high-rate rape offenders are declining as a proportion of the state's overall population). [11]

Several recent studies have attempted to sort out the relationship between imprisonment and crime. The research results are surprisingly consistent: prison has a marginal crime prevention/ incapacitation effect, but it is not large enough to reduce overall crime levels significantly.

A recent study attempted to assess the impact of imprisonment on crime rates in California by comparing California to Texas. The two states were experiencing rather similar crime and incarceration patterns until the mid-1980s, when the Texas recession led the state to reduce prison construction and prison commitments. California, on the other hand, continued to build prisons and increase commitments. Comparing the two states provides a kind of natural experiment to judge the impact of incarceration on crime rates. The analysis suggests that the much higher imprisonment rates in California had no appreciable effect on violent crime and only slight effects on property crime. [12]

Commenting on such research, Professor Franklin Zimring, University of California, Berkeley, stated:

> The data indicate that the money spent in California on prison construction was money wasted. The almost quadrupling of prison capacity seemed to make little difference when it came to curbing the rate of violent crime. [13]

Several recent studies have investigated the impact of incarcerating so many drug offenders. Again, the results are consistent: increased sentencing of drug offenders to prison has had little impact on curbing drug-related crime because the offenders taken off the streets seem to be immediately and completely replaced by other drug offenders. [14,15,16]

A National Academy of Sciences panel reviewed all available data on the incapacitation effects of prison and concluded that doubling the U.S. prison population between 1973 and 1982 probably reduced the number of burglaries and robberies in the United States by 10–20 percent. The panel concluded, "For general increases in incarceration to reduce index crimes by an additional 10 to 20 percent from 1982 levels, inmate populations again would have to have more than doubled." The panel went on to state: "The increments to crime control from incapacitation are modest, even with very large general increases in inmate populations." [17]

In June 1992, 450 criminal justice leaders signed a statement criticizing the "lock 'em up" approach and urged public officials to be more honest with the public about the failure of prisons to control crime and the enormous financial burden prison building and operations places on taxpayers. The statement was signed by prison officials, governors, attorneys general, prosecutors, police chiefs, academics, and legislators.

In signing the statement, Morris L. Thigpen, director of corrections in Alabama, said: "We are on a train that has to be turned around. It just doesn't make sense to pump millions and millions into corrections and have no effect on the crime rate." A California district attorney said: "Somebody should confront and educate the public on whether it is in the public's interest to keep incarcerating larger numbers of people at enormous cost and diversion of scarce resources from other social goals."

Dozens of states have also recently issued commission reports on crime and corrections and each reached similar conclusions: the "quick fix" approach to crime did not produce the hoped for crime-reduction benefits. California's own Blue Ribbon Commission declared the justice system "hopelessly out of balance," saying it relied too heavily on prisons as the major response to crime while ignoring more promising community-based alternatives. [4]

WHY DON'T PRISONS MAKE MORE OF AN IMPACT ON CRIME?

The short answer is that we expect too much of our prisons. Prisons—and criminal justice agencies more generally—have really very little impact on the amount of crime experienced in local communities. To those unfamiliar with criminal justice research, this may seem self-contradictory. After all, simple logic suggests that when offenders are incarcerated, they cannot commit new crimes in the community. However, it is one thing to say that a person will not commit a crime while incarcerated and quite another to say that society's overall crime rate will be affected, for a number of reasons.

First, much predatory crime is committed by juveniles too young to be eligible for prison or by very young adult offenders who are unlikely to be sent to prison for most first-felony convictions.

The general pattern is quite familiar. Persons under the age of 18 constitute about one-fifth of the total population, but they account for one-quarter of all persons arrested and nearly one-half of all those arrested for one of the seven serious "index" crimes. And official arrest data probably understate the contribution of juveniles to the general level of crime because the chances that a juvenile will be arrested for a crime are lower than for an adult. They are especially low for chronic juvenile offenders, who account for a large proportion of all serious crime. [18]

Second, prison terms are usually imposed late in an offender's criminal career, when criminal activity, on average, is tapering off.

Criminal career research shows that criminal activity usually begins at about age 14, increases until the early 20s, and declines thereafter until age 30, when the majority of careers terminate. [17] By the time the criminal justice system has enough evidence to identify a person as a serious career criminal, the individual's criminal career has probably reached its "maturation phase." In California, the average age of arrest is 17; the average age of first commitment to prison is 26 years of age. In 1990 the median age of new admissions to prison was 29. Imposing a prison term at this stage serves to *punish* that individual, but it may have little impact on that person's overall contribution to crime in the community.

Third, because the justice system only deals with a small proportion of crime, its ability to affect crime levels through incapacitation is limited.

Of the approximately 34 million serious felonies committed in the United States in 1990, 31 million never entered the criminal justice system because they were either unreported or unsolved. This means that 90 percent of serious crime remains outside the purview of police, courts, and prison officials. The remaining 10 percent are further eroded as a result of screening by prosecutors and dismissals or acquittals. In California, 65 percent of adults arrested for felonies are convicted, and of these, 20 percent are sent to state institutions. It was recently estimated that nationally fewer than one in seven arrests for serious crime results in imprisonment. [20]

Of course, offenders commit more crimes than they are arrested for, so these figures underestimate the proportion of criminals (as opposed to crimes) who come into contact with the criminal justice system. The challenge is to distinguish higher-rate from lower-rate offenders so that prison space can be reserved for the most criminally active, a point discussed more fully below.

Fourth, our ability to accurately identify the most criminally active offenders at sentencing is hampered by legal, ethical, and practical constraints. More accurate identification of high- and low-rate offenders would allow us to selectively *incapacitate, increasing the crime-prevention effects of prison.*

RAND research has confirmed that offenders commit many more crimes than they are officially arrested for and that certain characteristics are associated with high-rate offending. Chaiken and Chaiken [21] found, for example, that 50 percent of robbers committed an average of fewer than five robberies per year, but the most active 10 percent committed more than 85 robberies per year. Furthermore, high-rate robbers were more likely than low-rate robbers to have juvenile criminal records, poor employment histories, and a history of alcohol and drug use. [22] Such findings have tremendous policy appeal: if we can identify high-rate offenders at sentencing, they could be *selectively* incapacitated, thereby significantly reducing crime without necessarily increasing the total number of offenders incarcerated. Unfortunately, RAND research has shown that our ability to predict high-rate offending is poor. The most important problem is the presence of "false positive" predictions—predictions that persons will engage in criminal behavior when in fact they do not.

Selective incapacitation, based on predictions about future behavior, also raises substantial ethical and constitutional issues. For example, males are more likely to be high-rate offenders, as are younger persons and persons from identifiable ethnic and racial groups. Most would find it objectionable to use ethnic and racial characteristics to enhance punishment, even if these characteristics are associated with high-rate offending. Hence the dilemma: we want to incapacitate offenders who are likely to commit the most crime if free, but to make more accurate predictions raises troublesome ethical and legal problems. As a result, our imprisonment policy tries to implement an incapacitation strategy based on crimes (not criminals), limiting crime prevention/incapacitation effects.

Fifth, studies have shown that much individual crime (particularly violent crime) is an impulsive response to an immediate stressful situation and is often committed under the influence of drugs and/or alcohol. [19]

If crime is highly impulsive, then rational choice models, which attempt to convince the offender that crime doesn't pay by increasing penalties, have limited utility for crime control. They require an offender to think clearly about the costs and benefits of committing crime, weigh those costs, and determine that the costs outweigh the benefits. Yet more than half of all violent offenders are under the influence of drugs or alcohol at the time of their crime, a state of mind with little affinity for rational judgment. [23] Thus, the hoped-for deterrent benefits of increasing imprisonment may be less substantial than originally anticipated—and may increase over time as more criminals routinely use drugs and/or alcohol.

Sixth, for prison sentences to deter offenders and potential offenders, it must be stigmatizing and punishing, and there is evidence that it is becoming less so.

Prison is most likely to deter if it meets two conditions: social standing is injured by the punishment and the punishment is severe in comparison to the benefits of the crime. It seems that prison incorporates neither of these aspects, particularly for repeat offenders. Possessing a prison record may not stigmatize to the same extent as in the past because many of the offender's peers and other family members have also done time. Forty percent of youths incarcerated in state training schools in 1988 reported that their parents also had been incarcerated. Further, estimates show that about a quarter of all males living in U.S. inner cities will be incarcerated at some point in their lives, so the stigma attached to having a prison record in these high-crime neighborhoods may not be as great as it was when prison terms were less common.

In fact, far from stigmatizing, imprisonment appears to confer status in some neighborhoods. Jerome Skolnick, at UC-Berkeley, has been interviewing imprisoned drug dealers in California since 1989 and reports that imprisonment may confer a certain elevated "home boy" status, especially for gang members for whom prison and prison gangs can become an alternative site of loyalty. According to California corrections officials, inmates frequently steal state-issued prison clothing for the same reason: wearing it when they return to the community lets everyone know they have done "hard time."

And, while more people are being sent to prison, the length of time an offender can be expected to serve in prison has decreased slightly over time. Offenders on the street seem to be aware of the short sentences, even to a greater extent with the wide media coverage such issues now receive. For these reasons, it seems at least plausible that prison terms (on average) are not perceived as being as severe as they once were; hence their deterrent potential is diminished.

Seventh, prison must not increase the postrelease criminal activity of those who have been incarcerated sufficiently to offset the crimes prevented by their stay in prison.

Some criminologists argue that prisons breed crime and act as schools for criminal learning. If true, and prisoners simply make up for lost time once released, then prison may actually *increase* crime in the community. RAND analysts recently studied the impact of serving a prison term on future criminal behavior by studying a matched sample of offenders who were similar at sentencing (in terms of type of crime convicted of, demographics, and criminal record) but were sentenced differently—one to prison, one to probation. [24] After tracking the matched groups for three years, the researchers found higher subsequent crime rates for offenders sentenced to prison. Drug offenders who had been imprisoned were

11 percent more likely than comparable probationers to have new criminal charges filed against them, violent offenders were 3 percent more likely, and property offenders, 17 percent more likely.

The higher recidivism of the imprisoned offenders can be interpreted in several ways. It may mean that, while the two groups were statistically matched, significant differences remained, and that the imprisoned offenders had a greater preexisting propensity toward crime—a selection effect. Another explanation is that prison may have made offenders worse, that is, more likely to commit new crimes than they would have been without the prison experience. Alternatively, it may be that the offender did not change as a result of prison but that society's response did. Employers may be more reluctant to employ exprisoners than probationers, landlords more reluctant to accept them, and families less likely to reconcile with them. If society's response makes it more difficult for the offender to resume (or establish) a noncriminal life-style, imprisonment may still be said to have increased the probability of recidivism.

Eighth, and most important, for imprisonment to reduce community crime levels, those in prison must not be immediately and completely replaced by new recruits.

Although studies have shown that most criminal behavior is not organized in the usual sense of the term, some crime, for example, car theft rings, fencing stolen property, and distributing illegal drugs, does appear organized along the lines of a labor market. [16] In these instances, when an arrest is made and a prison sentence imposed, a vacancy opens. This vacancy is filled, and crime in the community continues unabated.

It is also true that regardless of the labor market analogy, new "recruits" constantly refresh the ranks of active criminals. A recent study of a cohort of California-born males discovered that, by the time they had reached age 29, 35 percent had been arrested (66 percent for blacks). [25] As more young people are recruited into and retained in a criminal life-style, the ability of back-end responses (such as imprisonment) to increase public safety is severely limited because of the replenishing supply of young people who are entering into criminal careers.

ALTERNATIVES TO CURRENT POLICY

As we have seen, California's experience over the last decade fails to show that the "get tough" policy of dramatically increasing imprisonments has significantly reduced crime rates, despite the enormous expenditures on law enforcement and prison building. The challenge is to develop a new approach that will make better use of taxpayer funds, a new approach that recognizes that incarceration may have an impact, albeit limited, on crime rates; that focuses imprisonment on those most likely to pose a threat to society; and that redirects some resources into other promising approaches for reducing crime rates. As with all policy prescriptions, this comes with no guarantees, but the recommendations outlined here seem more consistent with what we have learned from research and experience.

1. *Begin by acknowledging the limits of a "get tough" policy on reducing crime.*

It is vital that political leaders and criminal justice professionals publicly acknowledge that justice agencies play a relatively limited role in crime control. Failure to do so means that the debate becomes misdirected. We spend inordinate amounts of time and energy debating how best to punish and how punitive various states and nations are in comparison to one another, even though the evidence suggests that punishment may be of limited relevance for crime control. [26, 27] Moreover, those who focus on the criminal justice system are offering the public a false hope, the hope that if the criminal justice system just did its job more competently—and criminals were punished more often and harsher—the public would be safe from most crime. The public gets some comfort from statistics showing that arrests and imprisonments are going up. But if 34 million crimes are being committed in this country, and only 31 million are ever detected, the only way to truly reduce crime is to find some way to stop some of the crime from being committed in the first place.

Of course, there are other reasons for putting people in prison besides the desire to deter and incapacitate. One of the most important is the moral one of retribution—delivering to the convicted criminal his "just deserts." Imprisonment also serves an important symbolic function by publicly defining the limits of appropriate behavior. For those reasons as well as the contribution that prisons *do* make to crime control, imprisonment remains an important and necessary component of the criminal justice system.

2. *Refocus who we put in prison.*

The earlier discussion showed that probation and parole violators account for a considerable part of the increase in California's inmate population.   Such persons account for about 20 percent of California's prison population on any given day, or about 21,200 inmates based on today's prison population. We could alleviate the pressure on California's crowded prison system by imprisoning far fewer of these persons. In the past, parole/probation revokees used to spend their two-to-six-month revocations periods in local jails, but as jails became crowded, violators have been increasingly returned directly to prison.

These short-term commitments serve to increase the size of the prison population, reduce the average length of terms served, and create security and administrative burdens on staff. Such a policy is also not cost-effective, since prison beds (with their added security and programming costs) are more expensive than jail beds. But some argue that imprisoning an offender for a "technical" violation is often used as a less costly and more effective substitute for a new criminal prosecution. In other words, those who are revoked for rule violations were actually being removed from supervision due to the commission of new crimes, but because of the expense and time involved in prosecuting a new offense, the revocation route is pursued instead. There is no data to reveal how many revocation cases were motivated by new crimes, but if crime prevention is the goal with such policies, it is not being achieved through this process because revocation cases will spend only a few short months behind bars upon their return. Moreover, recent RAND research failed to reveal a relationship between having a technical violation and having a new arrest. In other words, those who violate technical conditions are not necessarily the ones committing new crimes. [28]   If California wishes to reduce its reliance on prisons, a logical target population for alternative handling would be these very short-term probation and parole violators.

At the same time, we should continue our efforts to identify the most likely repeat offenders, consistent with constitutional principles and other legal safeguards. This is an area where additional research could help improve the crime reduction impact of the penal system.

3.   *Divert some resources to nonpenal strategies for crime prevention.*

Imprisonment is not the best nor the most efficient way to reduce crime. Drug clinics do more to rehabilitate drug addicts than prison, job training does more to reduce recidivism than jails, and early childhood prevention programs do more than any other factor to reduce a propensity to crime. [29] Of course, there are many obstacles to implementing effective programs, but as Peter Greenwood and Phyllis Ellickson discuss elsewhere in this book, several such programs have already moved a considerable distance in the right direction.

When the public debate focuses so heavily on punishment, it creates a false dichotomy between tough law enforcement and "soft on crime" social programs. The choice is not one or the other—it must be both. Californians have to create enough prison space to incarcerate the truly violent and also support programs to reduce the flood tide of criminals that current conditions create. Our expectations of what justice agencies can do should be lowered and our expectations of what social programs *must* do should rise.

Instead of calling for tougher crime control measures, policymakers should have used the opportunity of Los Angeles's recent civil disturbance to educate the public about the limited role that criminal justice agencies play in crime control. Particularly now, in the midst of the state's worst recession since the Great Depression, when every additional prison guard may mean one fewer teacher and every prison cell constructed may mean a gang prevention program unfunded, public education is essential to meaningful change in our approach to the crime problem.

NOTES

*The laws are: 1977 Determinate Sentence Law (specified fixed length prison terms for each felony); 1981 Beverly Burglary Bill (denied probation sentences to offenders convicted of residential burglary); 1982 Victims' Bill of Rights (gave more rights to victims); 1986 Domestic Violence Law (domestic violence was classified as a felony).

†In fact, in recent years, 30 percent of the CCI total figure stems from auto theft. It appears that auto theft has changed from the historically established pattern of youthful joyriding to a crime increasingly committed for commercial reasons. Such activities are taken more seriously by the police and the courts.

‡The major drop in drug arrests shown in Figure 7 in the mid-1970s is the result of the decriminalization of marijuana in 1976; increases since 1983 have been primarily cocaine and methamphetamine-related arrests.

REFERENCES

1. Lieberman, Paul, "40% of Riot Suspects Have Criminal Records," *Los Angeles Times,* May 19, 1992, p. B1.

2. Simpson, Richard, *Jailhouse Blues: Hard Time for County Taxpayers: A Study of Rising County Costs of Incarceration in California,* Sacramento: California Counties Foundation, 1991.

3. California Department of Corrections, Offender Information Services Branch, *California Prisoners and Parolees, 1990,* Sacramento, 1991.

4. California Commission, *California Blue Ribbon Commission on Inmate Population Management,* Final Report, Sacramento, 1990.

5. California Department of Justice, Bureau of Criminal Statistics and Special Services, *Crime and Delinquency in California, 1990,* Sacramento, 1991; California Department of Justice, Law Enforcement Information Center, *Crime and Delinquency in California, 1991,* Advance Release, Sacramento, 1992.

6. Bureau of Criminal Statistics and Special Services, *Crime in California and the United States*, Sacramento, 1990.

7. Thomas, J. B., "Motor Vehicle Theft in the Eighties," in Bureau of Criminal Statistics and Special Services, *Crime and Delinquency in California, 1980–1989*, Sacramento, 1990.

8. Bureau of Justice Statistics, U.S. Department of Justice, *Criminal Victimization 1990*, Washington, D.C., October 1991.

9. Langan, Patrick A., "America's Soaring Prison Population," *Science*, Vol. 251, March 29, 1991, pp. 1568–1573.

10. Wilson, James Q., *Thinking About Crime*, New York: Basic Books, 1975.

11. Cross-Drew, Candace, "Forcible Rape in California in the 1980s," in Bureau of Criminal Statistics and Special Services, *Crime and Delinquency in California, 1980–1989*, Sacramento, 1990.

12. Ekland-Olson, Sheldon, William R. Kelly, and Michael Eisenberg, "Crime and Incarceration: Some Comparative Findings from the 1980s," *Crime and Delinquency*, Vol. 38, No. 3, July 1972, pp. 393–416.

13. Zimring, Franklin E., "Correctional Growth in Context," Conference on California's Blue Ribbon Commission, Presentation, University of California, Berkeley, May 10–11, 1990.

14. Stutman, Robert M., and Richard J. Esposito, *Dead on Delivery: Inside the Drug Wars, Straight from the Street*, New York: Warner Books, 1992.

15. Austin, James, *The Consequences of Escalating the Use of Imprisonment: The Case Study of Florida*, San Francisco: National Council on Crime and Delinquency, June 1991.

16. Kleiman, Mark A. R., *Against Excess: Drug Policy for Results*, New York: Basic Books, 1992.

17. Blumstein, Alfred, Jacqueline Cohen, Jeffrey A. Roth, and Christy A. Visher, eds., *Criminal Careers and "Career Criminals,"* Vol. 1, Washington, D.C.: National Academy Press, 1986.

18. Wolfgang, Marvin E., Terence P. Thornberry, and Robert M. Figlio, *From Boy to Man, from Delinquency to Crime,* Chicago: University of Chicago Press, 1987.

19. Gottfredson, Michael R., and Travis Hirschi, *A General Theory of Crime,* Stanford: Stanford University Press, 1990.

20. DiIulio, John J., Jr., "Crime Policy," in *Setting Domestic Priorities,* Washington, D.C.: Brookings Institution, 1992.

21. Chaiken, Jan M., and Marcia R. Chaiken, *Varieties of Criminal Behavior,* Santa Monica, Calif.: RAND, R-2814-NIJ, 1982.

22. Greenwood, Peter W., and Allan F. Abrahamse, *Selective Incapacitation,* Santa Monica, Calif.: RAND, R-2815-NIJ, 1982.

23. Wilson, James Q., and Richard J. Herrnstein, *Crime and Human Nature,* New York: Simon & Schuster, 1985.

24. Petersilia, Joan R., Susan Turner, with Joyce E. Peterson, *Prison Versus Probation in California: Implications for Crime and Offender Recidivism,* Santa Monica, Calif.: RAND, R-3323-NIJ, 1986.

25. Tillman, Robert, "The Prevalence and Incidence of Arrest Among Adult Males in California," *BCS Forum,* Sacramento: California Bureau of Criminal Statistics, 1987.

26. Lynch, James, *Imprisonment in Four Countries,* Washington, D.C.: Bureau of Statistics, Special Report, February 1987.

27. Selke, William L., and Steen A. Andersson, "A Model for Ranking the Punitiveness of the States," *Journal of Quantitative Criminology,* Vol. 8, No. 2, 1992, pp. 217–232.

28. Petersilia, Joan R., and Susan Turner, *Intensive Supervision for High-Risk Probationers: Findings from Three California Experiments,* Santa Monica, Calif.: RAND, R-3936-NIJ-BJA, 1990.

29. Tonry, Michael, Lloyd E. Ohlin, and David P. Farrington, *Human Development and Criminal Behavior: New Ways of Advancing Knowledge,* New York: Springer-Verlag, 1991.

Chapter Eight

Reforming California's Approach to Delinquent and High-Risk Youth

Peter W. Greenwood

INTRODUCTION

The problem of adolescent crime in California and in Los Angeles in particular has increasingly captured the attention of the public and the media. To a large extent, both the state and county have responded to this problem with punitive policies instead of focusing on prevention and with a heavy emphasis on residential rather than community-based programs. On a variety of measures, California ranks among the most punitive or neglectful of states in how it treats its high-risk youth. For example, California, with 11 percent of the U.S. population, accounts for more than 20 percent of the juveniles locked up in the entire nation.

Over the past 10 years, other states have been experimenting with a variety of programs to prevent adolescents from becoming delinquent or to rehabilitate them if they are. In their structure and content, these programs better reflect what we have learned about the roots of juvenile delinquency, and many of them have had promising results. California should learn from the experience of other states and move beyond punitiveness as its primary response to adolescent crime. Doing this will require substantial changes throughout the juvenile justice system.

JUVENILE CRIME

Predatory street crime is a young man's game. Most offenders begin their active criminal careers in their early teens, and the vast majority quit by their early 20s. Arrest rates (the fraction of a given age group arrested in any one year) for all types of crime peak before the age of 18 and decline sharply thereafter. As a consequence, the higher the proportion of young men in the general population, the higher the expected crime rate. In 1990, 9 percent of California's population were juveniles aged 13 through 17. In that year, juveniles accounted for 26 percent of all felony arrests for property offenses and 14 percent of all felony arrests for violent offenses.

There have been significant changes in juvenile arrest patterns over the past 10 years. Arrests for burglary, the most frequent type of juvenile crime, have fallen. In contrast, arrests for violent offenses and for drugs have substantially increased. For example, between 1985 and 1990 the rate of homicide arrests among juveniles increased by 151 percent.

Involvement in street crime is not equally distributed by social class and race; both offenders and victims are concentrated among those who are raised in impoverished communities and households. Since rates of poverty are strongly related to race (see chapters by Karoly and DaVanzo in this volume), it is no surprise that the rate of offending and victimization is high in the black community. In 1988 blacks accounted for 11 percent of the population in California; 20 percent of all arrests; 38 percent of all arrests for homicide; and 31 percent of all homicide victims. A study of the state's juvenile crime problems in the early 1980s estimated that, among black teens, the probability of being arrested for robbery was 17 times that of similarly aged whites. [1]

Arrest figures provide only crude estimates of the offender population since the probability of arrest for any one offense is only about 5 percent for most street crimes. In addition, arrest rates reflect to some degree the priorities and policies of the police. An alternative and more-detailed measure is provided by surveys that ask individuals to report their involvement in particular categories of offending. Recent self-report surveys suggest that between 28 and 38 percent of all males residing in high-crime neighborhoods participate in some form of street crime during their 16th year; those who are active (report at least one crime) commit between 20 and 40 serious offenses per year.

In recent years, concerns about traditional forms of juvenile delinquency have been overshadowed by concerns about the involvement of minority youth in drug dealing and gang violence. It is not clear whether the dramatic increase in cocaine sales that began with the introduction of crack in 1982 is the primary cause of the simultaneous increase in gang violence or just one of its many contributing factors. Juvenile arrests for drug offenses grew steadily during the 1980s, as did those for gang-related violence, but began to decline, along with those for adults, at the end of the decade.

Whatever the link between gangs and drugs, Los Angeles County now has the largest concentration of gang activity anywhere in the country, with estimates of the number of active gang members ranging from 50,000 to 100,000. Although most of the hundreds of individual gangs are associated with particular black or Hispanic neighborhoods, there are also gangs consisting primarily of various Asian nationalities, such as Cambodians and Vietnamese.

CALIFORNIA AND LOS ANGELES: RESPONSE TO JUVENILE CRIME

In recent years, both the state and the county have taken an increasingly punitive approach to juvenile crime. This approach is reflected in high incarceration rates and in the limited options for correctional placement.

Felony juvenile arrests in California declined in the early 1980s and then gradually rose again toward the end of the decade, reaching more than 238,000 in 1989. About 60 percent of these juvenile arrests resulted in a prosecutor filing charges in juvenile court; the other 40 percent were released by the police without any further action.

Analysis of a random sample of juvenile arrests selected from Los Angeles County in 1981 revealed that 38 percent of these arrests resulted in the filing of a petition with the juvenile court; 30 percent (76 percent of filings) were found delinquent; 11 percent (35 percent of those found delinquent) were placed in some type of residential program; and 4 percent were placed with the California Youth Authority (CYA). [1] The rate of CYA commitments from Los Angeles County reached a high of more than 1,600 in 1986; since then, it has remained fairly constant at around 1,350 per year.

National surveys of juvenile correctional facilities show that California has the highest per capita rate of male juveniles of any state in the country (1,099 per 100,000 versus a national average of

546 in 1987). The higher rate of incarcerating youth in California can only be partially explained by a higher arrest rate. The number of youth in custody in California per 1,000 juvenile arrests (84 in 1987) is 56 percent higher than the national average.

Juvenile courts in Los Angeles do not have the variety of privately run community-based options for placing youth that are available in many other parts of the country. The primary placement options are, in increasing order of severity, (1) general probation, which means little or no supervision; (2) placement in one of a small number of privately run group homes, which are licensed by the state and monitored by the county; (3) placement in one of a group of camps run by Probation in outlying areas of the county; or (4) commitment to the CYA for placement in one of their secure institutions. Youth who are confined prior to placement are held in one of several severely overcrowded juvenile halls.

Most of the probation camps, which are scheduled for closure in the Probation Department's fiscal year 1993 budget, are minimum security facilities housing 50 to 100 youth for stays averaging between six to nine months. The CYA facilities, each of which houses from 600 to more than 1,500 youths, are much more secure and provide a much greater range of educational and vocational programming. During recent years, the average length of stay for CYA youth has been about 24 months, double what it was a decade ago and twice the national average.

In general, California has resisted the national trend toward more flexible correctional facilities and is now among the states lowest in the use of private providers—19 percent versus a national average of 41 percent. A recent analysis of juveniles in custody from Los Angeles County revealed that only 9 percent were in private facilities and that the proportion of juveniles in different types of facilities varied significantly by race. Only 8 percent of black youth in custody were in private facilities compared with 21 percent of white youth.

The incarceration rate for juveniles and the limited choice of correctional facilities are not the only dimensions on which California compares unfavorably to the nation. An index designed to measure several aspects of child well-being places California near the bottom in several other categories, including the percentage of children living in poverty (35th) and the percentage graduating from high school (42nd).

Other indicators of the declining investment in youth include increasing class sizes and elimination of many special programs (arts, music, sports, etc.) in the public schools; closing emergency health care and community mental health centers; reductions in programs, maintenance, and hours of operation for parks and recreation facilities; and reductions in summer youth employment programs.

CAUSES AND CORRELATES OF JUVENILE DELINQUENCY

California's punitive treatment of juvenile criminals is troubling because it is inconsistent with a growing body of evidence about the causes of juvenile delinquency. In recent years, a series of carefully designed studies have documented the progressive effects of dysfunctional and abusive families, inadequate child care and early childhood education, academic and behavioral problems in school, association with delinquent peers, and differential opportunities for participation in illegitimate versus legitimate employment.

Theorists have developed and tested a number of models to explain why some youth become delinquent. Since delinquency was observed to be more prevalent among youth residing in poorer neighborhoods, strain theorists argued that a primary cause was the frustration these youth faced in their inability to satisfy their normal needs and aspirations through legitimate means.

Control theorists countered with the argument that most individuals experience some degree of strain and frustration in meeting their needs. They believed that the primary factor distinguishing those who turn to crime from those who do not was the strength of their bonds with conventional institutions such as their families, schools, and churches. Control theorists believe that it is the social pressure created by these bonds that keeps most of us in check.

Social learning theorists assume neither a constant motivation (strain) for delinquency nor a constant restraining (social control) influence. Rather, they argue that decisions to engage in conforming or deviant behavior are promoted by social reinforcement—a constant stream of rewards and punishments in response to behavior.

Social learning theory emphasizes the importance of role models in influencing behavior and suggests that youth are more likely to be delinquent if they grow up in an environment where such behavior is condoned or engaged in. Many leading theorists now favor an integrated model that combines the effects of strain, control, and social learning.

From a statistical standpoint, the factors that predict delinquency include the following:

- Having parents with histories of dysfunctional behavior (crime, or substance abuse)

- Inadequate or inappropriate parental supervision and discipline

- Early involvement in high-risk behaviors (delinquency, substance abuse, sex)

- Behavioral or academic problems in school

- Association with delinquent peers [2,3]

ALTERNATIVES TO PUNITIVENESS: EFFECTIVENESS OF PROGRAMS

Although criminologists argue about which types of programs are most effective in addressing the root causes of juvenile delinquency, most agree that improving prenatal health care, early childhood education, parent training, public schools, and youth employment opportunities are steps in the right direction. Additional candidates include programs that help families improve their problem solving, communications, and ability to manage their kids' behavior; after school recreational programs; and special outreach programs targeted on high-risk youth. For youth identified as active delinquents, community-based and residential programs can respond to each adolescent's needs and capabilities. [4]

A number of states have adopted programs along these general lines. Some of the programs have yet to be rigorously evaluated, but the assessments we have seem promising. The programs are of three basic types: prevention, supervisory, and custodial.

Prevention Programs

Since problems in early childhood health status and socialization have consistently been associated with increased risk of delinquency and of school failure, most experts believe that preventive efforts should focus on these areas. The strongest evidence in support of this approach is provided by long-term evaluation data for the Perry Pre-School Program, a precursor to Head Start. These data showed that the program substantially reduced the probability of arrest for high-risk youth participating in the program compared with a matched group of nonparticipants.

Problems in family management also increase the risk of delinquency. A number of programs have been developed to help parents learn techniques, such as the use of time-outs and behavioral contracts, for dealing with problem behavior in their children. Participation in these programs reduces subsequent delinquency and antisocial behavior. [5]

A third area for potential intervention is the school, which is second only to the home in terms of its influence on youth. Historically, the strategies that school systems have devised for dealing with disruptive youth feature increasing forms of punitive suspension and segregated programming. We have little evidence that these approaches change problem behaviors.

In recent years, a number of innovative programs have been fielded that appear to reduce the level of drug use among the general population and to improve the prospects of high-risk youth. As Ellickson discusses in her chapter, the best known of these programs use the "social influences" model to provide youth with accurate information about the health risks of using tobacco and illegal drugs, the true prevalence rate of use among their peers, and training in effective techniques for resisting peer pressure to use. These programs have been shown to significantly reduce initiation of cigarette and marijuana use, two activities predictive of subsequent delinquency.

Less well known are programs designed to reduce antisocial and non-drug-related forms of deviant behavior in school settings. Over the past decade, the Federal Office of Juvenile Justice and Delinquency Prevention supported a number of these programs. Those that appeared most effective in reducing delinquency for general school populations (1) involved staff, students, and the community in designing and managing school change; (2) involved schoolwide organizational changes aimed at increasing academic performance and enhancing school climate; and (3) included career education components. Although several programs tried to target high-risk youth, the only one that proved effective involved a special alternative class organized around a small number of learning projects that increased participation and group interaction. Programs that simply provided extra attention or services did not show positive results. [6] Other techniques that have been tried and found ineffective include programs designed simply to educate youth about the consequences of certain high-risk youth behavior or to scare them with dramatic portrayals of dire consequences.

Custodial and Supervisory Programs

Although most criminologists would argue that we should spend the bulk of our public funds trying to keep youths from becoming delinquent rather than rehabilitating them if they are, that is not the way we spend our money. The vast majority of public delinquency funds go to support custodial and supervisory programs designed for youth whom the juvenile courts have found to be delinquent. These include programs that provide various degrees and types of community supervision, daytime programming, group homes, and long-term residential placements in institutional or isolated wilderness settings.

During the past 25 years, expectations regarding the effectiveness of preventive or rehabilitative programs for juvenile delinquents and adult criminals have veered from extremely optimistic, to extremely pessimistic, to mildly hopeful. In 1967 President Johnson's Commission on Law Enforcement and the Administration of Justice proclaimed that recidivism (returning to criminal behavior) among juvenile and adult offenders could be greatly reduced by improving the educational background and training of correctional workers, placing a much higher percentage of offenders in community-based settings (on probation or in group homes), and emphasizing remedial education and job training. The commission's enthusiasm for these recommendations was based in part on preliminary evaluation reports from the CYA's Community Treatment Project, which was experimenting with new techniques for programming youth in the community based on a careful evaluation of their characteristics and needs.

Ten years later the consensus among criminal justice officials and scholars regarding the effectiveness of rehabilitative programs had switched dramatically, based primarily on the findings of several widely reported reviews of the corrections literature but also on the revelation that the CYA had not been reporting the results of its Community Treatment Project accurately. [7]

In the last few years, enthusiasm for rehabilitative programs has been rekindled by new evidence regarding factors that contribute to program effectiveness and by improvements in our knowledge about causal influences. Better analytic methods, which synthesize results across evaluations, make it possible to identify relatively small but consistent effects that would not be detected with conventional hypothesis testing and to explore the relationship between these effects and characteristics of the experimental programs and their subjects. We have learned the most about causal influences in the areas of identifying and measuring antisocial behavior in early childhood, and understanding the importance and mechanisms of social learning processes in shaping human behavior. Some of the key programs from which we have learned are described below.

Two recent studies that synthesized results across evaluations identified several characteristics associated with higher success in reducing recidivism. [8,9] These characteristics include focusing efforts on high-risk offenders; focusing programs on factors associated directly with delinquent activity, such as antisocial attitudes, anger management, substance abuse, etc.; avoiding the development of antisocial cliques; and utilizing cognitive/behavioral and social learning approaches that provide youth with frequent opportunities to confront real challenges and to practice appropriate coping skills. All the successful techniques produce larger effects when applied in community rather than institutional settings. This latter finding argues strongly for placing youth in community-based rather than institutional settings, whenever it is practical to do so.

The components generally thought to be necessary for these types of programs include an initial assessment to identify each youth's problems and assets; a process for developing and monitoring individual treatment plans; a positive peer culture, which supports prosocial and discourages antisocial behavior; remedial education programs; cognitive-behavioral programs to help youth deal with anger, substance abuse, sexual offending, and other problem behaviors; social and survival skills training to help adolescents cope with the outside world; efforts to educate other family members about their role in the youth's delinquency and to identify steps they can take to support more prosocial behavior; graduated release; and intensive aftercare following release to the community.

Trends in Correctional Institutions

Juvenile courts and specialized juvenile correctional institutions were developed at the beginning of the 20th century as alternatives to regular criminal prosecution and correctional programs. However, by the late 1960s, many large state juvenile institutions had become more custodial and punitive than the adult institutions they had been designed to replace. Starting with Massachusetts in 1971, a number of states (Pennsylvania, Colorado, Utah, New Jersey, Florida, and Michigan) have moved to decrease their use of large institutions, relying instead on a mix of community-based programs, many of which are operated by private providers. Although there is little evidence to suggest that such programs are more or less effective than those run by public agencies, officials in these states believe that this mix of public and private providers offers them a wider range of alternatives to meet the needs of individual youthful offenders.

In Massachusetts, more than 80 percent of the youth committed by the courts to the Department of Youth Services are now placed in programs run by private agencies. In New Jersey, about half of the youth committed to the state by local juvenile courts are placed in small (20–30 bed) community-based programs. Florida has recently contracted with a variety of private providers to provide specific programs or to manage institutions formerly operated by the state.

Periodic federally sponsored surveys of juvenile correctional facilities reveal the following trends in the use of private facilities:

- Between 1975 and 1986 admissions to public facilities declined by 7 percent, while admissions to private facilities increased by 122 percent.

- Private facilities tend to be smaller, provide more services, and have a longer average length of stay.

- Public facilities are more apt to be overcrowded.

- Costs of public and private facilities are about the same within geographic regions.

HOW IT GOT THIS WAY

We have seen that many other states have developed programs for juvenile offenders that are less punitive, more flexible, and more reflective of what we understand about the roots of, and potential remedies for, juvenile delinquency. Why has California remained so punitive? The answer is a complex blend of fiscal realities, politics, and red tape.

The Proposition 13 taxpayer revolt severely restricted the level of funding available to counties, including Los Angeles County. And, as surrounding counties have continued to grow by attracting Los Angeles County's wealthier middle class residents, they are being replaced by immigrant populations who place more of a burden on Los Angeles County services.

Proposition 13 was particularly hard on county probation departments, which are politically the weakest members of the county criminal justice systems. In earlier days, the state provided the counties with funds to support the development of innovative local programs. But as the subsidy payment failed to keep pace with inflation and as Probation had to absorb disproportionate Proposition 13 cuts, Probation has been forced to cut programs and services almost every year.

However, declining funding for probation services does not completely explain the limited availability of community-based programs for juvenile offenders in Los Angeles County. Other political factors have severely limited private sector participation, which in other states provides innovative alternatives. One impediment is simply bureaucratic red tape. Many of the private providers see Los Angeles County as being more difficult than any of the surrounding counties to do business with. Its staff are said to be more demanding in terms of their initial certification; the youth they send tend to be more difficult; and the county is much less prompt in paying its bills. No wonder private juvenile program providers in Southern California, who get paid the same daily rate for youth from any county, often prefer receiving youth from Ventura or Riverside County over those from Los Angeles.

Even beyond these bureaucratic roadblocks, Los Angeles County Probation has policies that exclude private programs used by many other counties throughout the state. Probation officials will not send youth to programs in the northern part of the state because they feel the youth will be too difficult to monitor; and they will not allow another county to monitor their youth on a courtesy basis, as many other counties do. Granted, county probation departments have an obligation to ensure that youth they place in private programs are treated appropriately. However, it appears that Probation's overly rigid requirements in Los Angeles prevent it from utilizing a wide range of programs like VisionQuest, which are receiving hundreds of youth from surrounding counties. [10]

Several years ago, the Los Angeles County–based Seaver Institute provided funding for the National Center for Institutions and Alternatives, a nationally recognized private organization, to prepare private presentence reports for youth whom Los Angeles County Probation had recommended for placement in the CYA. Even though the private program experienced a number of management problems and continued resistance from Probation staff, its reports and advocacy efforts still managed to reduce the CYA commitment rate among participating youth by about 50 percent. Nevertheless, the county showed no interest in continuing the program or adopting any of its approaches after the grant funds ran out. [11]

The state also impedes the development of quality programming for juvenile offenders. A private provider, Associated Marine Institutes (AMI) based in Tampa, Florida, has developed an innovative program model that integrates scuba (underwater diving) training and certification with more traditional remedial education and social skills training programs to provide a higher degree of physical challenge and excitement than is found in most traditional correctional programs. Over a period of 15 years, AMI has developed a highly respected network of about 30 local programs throughout Florida and the Southeast, with each institute providing daytime programs for 20–30 youth.

Several years ago, the California-based Packard Foundation agreed to underwrite the initial start-up and pilot testing costs for an AMI program in Monterey County, contingent on the state's developing a funding mechanism for supporting the program after the initial test period. Under the state's current funding rules, only the county's costs for a "residential placement" could be reimbursed by state Aid to Families with Dependent Children (AFDC) funds; those for a day program could not. For several years, the state legislature passed bills to allow reimbursing the program's costs, but each year the governor vetoed the legislation. California has yet to implement a program like the one offered by AMI.

Just as funding regulations limit the county's ability to innovate, experimentation with new programs by the CYA is limited by the Youthful Offender Parole Board, which has the final word on time served. This limitation recently prevented the CYA from competing for federal funds that were made available for developing experimental "boot camp" programs for juveniles designed to reduce their length of stay.

A PATH TO REFORM

Youthful criminality and gang problems are as serious in Los Angeles as they are anywhere in the country. The punitive response of both the state and county conflicts with what we have learned about juvenile delinquency. California should learn from the experience of other states and begin to develop and evaluate more appropriate programs for high-risk youth. To do that will require strong leadership to bring about needed reforms.

There is no evidence to suggest that any one program or policy reform will have more than marginal effects on the interrelated problems of juvenile delinquency, drug use, and gang involvement. Rather, any substantial improvement in this area will require a comprehensive and sustained campaign to improve the quality of childhood for youth in high-risk neighborhoods and to raise their expectations about their future. Here are what I perceive to be four basic ingredients of that campaign.

First, the state must take the lead in bringing about change. Although a few counties have been successful in developing innovative programs, it is the state as a whole that has fallen behind other states in its investment in youth. Both the executive branch, which needs to develop the programs, and the legislative branch, which needs to see that they are adequately funded, must be active change agents.

Leadership must come from the top. None of the states that have recently reformed their juvenile corrections programs has done so without strong support from the governor's office. In fact, in most cases, the governor's office was the primary instigator of change.

The inadequate care, dangerous environment, and limited opportunities faced by many California youth should be continuing issues for governmental concern, not just the subject of one-shot reforms or editorial hand-wringing. The governor and legislature should appoint a standing Commission on Youth to ensure that these issues receive the consistent attention they deserve and to guide the development of an effective reform agenda. The commission's charter should be to investigate and monitor the quality of care, services, and opportunities available to youth in various parts of the state; to develop and assess new ideas for proposed reforms; and to monitor and evaluate their implementation over time. The commission should be composed of representatives from the health, education, social welfare, mental health, and juvenile justice professions as well as parents, researchers, and representatives from the executive, legislative, and judicial branches.

Second, we must reform the juvenile justice system and the kind of dispositional alternatives it offers. Several directions should be pursued.

- *Increase the role of private agencies in developing and operating programs.* This initiative does not imply that public agencies are incapable of running effective programs or that privately run programs are inherently superior. Rather, experience in other states suggests that greater participation by the private sector expands the variety of options available, improving the likelihood of finding an alternative that will work for any particular youth. The diversity across programs also appears to encourage healthy competition among them.

- *Develop funding mechanisms so that private providers can participate with publicly run residential facilities on an equal basis.* Currently the state only subsidizes residential care, while the counties must bear the full costs of any form of intensive supervision or day programs. We need to eliminate the bias against cheaper, and probably equally effective, nonresidential programs.

- *Increase the range and number of community-based placements.* Options that other states have developed and are productively using include intensive supervision and tracking; nonresidential programs, such as the marine-based programs run by AMI; short-term wilderness challenge or boot camp programs followed up by intensive community supervision; long-term wilderness challenge programs like VisionQuest; long-term community residential programs in which youth can develop and maintain links with their home community; and independent living programs for youth who have no other appropriate residential options following residential placement.

Developing these options should decrease the state's reliance on large, overcrowded, and outmoded institutions. These impersonal institutions impede the development of the close personal bonds and relationships essential to the rehabilitative process and inevitably become places that continue and even reinforce the kinds of gang conflict and confrontations with authority that these youth continually experience on the streets.

Third, we need to structure programs that more realistically reflect both the causes of and the course of treatment for delinquency. We know from a number of well-designed studies that chronic delinquency usually has its origins in early childhood experiences. We also know from experience with therapies for other types of behavioral disorders (overeating, smoking, substance abuse, etc.) that there are no quick cures for behavior patterns that have been allowed to develop over many years. Many chronic delinquents will require sustained periods of rehabilitative programming and supervision as they make the gradual transition from antisocial to responsible and productive adult behavior. To capture the cumulative benefits of sustained intervention efforts, some programs should be encouraged to provide a full continuum of care over an extended period rather than having the court treat each relapse as a total failure and initiate a new type of programming that ignores everything that has gone before.

Fourth, to ensure that we have the most effective programs possible, we must develop ways to collect outcome data for each provider and type of treatment program. Currently programs are evaluated by their compliance with state-mandated operational requirements and standards rather than on the basis of what they achieve. A number of states and programs have demonstrated that it is possible to routinely collect outcome measures, such as recidivism and academic achievement, in a way that permits comparing programs over time and with each other.

IMPEDIMENTS TO REFORM AND REALISTIC EXPECTATIONS

Two chronic problems in juvenile justice will always hamper reform attempts.

The first is the nature of juvenile delinquency. Juveniles who rebel against or reject adult values are extremely difficult to deal with, even when their behavior is not criminal. Teenage rebels can be difficult to turn around, whether in a school or in a correctional institution. Any parent who has tried to deal with a teenage drug problem, poor performance in school, or a turbulent teenage romance is aware that patience is required. For this reason, juvenile delinquency prevention or treatment programs will never have smooth sailing. Failure rates will always be high.

The second problem is rooted in the nature of the juvenile justice system. It is a large, complex bureaucracy made up of diverse philosophical and political interests. Each of the constituent agencies—police, prosecutor, court, defense, probation, CYA, private care providers—looks at juvenile delinquency problems from a different perspective and favors a different set of reforms. System reforms often produce outcomes different from what their proponents intended because of the compromises required to gain acceptance by the system's other constituents or because the program was sabotaged outright.

Those who work in the juvenile justice system are best equipped to recommend or evaluate the changes needed. No legislative committee or task force can develop the expertise and insight possessed by respected representatives of the juvenile bench, prosecution, defense bar, probation, corrections, and various juvenile advocacy groups. I believe the state should appoint a standing Juvenile Justice Commission, consisting of experienced representatives of the various practitioner and advocacy groups with an interest in the system. The purpose of this commission would be to develop more-detailed proposals for bringing about the kinds of reforms described in this chapter, monitoring their implementation, and developing detailed policy guidelines for their use. This type of commission has proved useful in guiding the reform of sentencing practices in both the juvenile and adult systems in a number of states.

Some readers may conclude that these recommendations merely repeat the usual "liberal" nostrums in favor of treating the "root causes" of crime and juvenile delinquency, an approach largely discredited in the eyes of the current political consensus by the perceived failure of President Lyndon Johnson's War on Poverty.

In my view, this popular perception is inaccurate. Far from being discredited, many of the programs recommended here, such as early childhood education and community-based corrections, have been validated by careful evaluations or experience in other states. Rather, it is the "neglect of fundamental services" and "get-tough-on-crime" approaches of the past decade that appear to be discredited both by current conditions and by research. As a state that now leads the nation in its rates of incarceration and crime, but is ranked at the bottom on important measures of youth welfare, California should recognize that some changes in funding priorities are in order.

REFERENCES

1. Greenwood, Peter W., Albert J. Lipson, Allan F. Abrahamse, Franklin E. Zimring, *Youth Crime and Juvenile Justice in*

California: A Report to the Legislature. Santa Monica, Calif.: RAND, R-3016-CSA, 1983.

2. Elliott, Delbert S., David Huizinga, and Scott Menard, *Multiple Problem Youth: Delinquency, Substance Use, and Mental Health Problems,* New York: Springer-Verlag, 1989.

3. Hawkins, David J., Denise M. Lishner, Jeffrey M. Jenson, and Richard Catalano, "Delinquents and Drugs: What the Evidence Suggests About Prevention and Treatment Programming," in Barry S. Brown and Arnold R. Mills, eds., *Youth at High Risk for Substance Abuse,* National Institute on Drug Abuse, DHHS Publication No. (ADM)87–1537 ADAMHA, 1987.

4. Greenwood, Peter W., and Franklin E. Zimring, *One More Chance: The Pursuit of Promising Intervention Strategies for Chronic Juvenile Offenders,* Santa Monica, Calif.: RAND, R-3214-OJJDP, 1985.

5. Patterson, Gerald R., P. Chamberlain, and J. B. Reid, "A Comparative Evaluation of a Parent-Training Program," *Behavior Therapy,* Vol. 13, 1982, pp. 638–650.

6. Gottfredson, Denise, "An Empirical Test of School-based Environmental and Individual Interventions to Reduce the Risk of Delinquent Behavior," *Criminology,* Vol. 24, No. 4, 1986.

7. Sechrest, Lee, Susan O. White, and Elizabeth D. Brown, eds., *The Rehabilitation of Criminal Offenders: Problems and Prospects,* Washington, D.C.: National Academy of Sciences, 1979.

8. Andrews, D. A., Ivan Zinger, R. D. Hoge, James Bonta, Paul Gendreau, and Francis T. Cullen, "Does Correctional Treatment Work? A Clinically-Relevant and Psychologically-Informed Meta-Analysis," *Criminology,* Vol. 28, No. 3, 1990, pp. 369–404.

9. Lipsey, Mark W., "Juvenile Delinquency Treatment: A Meta-Analytic Inquiry into the Variability of Effects," in *Meta-Analysis for Explanation: A Casebook,* New York: Russell Sage Foundation, 1991.

10. Greenwood, Peter W., and Susan Turner, *The VisionQuest Program: An Evaluation*, Santa Monica, Calif.: RAND, R-3445-OJJDP, 1987.

11. Greenwood, Peter W., and Susan Turner, "The Impact of Private Pre-Sentence Reports on Dispositions of Serious Juvenile Offenders," *Justice Quarterly*, forthcoming.

Chapter Nine

Street Drug Markets in Inner-City Neighborhoods
Matching Policy to Reality

Peter H. Reuter and Robert J. MacCoun

INTRODUCTION

In the last 10 years, public opinion surveys, the news media, and Hollywood films like *Colors, Boyz 'n the Hood,* and *New Jack City* have all portrayed street drug markets as a major urban problem. Associated with hard drug use and violence, the markets have come to symbolize the decay of American cities. While drug problems are by no means unique to the inner cities—indeed, some surveys suggest higher rates of drug use among suburban populations—inner-city drug markets have an insidious effect that goes beyond the fact of drug use. First, urban street markets are more visible and more violent than other types of drug selling. Second, the attraction of fabulous profits from the drug trade appears to offer urban youth a tantalizing alternative to staying in school and finding legitimate jobs, especially in communities where jobs are scarce and pay low. Street markets seem to have made drug dealing an essential feature of the economic life of inner cities.

In Los Angeles, the emergence of large-scale drug markets appears, at least on the surface, intertwined with the growing power and visibility of street gangs that actively participate in the cocaine trade. Indeed, drug dealing has led the gangs to extend their activities to wholesale and street distribution of drugs to other cities in the West and Southwest. Some believe that the two phenomena feed on each other: the potential profits from drug selling increase the strength and violence of the gangs, while the highly organized gang structure increases the efficiency and violence of the drug trade.

The primary national policy response to the markets, mirrored in Los Angeles, has been to get tough. Between 1981 and 1991, for example, state prison commitments for drug offenses rose eightfold. Law enforcement is the most direct response to what manifests itself most visibly as a crime problem; however, as we shall see, the enforcement campaign has had a very limited effect.

Alternatives to enforcement have been proposed. For example, in the long run, drug prevention programs may dampen the future demand for drugs. Drug treatment could reduce both the number of buyers and sellers. Rebuilding the economic structure of the inner city, devastated over the last two decades by the decline of American manufacturing, could provide better paying jobs, thus reducing the supply of young men eager to make more than minimum wages by selling drugs. Better schooling for inner-city children could give them marketable skills.

Choices among these policies should have a sound empirical basis. But so far they have been based on vague impressions rather than on systematic evidence about the causes, extent, and dynamics of street-level drug selling. Because we haven't known enough about how street markets worked, we haven't known how to design programs that might change the behavior of buyers and sellers.

Our own recent research, and that of others, has begun to fill in some of the gaps in our understanding. The results of this research lead us to believe that enforcement will not substantially reduce either drug use or drug dealing below current levels. However, what we have learned suggests that the street markets of the 1990s will be different from those of the 1980s, as shifting social norms reduce the number of middle class cocaine users. As the demand for drugs declines, street markets will no longer offer sellers such attractive profits, and legitimate jobs may become more competitive.

But changes in the market will not discourage older dealers, who are more likely to be addicts. If drug selling becomes less profitable, they may need to commit more crimes to finance their habits. Drug treatment programs are the only potentially effective intervention for older dealers.

To understand how this scenario could unfold, we shall discuss why street drug markets emerged in the 1980s, who buys and sells in them, how the markets affect the economies of their communities, and how the characteristics of the markets themselves become the seeds of change.

DRUG MARKETS IN HISTORICAL PERSPECTIVE

Although drug use has been a prominent public concern since the explosion of marijuana and LSD use during the late 1960s, drug selling has been a distinctive problem only since the emergence of mass cocaine markets in the 1980s. Marijuana was so accessible and relatively cheap that it has always attracted a large number of part-time sellers, working in a wide array of socioeconomic settings. For example, college students typically bought their drugs from campus friends in dormitories; the sellers in turn bought it from wholesalers in private transactions away from the streets or, in recent years, from local growers. High-level figures in the industry, particularly those who ran smuggling operations for marijuana imported from Colombia, amassed huge fortunes, but most sellers made modest profits. Marijuana was certainly available on inner-city streets, but it was a small economic activity and generated little violence or disorder.

Heroin, which emerged as a significant problem at the end of the 1960s, also generated small incomes for most retailers but for very different reasons. Heroin is sold mostly by addicts, for whom the sale is less important as a method of generating cash than as a source of the drug for personal use. A typical retailer might get five bags of heroin for $80 (each containing 10 milligrams of pure heroin and 90 milligrams of some diluting agent) and sell four of them for $20 each, keeping the fifth bag for his own use. Though the theoretical estimates of heroin revenues are quite large (perhaps $10 billion nationally each year), actual net cash earnings are much smaller, and a number of studies show that most addict/retailers make only a few thousand dollars a year. Heroin selling was always concentrated in the inner city and attracted a certain amount of crime and disorder, but the markets themselves tended to be small and local.

The cocaine market that emerged in the 1980s was very different. In the 1970s, cocaine was an expensive drug with a relatively benign reputation. As a result, there was a substantial middle class demand for cocaine in the late 1970s and early 1980s. By the mid-1980s, however, considerable stigma had become associated with its sale and use. At the same time, however, *crack,* or "rock," a new form of smokable cocaine, began to appear in major cities. Because crack is easily sold in smaller and hence cheaper packages, it was more accessible than powdered cocaine to lower-income populations. As the demand for crack exploded, crack selling provided the lure of quick cash, status, and excitement for many young males with poor job prospects. And because the drug tends to be sold in repeated transactions involving small doses, crack markets tended to form in or near city street locations, where buyers could readily locate sellers and quickly consummate anonymous transactions. Thus, crack stimulated a rapid expansion of inner-city drug markets.

A PROFILE OF DRUG MARKETS IN WASHINGTON, D.C.

Until recently, we knew little about who actually participates in inner-city drug markets and how much they earn selling drugs. [1] The most comprehensive data on the extent of drug selling in a city and on the earnings and careers of low-level drug sellers come from a study that we conducted in Washington, D.C., in the late 1980s. [2] What we found partly confirmed and partly contradicted the conventional wisdom. It is true that drug selling has attracted a significant share of young black males in the District's inner city, but their earnings from drug selling are surprisingly low and their involvement in the legitimate economy surprisingly high.

Unfortunately, the scarcity of systematic empirical research on drug dealing makes it difficult to know how well our findings from Washington in the late 1980s characterize other American cities or more recent years. Where possible, we can compare our findings to those of recent studies in other cities, but such studies are scarce, and the sheer difficulty of observing this illicit activity makes comparison across different methodologies problematic. Washington differs from Los Angeles in some important respects; most notably, it lacks the extensive and highly developed gang structure found in areas like South Central and East LA. But both LA Sheriff Sherman Block and District Attorney Ira Reiner have recently suggested that the local gangs/drugs connection has been overstated, and indeed, recent research suggests that the majority of local drug selling arrests involve nongang members. [3] Moreover, Washington and Los

Angeles have many things in common, including social strife; in the late 1980s, Washington and Los Angeles rated first and second among major American cities in homicide rates for black male adolescents. [4]

Who Participates in the Washington, D.C., Drug Market?

The District of Columbia has a population of about 625,000. Data from the Pretrial Services Agency (PSA) in Washington for all persons charged with a criminal offense between 1985 and 1987 showed that 11,430 residents were charged with drug selling in that three-year period; another 5,600 were charged with a drug possession offense.

Most of those charged with drug selling were young, male, and black; in a city that is 66 percent black, 99 percent of residents charged with drug selling were black. We estimated that of those black males born in 1967 and living in Washington in 1987, approximately one out of six was charged with selling drugs between 1985 and 1987—that is, one out of six black males between the ages of 18 and 20. [2] This estimate is almost certainly low because the PSA only counts those sellers who were arrested; presumably others managed to evade arrest. Those in their late teens and early twenties were more involved than older groups during the same period, but even among those born in 1957, nearly 10 percent were charged with drug selling in the three years from 1985 to 1987—that is, nearly 10 percent of black males between the ages of 28 and 30.

Indeed, drug selling came to dominate the criminal activity of young adults in the late 1980s. Nearly two-thirds of the group born in 1967 had at least one drug charge. Moreover, it appears that groups born later were even more involved in drug selling than were previous groups at the same age.

Contrary to the popular stereotype, two-thirds of Washington, D.C., drug sellers were legitimately employed at the time of their arrest. In this respect, they did not look much different from those arrested for other crimes. However, drug sellers at any age were much less likely to have finished high school than other arrestees—only 35 percent compared to about half for other offenses.

How Much Do Dealers Earn?

The media provide numerous accounts of fabulous earnings from selling drugs on the street corners of the nation's cities. For example, a 1991 article in *U.S. News and World Report* suggested that "crack's hold on inner-city kids is logic. . . . High-wage, low-skill manufacturing jobs have disappeared from the inner cities. Crack selling became rationalized as the only ticket to prosperity." [5] *Time* reported that "lookout is the entry-level position for nine- and ten-year olds. They can make $100 per day warning dealers when police are in the area. . . . The next step up the ladder is runner, a job that can pay more than $300 a day. . . . Finally, an enterprising young man graduates to the status of dealer, king of the street. In a hot market like New York City, an aggressive teenage dealer can make up to $3,000 per day." [6] If such reports are true, it is hard to imagine that giving kids access to jobs paying $10 per hour rather than $5—surely a very ambitious goal in itself—would coax them away from drug selling.

To learn what low-level drug dealers really earned, we interviewed 186 adult dealers who were sentenced to probation for some offense, mostly an offense other than drug selling. [2] These interviews suggest that most dealers sell only on a part-time basis and, consequently, do not have large monthly incomes from their drug deals. Indeed, the vast majority of them put in many more hours at a legitimate job than at drug selling. However, drug selling paid much better on an hourly basis and also provided access to cheaper drugs. Even though nearly half reported keeping some of their drug consignment for their own use, a similar fraction also spent some of their earnings on buying drugs.

Tables 1 and 2 present some of the major findings from our survey. Dealers grossed about $3,560 a month selling drugs, a figure quite similar to the reported gross monthly earnings of a sample of New York City drug sellers during roughly the same time period. [7] But after subtracting the often sizable expenses of the drug business, the average dealer in our sample netted only about $1,800 a month. And the median, which is less sensitive to a few large reports, suggests that the *typical* dealer in our sample only netted about $721 a month—less than $9,000 a year. This is hardly the kind of profit that purchases extravagant cars and houses. Clearly, the media images of

Table 1

Monthly Income of Street-Level Drug Sellers in Washington, D.C. (in dollars)

		Percentile		
Source	25th	50th (median)	75th	Average (mean)
Nondrug criminal income	0	0	50	215
Gross income from drug-selling activity[a]	300	1,333	3,733	3,558
Net income from drug-selling activity	25	721	2,500	1,799
Total criminal income	33	833	2,617	2,015
Total legal income	237	715	1,000	849
Total income (all sources)	836	1,647	3,830	2,863

[a]Gross drug-selling income minus total drug-business expenses.

SOURCE: Peter H. Reuter, Robert J. MacCoun, and Patrick J. Murphy, *Money from Crime: A Study of the Economics of Drug Dealing in Washington, D.C.*, Santa Monica, Calif.: RAND, R-3894-RF, 1990.

dealers hauling in thousands of dollars for a night's work are greatly exaggerated or at least unrepresentative of the typical experience.

Table 2 helps to explain why dealers earned relatively little. Only about three out of eight of the dealers sold five days a week or more often, typically earning about $2,000 a month. Nearly one-quarter sold no more than once a week. When they did sell, most reported selling only about three hours a day. About two-thirds were legitimately employed during the six-month period prior to probation, and three-quarters reported at least some legitimate work earnings. Their legitimate jobs were frequently semiskilled, but many had experienced frequent job changes. We estimated that they made about $30 per hour during the time they sold, as compared with $7 per hour during their legitimate jobs.

Why did sellers spend less time at the better paying business of drug selling than at their legitimate job? Drug selling seems to be an underground form of "moonlighting" with which poorly educated males supplement their primary jobs, and they choose to do their moonlighting at those times when they can maximize earnings. There are a few hours each day and a few days each week and month

Table 2

Sales Activity, by Major Drug, for Street-Level Drug Sellers in Washington, D.C.

Characteristics	All	Major Drug Sold				
		Crack	Cocaine	PCP	Marij.	Heroin
Number	182	61	59	30	16	16
Participation frequency (%):						
Daily	37	41	39	37	21	38
Several days/wk.	40	39	41	37	43	31
1 day/wk. or less	23	20	20	27	36	31
Median hours spent selling[a]	3	4	4	3	1	4
Median # sales[a]	13	16	15	10	4	14
Kept drug for self (%):	41	39	33	36	56	69
Half or more	11	11	12	13	6	6
Less than half	30	28	21	23	50	63

[a]On last regular day of selling.

SOURCE: Peter H. Reuter, Robert J. MacCoun, and Patrick J. Murphy, *Money from Crime: A Study of the Economics of Drug Dealing in Washington, D.C.*, Santa Monica, Calif.: RAND, R-3894-RF, 1990.

when earnings are high. For example, few transactions take place in the middle of the day, except perhaps at lunch breaks. Most purchases occur in the morning—for heroin—or in the evening or at night—for cocaine. Business gets brisker near the weekends or perhaps even near paydays. This would explain why so many of those we interviewed reported selling only one day a week or a couple of days each month. Being the only dealer on a street corner at 2 P.M. on Tuesday afternoon is likely to generate few sales and might attract a lot of police attention. There is some safety in numbers here and perhaps safety in darkness as well.

Balancing the Risks and Benefits of Drug Dealing

Drug dealing is a risky business, and a dealer's perception of risk must also play a role in how many hours to spend selling. We estimated that a regular drug dealer in Washington (selling at least two days a week) faced almost a one in four chance of going to prison. The more time a dealer puts into the business, the higher the probability that he is arrested and incarcerated. We estimated that a street-level Washington dealer might expect to spend about one-third of his time incarcerated. He also had an annual probability of one in 70 of being killed in the course of dealing and one in 14 of being seriously injured. These high risks may explain why people earning $7 per hour in legitimate work were able to earn $30 per hour in the criminal market place; the surplus is their reimbursement for risk.

Balancing these risks are the benefits obtained from selling, not limited just to money. Nearly 80 percent of the dealers we interviewed used an expensive drug during the six months before their last arrest, and they spent about one-quarter of their drug earnings on drugs for themselves. In addition, one-quarter kept some of the drugs they were supposed to sell for their personal use; to that extent, our estimates of earnings underestimate what dealers get from participation in the trade.

In sum, legitimate work and drug selling were complementary for many dealers: drug money supplemented their relatively modest legitimate wages, and the greater time spent in legitimate work helped limit their exposure to the risks associated with drug markets.

Drug Selling by Adolescents

So far, we have described only the behavior of adults. In collaboration with the Urban Institute, we also obtained data on adolescent drug dealers. [2]

Interviews with about 400 ninth and tenth graders in the poorest part of the District of Columbia revealed that almost one-sixth reported at least occasional drug selling. For those older than $16\frac{1}{2}$, the prevalence rate was closer to one-third. Surprisingly, more of the total sample reported selling drugs than using drugs; 16 percent versus 11 percent. Moreover, there was little overlap between the two groups; only 20 percent of the sellers reported use in the previous year. From the interviews it seemed that these young sellers saw drug distribution as very profitable and only moderately risky in terms of jail. Indeed, compared to the true figures, adolescents appear to overestimate both the profits associated with drug selling and the risk of getting killed or seriously injured in the course of a year's dealing, but they underestimate the risks of arrest and imprisonment.

The interview data reveal a significant difference in the drug-using behavior of adolescent and adult dealers. The vast majority of the adult dealers were themselves users of expensive drugs, and their street dealing seemed strongly motivated by that use. However, the adolescents seemed to have chosen drug selling as a way to make a lot of money. A recent study of adolescent dealers in Tampa, Florida, also found that drug selling tended to precede drug using. [8] Apparently, youngsters start peddling drugs because they see it as a path to economic mobility; unfortunately, selling brings contact with a drug-using subculture that may be hard to resist.

EFFECT OF DRUG MARKETS ON NEIGHBORHOODS

The Washington, D.C., study and other recent research have provided valuable information about the background, earnings, and activities of drug sellers. We need equally reliable data about the dynamics of street markets and how they affect the neighborhoods in which they are located.

Unfortunately, we lack empirical information on these topics. For example, the conventional wisdom holds that inner-city markets are fueled by middle class suburban buyers. Anecdotes certainly show that such buyers are found in the market, but unfortunately anecdotes provide no sense of how much of the market these buyers constitute. Survey evidence that most drug users are middle class does not help much here, because the question is what share of all sales in inner cities are to buyers from a particular socioeconomic background. The economic effect on neighborhoods also depends on the extent to which dealers reside in the neighborhoods in which they sell drugs. Again, there has been no systematic empirical research on this question. Ethnographic and anecdotal evidence suggests that dealers are generally more likely to be neighborhood residents but that nonresident dealers are also active in some neighborhoods.

Since we lack empirical data on these important dimensions of street markets, in the discussion that follows we suggest possible types of drug markets and explore the implications of each type. These categories illustrate how more-detailed knowledge about street markets could help us select effective policies to combat them.

Types of Drug Markets

All street markets have certain features in common. In each market, cash leaves the neighborhood via payments to drug importers and producers. Moreover, each market drains the human capital of the neighborhood to the extent that residents are exposed to the risks of addictive drug use, incarceration, and illicit activities that may interfere with schooling and legitimate work. However, the markets differ in the flow of cash for retail sales, and we believe they also differ in their economic effect, the violence they engender, and in their responsiveness to policy interventions.

We can distinguish four general types of markets, as seen in Figure 1. This distinction covers the possible combinations of resident and nonresident sellers and buyers; however, we can only speculate about the behavior of each market, and we cannot rank the relative frequency of each market type with any confidence.

We refer to markets characterized by mostly resident dealers and customers as *local markets*. Local markets are unlikely to provide a

		Customers	
		Mostly residents	*Mostly outsiders*
Dealers	*Mostly residents*	Local market	Export market
	Mostly outsiders	Import market	Public market

Figure 1—Types of Illicit Neighborhood Drug Markets

net economic gain for the neighborhood—they are more likely to generate a net economic loss. Nevertheless, because local markets meet a local demand and can readily relocate in covert settings, they may be difficult for the police to uproot.

Export markets exist when resident dealers sell drugs to nonresidents; these are frequently "drive-through" markets. So long as the inflow of cash exceeds the deleterious economic effects of market participation and drug use, export markets are potentially a net economic gain for the neighborhood. Thus, there may actually be some tacit neighborhood resistance to police intervention in export markets. Jeffrey Fagan has noted that, in such markets, "since neighborhood residents benefit from the secondary economic demand generated by drug selling, this undercuts efforts at formal and informal social control. Residents are likely to be less willing to disrupt drug selling when they directly benefit from it." [7, p. 26]

We characterize markets where mostly nonresident dealers sell to local residents as *import markets*, although perhaps a more apt (though value-laden) label would be "parasitic markets." Finally, markets where both sellers and customers are mostly nonresidents we call *public markets* because these tend to occur at large public locations like parks, train or bus stations, or schools. The effect of import and public markets on neighborhoods is likely to be particularly insidious—a net outflow of cash and other resources.

We would expect residents to demand, or at least cooperate with, police intervention in import markets. However, police intervention could have different effects in import and public markets. A disrupted import market may reappear in a new neighborhood, but public markets are likely to be particularly difficult to reestablish, at least in the short run, because sellers and buyers are generally strangers and may have difficulty locating each other at a new location.

Market-Related Violence

Paul Goldstein has distinguished three different ways in which illicit drugs are associated with violence. [9] *Psychopharmacological* violence results from aggression-promoting effects of a substance on behavior (e.g., high doses of cocaine appear to increase the likelihood of violent conduct). *Economic compulsive* violence occurs during crimes committed by addicted users in an effort to finance their drug use. Finally, there is the *systemic* violence associated with competitive illicit markets. [7,10] Systemic violence can involve turf battles among sellers and disputes with customers over transactions. In addition, sellers may use violence or the threat of violence in an effort to control their employees, intimidate neighbors, and protect their assets.

Goldstein and his colleagues found that just over half of a sample of New York City homicides in 1988 appeared to be drug related. Of these, almost three-quarters were classified as systemic and were likely to involve crack (61 percent) or powdered cocaine (27 percent). [9] The prevalence of systemic homicides illustrates how the crack market encourages and rewards violence and attracts violent individuals. A recent survey of urban adolescents [11] found that being a drug seller was one of the strongest predictors of handgun ownership and reported ease of access to guns.

Our four categories of neighborhood markets could help predict the amount and nature of systemic violence.

- We would expect local markets to be the least violent: informal social controls, ongoing social relationships, and established territorial boundaries should limit both dealer/dealer and dealer/customer conflicts.

- Export markets may also be relatively nonviolent but for a different reason: dealers have a strong incentive to discourage violence to avoid driving away customers, particularly upscale customers.

- On the other hand, import and public markets are both prone to violence. Import markets are likely to encounter neighbor/dealer conflicts, dealer/customer conflicts, and dealer/dealer conflicts. The lack of clear territorial boundaries in public markets promotes dealer/dealer conflicts, while the anonymous and impersonal transactions promote dealer/customer mistrust and conflict.

POLICY RESPONSE TO DRUG MARKETS

We have discussed why street drug markets emerged in the 1980s and who buys and sells in them. We have also proposed a way of classifying markets that helps us understand how they interact, economically and socially, with neighborhoods. We now describe and assess the governmental response to street drug markets. Unfortunately, neither the description nor the assessment is very complete. Relatively little is known about local responses across American cities and neighborhoods, and even less is known about how well different approaches work. This poor understanding complicates the task of making policy recommendations.

Enforcement

Number and composition of arrests. The primary response to the emergence of street markets has been increased enforcement. At least that is where most drug control money has been spent. Whether the increased enforcement has compensated for the growth in drug trafficking is harder to judge. We think it likely that drug markets grew faster than enforcement in the first half of the 1980s but less rapidly in the second half so that by 1990 drug selling was probably substantially riskier than it had been in 1980. [12]

The increased enforcement effort is reflected in the sharp increase in drug arrests nationally and in the changing composition of those arrests during the 1980s. In 1980 drug arrests by state and local police totaled 560,000; in 1990 the figure was 1.1 million. Even more striking was the changing composition of arrests. Arrests for the more serious offense of sale or distribution (rather than possession) rose from 127,000 to 345,000, and most of the increase was for offenses involving the more dangerous drugs of heroin and cocaine. Marijuana arrests fell from two-thirds of the total number to just one-third. The racial composition of drug arrests changed dramatically. In 1980, 23 percent of those arrested were black; the estimate for 1990 was 40 percent.

A large share of the arrests resulted in prison time. In 1988, the most recent year for which national figures are available, perhaps as many as 100,000 were incarcerated for at least one year, with larger numbers going to local jails to serve shorter sentences.

Los Angeles did not lag in enforcement activities. Data from the California Bureau of Criminal Statistics show the same surge in late 1980s drug arrests, the increasing share of minorities among the arrestees, and finally the increasingly severe punishments received by those arrested for drug selling (see Table 3). In 1982, 18 percent of all felony arrests (in Los Angeles County) were for drug offenses; by 1986 that figure had risen to 32 percent. Misdemeanor drug arrests, mostly for simple possession, actually fell sharply after 1985, while felony drug arrests rose from 29,000 in 1982 to a peak of 70,000 in 1989. Whites accounted for 29 percent of drug arrests in 1982; by 1991 that percentage had fallen to 21 percent. Finally, whereas in 1982 only a few hundred went to state prison, by 1990 that figure had risen to over 4,000.

These changes in enforcement reflected both changing realities and shifting perceptions of the drug problem in American cities, including Los Angeles. In the 1970s drug use itself was the central concern.

Table 3

Arrests and Convictions in Los Angeles County

	1982	1986	1990
Arrests, LA County			
Total arrests	99,499	517,737	585,524
Total drug arrests	64,867	05,334	86,844
White (%)	29	22	22
Black (%)	33	34	32
Hispanic (%)	37	42	39
Other (%)	1	2	6
Total felony arrests	159,662	189,097	215,804
Felony drug arrests	28,807	61,035	55,218
Total misdemeanor arrests	339,837	328,640	369,720
Misdemeanor drug arrests	36,060	44,299	31,626
Convictions, LA County			
Total felony convictions	39,685	55,909	51,837
Felony drug convictions	6,588	17,538	18,507
Prison (%)	7	16	25

SOURCE: Unpublished data from the California Bureau of Criminal Statistics.

By the mid-1980s it was the emergence of the street markets and the associated violence that dominated public fears. Certainly the poorer communities themselves were asking for aggressive enforcement to control those markets—hence the increasing share of arrests for drug selling in the rising total. Moreover, though whites constitute the majority of drug users and perhaps even of drug sellers, it is minorities who seem to dominate exposed drug selling in the inner city. Finally, the more severe sentencing for convicted drug sellers was consistent with the increased concern about drugs as a social problem.

Most of those arrested for drug offenses were low-level dealers. In part this reflects the sharply tiered nature of the drug distribution system. For every high-level dealer, there are literally hundreds of retailers and assistants steering customers to the seller, holding drugs, watching for police. So of the 345,000 people arrested nationally for drug distribution offenses in 1990, most must come from these lowest levels. The lowest levels are also where the most-exposed transactions take place and, thus, are where arrests are easiest to make. Finally, it is the retail trade that most directly generates the violence and disorder that so troubles communities; thus, it is a focus of police activity. Police do go after the big fish, but there simply are not many of them.

Effectiveness. How well has enforcement worked in suppressing street drug markets? Specifically, has it lowered drug use in the general population and has it reduced street drug markets and the harms associated with them?

On the whole, tough enforcement does not appear to have had a major independent effect on drug consumption, though it may well have reinforced other antidrug messages of society. National surveys showed sharply lower prevalence of drug use in the general population by the late 1980s. However, these same surveys also suggested that it was increasing social disapproval of drug use and concern about the dangers presented by the drugs themselves, rather than decreased availability or heightened legal risks, that produced this decline. [13] Except for marijuana, enforcement has not been notably successful in raising the price of illegal drugs, though increasing the price in order to lower consumption is usually taken as the primary short-term goal of enforcement. Cocaine is perhaps no longer quite as cheap as it was in 1988, but in inflation-adjusted prices, it costs a great deal less than it did at the beginning of the 1980s. Heroin is very much cheaper than it was 10 years ago. Marijuana is substantially more expensive than 10 years ago, reflecting the success of interdiction against the Colombian marijuana industry.

Even if enforcement did not lower drug use, it would still be valuable to communities if it caused the street drug markets operating in them to shrink. If this is the goal of enforcement, then it would be important to know if some police tactics are more effective than others against certain types of markets.

Our taxonomy of markets suggests which markets are most vulnerable to police intervention. Local markets may be the most robust because the buyers and sellers know each other from nonmarket contacts. There are many possible sites for these markets, and if the market is broken up, buyers and sellers can easily find each other again and reestablish it. On the other hand, public markets may be very fragile. There are relatively few good locations for these markets (e.g., near ramps of highways in poorer parts of the city) and almost no contact between buyers and sellers outside of the market. Breaking up the market, together with modest police pressure if similar locations show signs of becoming centers for drug transactions, may be sufficient to keep buyers and sellers apart. Export and import markets probably fall in between with respect to their ability to function under enforcement pressure. Information about which type of market is functioning in a community could help focus police intervention on the softest targets.

Police have been very innovative in their approaches to suppressing street drug markets. [14] In various cities they have adopted community policing approaches, prevented cars from coming in for purchases by encouraging the construction of concrete barriers around heavily patronized areas, razed abandoned buildings where drugs are sold, confiscated buyers' cars, sent postcards to the addresses of the owners of cars observed buying drugs, and used many different "buy and bust"—and even "sell and bust"—techniques. Each approach seems to have some success, but it is usually of a local and somewhat ephemeral nature. Drug dealers have shown considerable capacity to adapt, even if the adaptation is less than complete. Moving markets around makes them work less well, though it may also make them more violent as existing market-sharing arrangements are broken up.

The future of enforcement. After a decade of intense enforcement efforts that produced very mixed results, disenchantment with enforcement as a major policy response is growing. A recent authoritative review of local drug enforcement concluded that "[a] growing share of local law-enforcement budgets is . . . being committed to programs that are both unproven and implausible." [15, p. 102]

Indeed, all sectors of the criminal justice system—police, prosecutors, and judges—have visibly wearied of drug enforcement. By the end of the 1980s, drug arrests were declining both nationally and in Los Angeles. In Los Angeles, drug-selling arrests started to fall in 1989, and by 1991 the figure had declined to 18,000, barely the 1986 level; at the national level, the decline began a year later but was similarly steep.

Although there has been no systematic examination of this recent downturn, it is likely that we are observing a backlash against the dominance of enforcement in local criminal justice systems. For example, in 1987 more than 50 percent of felony indictments in Washington, D.C., were for drug offenses. One observer suggested that the criminal justice system of New York suffered from bulimia during its peak concentration on drug offenses, gorging itself beyond its capacity on these easy-to-catch offenses and offenders and neglecting some of its more important functions as a consequence. [16] There is growing support at local, state, and federal levels to shift energy and resources toward programs designed to reduce the demand for drugs rather than to punish users.

Yet even after the decline in drug arrests at the end of the 1980s and the growing disenchantment with enforcement as a policy response, enforcement continues to dominate government spending on drug control. At the federal level that is easily documented by the annual budget figures supplied by the Office of National Drug Control Policy: the percentage going to enforcement (including overseas programs) has never dropped below 68 percent, though it has been declining modestly since 1988. The federal drug control budget has increased massively in the last decade, rising from $1.5 billion in 1981 to $7 billion (after adjusting for inflation) in 1991. It is more difficult to construct comparable figures for state and local governments. Our rough estimate is that these governments spent, out of their own revenues, more than the federal government ($18 billion in 1990 compared with federal spending of $10 billion in current dollars) and that an even higher share of expenditures at these lower levels of government goes to enforcement. As federal funding for treatment and prevention has risen in absolute terms, state and local governments have actually cut back their own funding. The result is a hypothetical drug control budget in 1990 that probably totaled about $28 billion, of which at least $21 billion went to police, courts, and corrections.

Treatment and Social Services, Economic Development, and Prevention

Enforcement was not, of course, the only government response to drugs in the 1980s. However, it is difficult to succinctly describe the nonenforcement response because so many different program areas are involved.

Treatment and social services. The official estimates of the number of persons in drug treatment at any one time increased from 173,000 in 1982 to 351,000 in 1989, but this statistic captures only part of what is done to ameliorate drug problems. Associated with drug treatment is a wide array of services intended to help the addict continue the abstinence that he or she often achieves temporarily while in treatment. These services include work training, job placement, provision of halfway houses, and programs aimed at improving parenting and other social skills.

Data suggest that even as the reach of treatment has broadened, the services offered have become shallower. Taking inflation into account, expenditures per client fell in the late 1970s from their 1977 peak. Though expenditures started to rise in the mid-1980s, they had not reached that peak again even by 1987. [17] Nor does the comparison of per person expenditures capture the consequences of the increasingly dysfunctional population being treated and the growing difficulty of treatment. The 1980 treatment population was dominated by heroin addicts receiving methadone; by 1990 a greater share were cocaine abusers. These addicts had started using the drug earlier than the typical heroin addict, and there is no counterpart to methadone for cocaine addiction; thus treating these addicts required more expensive skilled labor-intensive services such as psychotherapy.

The outcomes from the current treatment system are hardly encouraging. Studies have shown that anywhere from 30 to 90 percent of those entering drug treatment drop out and that a high percentage who complete treatment lapse into drug use within the next year, although the amount of use is often reduced. [18] These findings are scarcely surprising. The addicts receive few services to wean them from an environment that reinforces their drug habits. The question of whether a high-quality public treatment system could make a major difference is one that has not been seriously explored.

Economic development. Young males become drug sellers to make money. As described in works such as Nicholas Leman's *The Promised Land* and Richard Price's recent novel about crack selling, *Clockers,* drug selling can appear to be a rational choice in an inner city characterized by increasing alienation, failing schools and public housing, and bleak job prospects. Drug selling seems to combine money and pleasure in a particularly mischievous way, offering the promise of immediate wealth and status for young men who can hardly see those as plausible rewards if they follow the socially approved path of school and work.

The decline of the inner-city industrial employment base has made the profits from selling drugs look especially attractive. The supply of semiskilled jobs that permitted inner-city residents to move into the lower middle class in the postwar era has shrunk dramatically. What remains are jobs that offer low wages, indeed scarcely above poverty incomes, and little prospect of upward mobility.

The Washington data provide some basis for assessing how effective employment programs might be in motivating drug sellers to change their occupation for a legitimate one. The high employment rate for adult sellers and their relatively high wage rates suggest that employment programs can have a major effect on the choice to sell drugs only if they can provide very substantial improvements in the wages available. Many are appropriately skeptical that such improvements can be achieved, particularly at a time when the urban economy continues to deteriorate.

On the other hand, the fact that younger sellers are not involved in drug use itself and have overly optimistic views of the economic rewards of drug selling may provide the basis for an intervention that is more targeted and less expensive, namely making them better informed about the medium-term risks associated with drug distribution. One can view this as secondary prevention aimed at drug selling rather than drug use.

Prevention. The drug programs with the longest time horizon are prevention programs. Programs aimed at seventh graders in 1990 will not reduce the number of adult drug addicts until the second half of the decade; after all, we have observed dramatic declines in drug initiation rates among high school students for the past decade and yet the problems of street drug markets continued to worsen until quite recently.   One could argue that the evidence favors a "naturalistic" theory of drug epidemics. In this view these epidemics follow their own paths, insensitive to government programs. A new drug is highly attractive, and its users are eager and effective proponents. Later, the drug's damaging effects become more visible, and that is what ends the epidemic of initiation. Prevention may accelerate that effect but perhaps only marginally. On the other hand, ongoing prevention efforts are likely to build the resistance of youth to future epidemics. In another chapter in this book, Phyllis L. Ellickson summarizes what has been learned over the past decade about the promise and the limitations of prevention programs.

The Future

We have reviewed and assessed the drug control policies of the last decade. What policies look most promising for the future?

- We see little evidence that tougher enforcement is likely to have a major effect on the street drug markets of American cities. The capacity to punish is already strained and there are other competing demands for that scarce capacity. Nor does the considerable imagination of police tactics seem able to defeat the economic realities of drug markets.

- Creating a significantly better set of job prospects for the next generation of potential sellers, whether by redeveloping the inner-city industrial base or by providing better schooling, is greatly desirable for a number of reasons, but we believe that wage increases would have to be fairly substantial to bring about a significant reduction in drug selling. We are not optimistic about the likelihood of such a major government investment in the near future.

- In our view, an effective and well-integrated public treatment system will be essential to cope with the drug problems of the

1990s, and building up our currently underfunded and neglected treatment institutions should be a major drug policy priority. The discrepancy between national enforcement and treatment expenditures is great enough that we can afford to redirect funds to drug treatment without jeopardizing the efficacy of drug enforcement.

Despite our somewhat bleak analysis of program effectiveness, some aspects of the drug problem should get substantially better over the next decade. There are likely to be many fewer middle class drug users. Since the middle of the 1980s, fewer middle class kids have become drug users; the decline is not specific to any race or ethnic group but is associated with education. There is also evidence that many middle class users have kicked their drug habits, though it is more difficult for those who were frequent users than for others.

This change in societal norms has an important trickle-down effect. The legitimate earnings of middle class users fueled the cocaine market. It permitted cocaine sellers, even adolescent retail dealers, to earn large amounts for each hour they sold. If that money is withdrawn from the market, then the cocaine market of the 1990s may come to resemble the heroin market of the 1980s, largely dependent on money generated by property crime and dominated by adult addicts who earn relatively little cash from their participation but who take their rewards primarily in the form of low-cost drugs.

This change in the market should reduce the returns from drug selling, and if selling no longer looks like a route to big profits, fewer adolescents will become dealers. Street markets will probably shrink; in particular, there should be fewer export and public markets, the market types that we conjecture are the easiest to break up.

Unfortunately, the change in the market will also have some adverse consequences. The violence associated with drug markets is likely to increase. The substantial population of adult cocaine addicts will no longer be able to finance their consumption by selling to nonaddicted middle class users. They will turn increasingly to property crime, which tends to engender violence. Thus, perversely, even as visible drug problems seem to be improving in inner-city neighborhoods, the crime problem may worsen. This situation should also increase the willingness of government to develop treatment and ancillary services to deal with the problems of adult addicts.

REFERENCES

1. Hunt, Dana, "Drugs and Consensual Crimes: Drug Dealing and Prostitution," in Michael Tonry and James Q. Wilson, eds., *Drugs and Crime: Vol. 13, Crime and Justice: A Review of Research*, Chicago: University of Chicago Press, 1990.

2. Reuter, Peter H., Robert J. MacCoun, and Patrick J. Murphy, *Money from Crime: A Study of the Economics of Drug Dealing in Washington, D.C.*, Santa Monica, Calif.: RAND, R-3894-RF, 1990.

3. Klein, Malcolm W., Cheryl L. Maxson, and Lea C. Cunningham, "'Crack,' Street Gangs, and Violence," *Criminology*, Vol. 29, No. 4, 1991, pp. 623–650.

4. Fingerhut, Louis A., Deborah D. Ingram, and Jacob J. Feldman, "Firearm Homicide Among Black Teenage Males in Metropolitan Counties," *Journal of the American Medical Association*, Vol. 267, No. 22, 1992, pp. 3054–3058.

5. *U.S. News and World Report*, August 19, 1991, p. 53.

6. *Time*, May 6, 1988, p. 22.

7. Fagan, Jeffrey, "Drug Selling and Licit Income in Distressed Neighborhoods: The Economic Lives of Street-Level Drug Users and Dealers," in George Peterson and Adele Harrell, eds., *Drugs, Crime, and Social Isolation*, Washington, D.C.: Urban Institute Press, 1992.

8. Dembo, Richard, Linda Williams, Werner Wothke, James Schmeidler, Alan Getreu, Estrellita Berry, Eric D. Wish, and Candice Christensen, "The Relationship Between Cocaine Use, Drug Sales, and Other Delinquency Among a Cohort of High-Risk Youths over Time," in Mario De La Rosa, Elizabeth Y. Lambert, and Bernard Gropper, eds., *Drugs and Violence: Causes, Correlates, and Consequences*, Rockville, Md.: U.S. Department of Health and Human Services, NIDA Research Monograph 103, 1990, pp. 112–135.

9. Goldstein, Paul J., Henry H. Brownstein, and Patrick J. Ryan, "Drug-Related Homicide in New York: 1984 and 1988," *Crime and Delinquency*, Vol. 38, No. 4, 1992, pp. 459–476.

10. Johnson, Bruce D., Terry Williams, Kojo A. Dei, and Harry Sanabria, "Drug Abuse in the Inner City: Impact on Hard-Drug Users and the Community," in Michael Tonry and James Q. Wilson, eds., *Drugs and Crime: Vol. 13, Crime and Justice: A Review of Research*, Chicago: University of Chicago Press, 1990, pp. 9–67.

11. Callahan, Charles M., and Frederick P. Rivara, "Urban High School Youth and Handguns: A School-based Survey," *Journal of the American Medical Association*, Vol. 267, No. 22, 1992, pp. 3038–3042.

12. Reuter, Peter, "On the Consequences of Toughness," in Melvyn Krauss and Edward Lazear, eds., *Searching for Alternatives: Drug Control Policy in the United States*, Stanford: Hoover Institution Press, 1992.

13. Jerald G. Bachman, Lloyd D. Johnston, and Patrick M. O'Malley, "Explaining the Recent Decline in Cocaine Use Among Young Adults: Further Evidence that Perceived Risks and Disapproval Lead to Reduced Drug Use," *Journal of Health and Social Behavior*, Vol. 31, pp. 173–184.

14. Conner, Roger L., and Patrick C. Burns, "The Winnable War: How Communities Are Eradicating Local Drug Markets," *The Brookings Review*, Summer 1992, pp. 26–28.

15. Kleiman, Mark, and Kerry Smith, "State and Local Drug Enforcement in Search of a Strategy," in Michael Tonry and James Q. Wilson, eds., *Drugs and Crime: Vol. 13, Crime and Justice: A Review of Research*, Chicago: University of Chicago Press, 1990.

16. Press, Aric, *Piecing Together New York's Criminal Justice System: The Response to Crack*, New York: New York Bar Association, 1987.

17. Gerstein, Dean, and Henrick Harwood, eds., *Treating Drug Problems: Vol. 1,* Washington, D.C.: National Academy Press, 1990.

18. Anglin, Douglas, and Yih-Ing Hser, "Treatment of Drug Abuse," in Michael Tonry and James Q. Wilson, eds., *Drugs and Crime: Vol. 13, Crime and Justice: A Review of Research,* Chicago: University of Chicago Press, 1990.

4

Public Services and Social Welfare

Chapter Ten

Financing Public Services in Los Angeles

Preston Niblack and Peter J.E. Stan

Like other cities across the country, Los Angeles faces demands for increased and enhanced public services. The scope and intensity of these demands have been brought into sharp focus by creation of a commission to help rebuild the city in the wake of last spring's civil disturbances. Against the backdrop of the recent recession, Los Angeles has been under particular budgetary pressure from a burgeoning population and a declining industrial base. Providing services requires access to resources—either the city's own or aid from the state or federal governments. What constraints will Los Angeles face in trying to rebuild and meet future demands for services, and what are alternative approaches to financing these services?

This chapter addresses this question by examining the fiscal situation of local governments in California since Proposition 13 was enacted. Our argument suggests that, in many ways, the current fiscal choices at the local level in California represent a continued playing out of the consequences of this landmark legislation, which in 1978 severely limited the role of property taxes in financing local government in the state.

In particular, the sources of revenue for public services and the jurisdictional responsibilities for providing those services shape the manner and degree to which the public sector responds to demands for services. Citizens who feel that the existing pattern of government spending is inappropriate must recognize that this pattern arises, not out of some political cost-benefit analysis, but rather through the complex interplay of demand and supply constraints on revenue. One goal of this chapter is to provide a picture of the supply constraints on local governments' revenue after Proposition 13 altered them so fundamentally.

A ROAD MAP

The chapter begins by reviewing the history of state and local fiscal relations over the last 15 years. The historical pattern of these relations was dramatically changed by passage of Proposition 13 in 1978 as well as by termination of federal general revenue sharing and aid to cities by the mid-1980s. We describe these changes and analyze their effects.

Not all local governments are alike. In particular, the revenue sources of California's counties differ substantially from those of its cities, and since Proposition 13 affected cities and counties differently, they have responded differently. Although the city and county of Los Angeles are each representative of its category within the state, they have experienced special problems associated with rapid growth in their populations over the past 15 years. We review the fiscal history of the county and city over this period. In addition, we examine the impact of changes in education finance on spending per pupil in Los Angeles.

In keeping with the focus of the book as a whole, we concentrate on four functions of local government: social services; primary and secondary education; health care; and public safety, which includes police protection, fire protection, and corrections. With the exception of education, these services are provided by either the city of Los Angeles or Los Angeles County; primary and secondary education are provided by the Los Angeles Unified School District in the geographic area of concern. Hence, except for remarks made in passing, our discussion is limited to the city, county, and school district, even though the development of special districts, like the Los Angeles County Transportation Commission and the South Coast Air-Quality Management District, is perhaps the most important innovation in local public finance in recent years.

Changing sources of revenue have affected both the mix of services provided and the vulnerability of local governments to economic downturns like the one California has been experiencing for the past two years. We examine the implications of these effects for the future and look briefly at several alternative strategies for responding to the demands on government in Los Angeles.

CALIFORNIA'S LOCAL GOVERNMENTS: SOURCES OF REVENUE SINCE PROPOSITION 13

California's local governments have traditionally provided a higher share of services—measured as a percentage of combined state and local expenditures—than do local governments, on average, in other states. As Figure 1 shows, local government spending in California typically accounts for more than 66 percent of total state and local general spending and thus exceeds the national average by about five percentage points.

Passage of Proposition 13 in 1978 rolled back property tax rates and capped their annual growth, generating a sharp imbalance between local expenditures and revenues. Even though the local share of combined state and local expenditures did not fall, the share of local own-source revenues dropped sharply after 1978, as Figure 2 suggests. Indeed, it fell below the national norm before recovering in the late 1980s, as we discuss below.

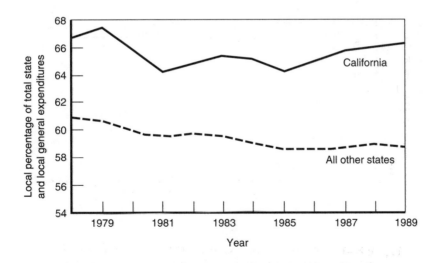

Figure 1—Spending by Local Government as a Share of State and Local Government Spending in California and Other States

To meet the budget crisis that Proposition 13 created, the state of California, which was in budget surplus at the time, stepped in with a massive infusion of aid to its local governments. This aid was especially directed toward school districts—the local function most affected by the drop in property tax revenues.

As Figure 3 illustrates, after passage of Proposition 13, local governments in California became much more dependent on state and federal aid while they sought new sources of revenue. Specifically, after 1978 the percentage of local government revenue derived from intergovernmental aid jumped by about 10 percentage points, or from just over 40 to just over 50 percent of total revenue, while tax revenue fell by over 10 points to about 27 percent of the total. A third revenue category that grew substantially after 1978 is user fees and charges. As we discuss later, this source of revenue has recently become especially important in the city of Los Angeles.

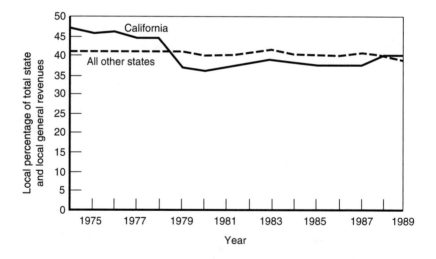

Figure 2—Local Government's Share of Combined State and Local Government Revenues in California and Other States

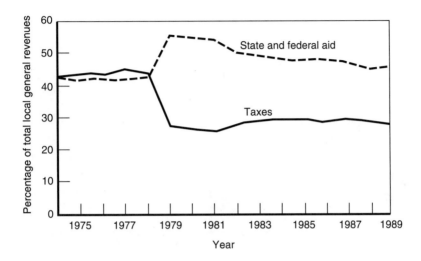

**Figure 3—Taxes and Grants as a Share of Total
Local General Revenue in California**

SERVICES IN CALIFORNIA'S COUNTIES AND CITIES

It is important to realize that in California, as in other states, there are many types of local government (e.g., counties, municipalities, school districts, and special-purpose districts). Proposition 13's cutback in property taxes and the rapid growth in state aid to localities that it engendered did not affect all of these entities equally, as Figure 4 shows.

California's counties act largely as agents for the state government, which also passes through some federal funding for federally mandated programs, such as Aid to Families with Dependent Children (AFDC), most often with matching grants. In this way, the federal government both sets minimum service levels and provides partial funding. Because of their agency role, the counties receive, on average, over 50 percent of their general revenues from the state. In contrast, the state's cities enjoy greater autonomy and receive less aid.

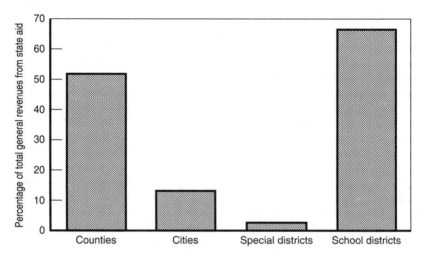

NOTE: Education spending set by Proposition 98.

Figure 4—Share of General Revenues Derived from State Aid in 1990 for Different Types of Local Governments in California

School districts rely more heavily on state funds than either counties or cities. Indeed, in 1990 fully 70 percent of school district revenue derived from state aid. After Proposition 13, state spending on primary and secondary education increased from roughly 12 to almost 20 percent of total state and local spending, even though the share of total spending going to education remained constant (Figure 5). Education finance is handled differently from other categories of public sector finance in California due to another ballot initiative, Proposition 98, which guarantees that a minimum percentage of state expenditures will go to primary and secondary education. We return to how education is financed in California below.

The basic services most affected by Proposition 13 differ across California's cities and counties, as Figure 6 suggests. On average, counties in California spend about half of their budgets on social services, health, and welfare. In contrast, cities direct most of their expenditures toward police and fire protection as well as toward

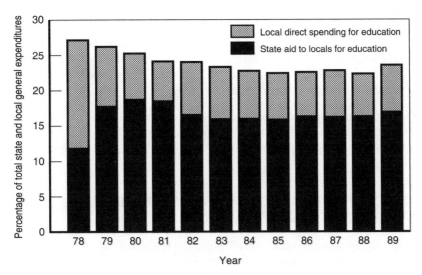

**Figure 5—Shares of Local Direct Spending and State Aid for
Primary and Secondary Education**

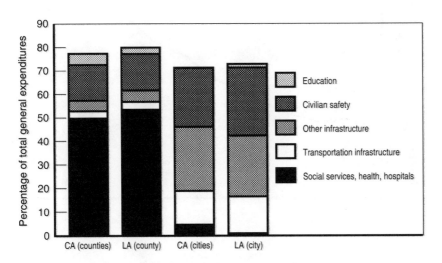

**Figure 6—Major Categories of Public Expenditure for
California's Cities and Counties, 1990**

traditional infrastructure programs like transportation, parks, housing, and disposal of sewage and solid waste. The remaining 20 to 30 percent of expenditures, in each case, goes to central government and interest payments as well as to a variety of smaller spending categories. Spending patterns in the city and county of Los Angeles generally resemble this statewide pattern.

Finally, Figure 7 shows that local debt burdens in California have expanded rapidly since 1978. This increased borrowing has, in part, made up for loss of property tax revenue at these levels of government.

THE COUNTY AND CITY OF LOS ANGELES: REVENUES, EXPENDITURES, AND SERVICES

Many of these statewide trends are likewise manifest in the county and city of Los Angeles. We discuss county patterns first.

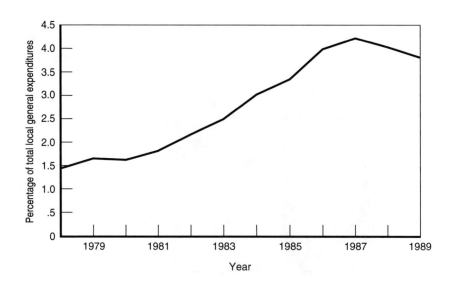

Figure 7—Interest on the General Debt as a Share of Total Local General Expenditures

Los Angeles County

Figure 8 shows the changes in per capita revenue and spending in Los Angeles County. Between 1977 and 1990, per capita revenue in the county made a comeback from its post–Proposition 13 low. Per capita expenditures have remained constant in the county, but the relative distribution of expenditures across functional categories has shifted.

Public welfare programs continue to dominate outlays in absolute terms. As Figure 9 shows, however, since 1977 they have decreased relative to other functions, particularly health and hospitals and public safety, which have grown at a rapid rate. (The bar labeled "All other" in the figure is made up of a large number of small expenditure categories, no one of which approaches the categories shown in its magnitude.)

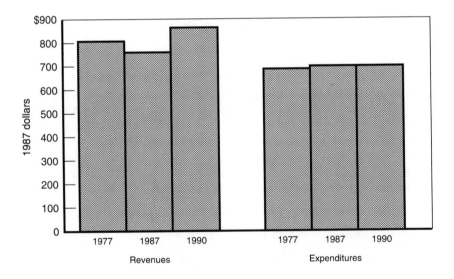

Figure 8—Per Capita Revenues and Expenditures for Basic Services in Los Angeles County (in 1987 dollars)

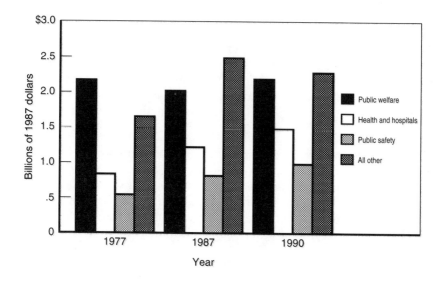

**Figure 9—Categories of Public Expenditure in Los Angeles County
(in 1987 dollars)**

The sources of revenue available at the county level have shaped the
character of county spending. Where did the funds come from that
substituted for lost property tax revenue? Figure 10 shows that, as
property taxes fell, the state's grants increased substantially, rising
from 45 percent of county general revenues in 1977 to 54 percent in
1990. These grants have largely gone to health and corrections, services that the state requires counties to provide. This constrains the
counties' ability to choose their mix of services.

To a lesser extent, the county replaced lost property tax revenue with
increases both in charges, particularly for sewerage and sanitation,
and in other revenue sources. These other sources include interest
receipts, fines and forfeitures, and special assessments. The last two
categories, which make up the bulk of the bar labeled "All other," increased nearly threefold between 1977 and 1990, although they remain a comparatively small share of the total.

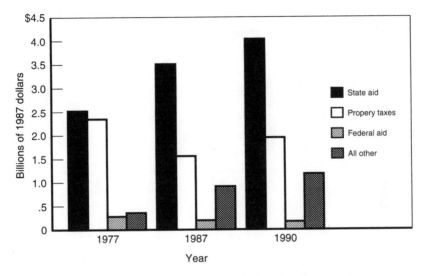

**Figure 10—Sources of Revenue in Los Angeles County
(in 1987 dollars)**

The City of Los Angeles

The fiscal situation in the city of Los Angeles differs from that in the county in several important respects. Figure 11 shows that, in contrast to the county, the city's per capita revenues and its expenditures for basic services have grown substantially in real terms. This growth may, at first blush, seem surprising in light of the blows dealt to urban revenues after 1978 by Proposition 13, the end of the federal general revenue-sharing program, and the termination of federal grants to cities, more generally. However, the city of Los Angeles has been remarkably innovative in finding new sources of revenue that have effectively replaced lost revenue in much the same way that state grants have replaced lost revenue at the county level.

Figure 12 shows that the relative shares spent on various functions also shifted in the midst of this per capita increase. Spending on police and fire protection fell from 37 percent of the budget in 1977 to 29 percent in 1990. In contrast, spending on environment and

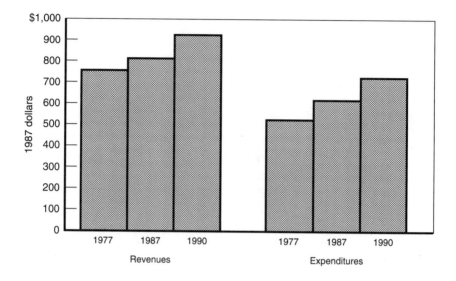

Figure 11—Per Capita Revenues and Expenditures for Basic Services in the City of Los Angeles (in 1987 dollars)

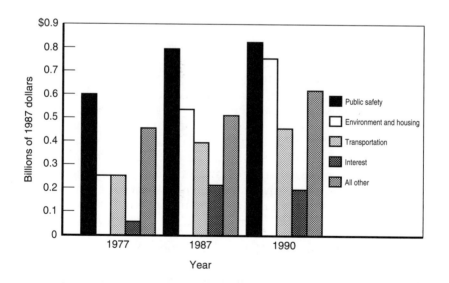

Figure 12—Categories of Public Expenditures in the City of Los Angeles (in 1987 dollars)

housing—principally housing, sewerage, and solid waste disposal—rose from 15 to 27 percent. Transportation spending has held constant as a share of the budget, with the real-dollar increase principally reflecting increased transit subsidies. Finally, interest payments have nearly doubled their share of the budget, moving to almost 7 percent.

Reliance on new sources of own-revenue instead of on increased grants constitutes the primary fiscal contrast between the city and county in the 1980s. Figure 13 shows the shifting sources of revenue. The decline in federal aid is striking: in 1977 the city received federal aid worth $370 million; by 1990 these grants had dropped to $60 million—or from almost 18 percent of the city's operating budget to less than 2 percent. The principal component of this aid was federal general revenue sharing, which disappeared in the mid-1980s. The decline was only partially offset by increased aid from state and local sources. As a whole, the city's reliance on its own revenues has increased from 73 percent of its general budget to 88 percent.

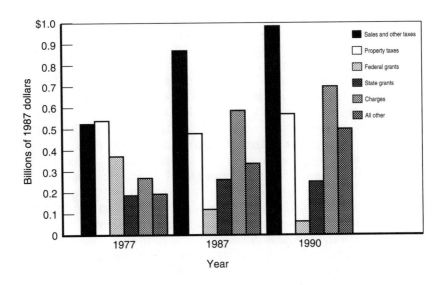

Figure 13—Sources of Revenue in the City of Los Angeles
(in 1987 dollars)

Because Proposition 13 allows assessments to increase when property is sold, inflation-adjusted property tax revenue actually remained roughly constant over this period after recovering from a slight decline. As a share of total general revenues, however, its importance diminished considerably, dropping from 26 percent to 18 percent of the total.

The city primarily compensated for the absolute loss of federal aid and the relative loss of property taxes by increases in two revenue sources—other taxes, especially sales taxes; and charges and fees. Sales tax revenue doubled in real terms between 1977 and 1990, and altogether, nonproperty tax revenues rose from 25 to 31 percent of general revenues. Similarly, by 1990 charges and user fees had grown in absolute real terms to more than two and one-half times their 1977 level, rising from 13 percent of the budget to 22 percent. Housing-related fees have seen the greatest percentage increase, rising from $0.7 to nearly $40 million between 1977 and 1990. The city has imposed other charges on parking, airports, and sewerage and solid waste disposal, although road and highway-related charges have fallen by roughly 75 percent in real terms.

Despite the city's many striking contrasts with the county, there is at least one respect in which their fiscal histories are similar— sources of revenue for public services and historical jurisdictional responsibilities have combined to shape the public services that each provides. In the city's case it is notable that expenditures have increased most quickly for categories of services financed by charges. This is the case for housing, sewerage, and sanitation, leaving aside the rapid growth of special districts that provide most of the latter services. Spending on police and fire protection has, in contrast, grown more slowly. Likewise, at the county level, those categories of expenditures that have grown most quickly—health and hospitals and public safety—are the ones that have received the most state aid, aid that often comes with a mandate to provide these services. Thus, the observed pattern of expenditures arises, not through unconstrained political choice, but at least partly through a complex interplay of constraints that are tied to sources of available revenue. Any proposals to alter the mix of expenditures must take these constraints into account.

The Los Angeles Unified School District

Throughout the nation, local governments administer primary and secondary education, and state governments provide for higher education. The ruling by the California Supreme Court in *Serrano v. Priest* (1971) limited disparities in spending across local school districts. Because of this ruling and local governments' loss of property tax revenues, the state now bears the principal responsibility for financing primary and secondary education and allocating these expenditures. In California the state government determines the spending level for all school districts and finances these expenditures with a mix of state and local funds. Two-thirds of primary and secondary education spending are paid for by the state, with only about one-fifth paid for by local property taxes. By contrast, the national average for the state share is around 50 percent.

One consequence of this shift to state financing is that spending on primary and secondary education has had to compete with spending for other state functions. In addition, the loss of property tax revenues after 1978 led to greater reliance on "procyclical" sources of revenue (i.e., sources of revenue that tend to fall when the business cycle falls), as we discuss at greater length below.

For both of these reasons, voters approved Proposition 98 in 1988. The purpose of this initiative is to ensure a stable spending floor for primary and secondary education. In fact, in the first two years that it was in effect, real spending per pupil fell, and in 1991–1992 the minimum funding level specified by the initiative was not met. [1] Nonetheless, between 1977 and 1990 real spending per pupil in the Los Angeles Unified School District rose from $3,475 to $5,483, or by 58 percent (Figure 14).

Although this growth in spending per pupil seems favorable, the underlying shift in revenue sources contains a hidden time bomb. In 1977 the school district financed 57 percent of its expenditures itself, principally through the property tax, and depended on state and federal aid for the remaining 43 percent. In stark contrast, by 1990 these proportions had become 15 and 85 percent, respectively. Moreover, Los Angeles schools receive 78 percent of their revenues from the state—the statewide average for school districts is 67 percent. This

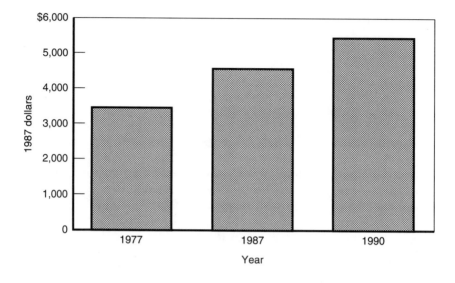

Figure 14—Spending Per Pupil in the Los Angeles Unified School District (in 1987 dollars)

fiscal year state spending per pupil will be the same as last year in *current* dollars, but even this level will be maintained only by borrowing against future appropriations guaranteed by Proposition 98 and by cutting funds for special education. With a projected growth rate of over 30 percent in the state's school-age population in the next decade, [2] it seems unlikely that state spending can keep up, and under current conditions, education expenditures per pupil are likely to fall.

A SUMMARY

We can briefly summarize the chapter's line of argument to this point as follows:

• With the exception of police protection, political jurisdictions tend to specialize in the public services they provide.

In the Los Angeles area and elsewhere in California, counties provide health and welfare services and corrections; cities provide environmental services and fire protection; and special districts provide a variety of services, including elementary and secondary education. However,

- Funds used to finance these services vary across jurisdictions, which have limited and differing capabilities to affect the level and mix of their funding.

Undoubtedly, there have been increased demands for virtually all public services in Los Angeles as population has increased, crime has risen, health care costs have increased, standards of care have improved, and people have sought better education for their children. However,

- To a significant degree, the way that government responds to demands for specific types of public services is shaped by which type of local government has historically provided the services in addition to that jurisdiction's current revenue constraints.

Some revenue constraints are specific to California. In particular, over the past decade and a half, California's voters have sharply curtailed several sources of funds through Proposition 13 and other limitations. By decreasing property tax revenues, Proposition 13 increased the share of state revenue in combined state and local revenue and led to increased state aid to Los Angeles County and the Los Angeles Unified School District. As a result,

- In the wake of Proposition 13, Los Angeles County and the Los Angeles Unified School District have come to depend heavily on state aid. The services that these jurisdictions provide is thus constrained by state revenue and state spending mandates.

- At the county level these grants and mandates have been focused largely in health and corrections, the spending categories that have shown the most rapid growth over the past 15 years.

Finally, California's cities have historically received smaller amounts of state aid than its counties and have instead relied for their revenue on federal urban aid; a variety of taxes, including sales and property taxes; and user fees and charges. Federal aid to cities effectively ended in the mid-1980s, and Proposition 13 has limited revenue available from the property tax. Consequently,

- Following Proposition 13 and the end of federal urban aid, the city of Los Angeles has come to rely heavily on the revenue source over which it exerts the most control—user fees and charges.

- Not surprisingly, the city has increased those services most that can be financed by fees and charges.

Above all, then, the fiscal context of public services in Los Angeles is one in which the city and county possess very limited capacities for reallocating resources to meet the needs of their citizens. It is also an environment in which "external" forces—largely those that shape state revenues and spending mandates—seem to play a larger role than local preferences in determining services offered by the local public sector.

THE OUTLOOK FOR THE FUTURE

Like current services, future services will be strongly shaped by the available sources of revenue. Hence, we close by examining three prospective revenue sources, the characteristics of each, and implications of those characteristics.

The Implications of Procyclical Revenue Sources

The state of California recently faced a $10 billion deficit in its $57.4 billion general budget, its worst fiscal crisis since the Great Depression. Part of the reason for this shortfall is that, like most states, California relies on income and sales taxes as its principal sources of revenue: since these taxes are procyclical, the revenue they produced declined sharply during the recent recession.

Property taxes, in contrast, are usually relatively stable sources of revenue since they are based on the assessed value of a home or business property; reassessments are made only when a property is sold. Property taxes therefore have tended to rise steadily and fall infrequently. Any fall in the market value of a property during a recession is not reflected in assessments unless the property is sold. But property sales are generally less frequent during a recession, and property tax revenues are thus shielded from fluctuations.

The county relies on the state for half of its revenue, and the city relies on the sales tax for just under a quarter of its revenue. Thus, each is more vulnerable today to revenue downturns during recessions than it was in 1977. The county is in a particularly tight squeeze since expenditures on many of its public welfare functions are *counter-cyclical*; that is, they rise during economic downturns just when revenues are falling.

The positive side of this picture is that California's economy will recover, and tax revenues will increase. Can local governments make provisions for the bad times during the good? The state government is obligated to retain a reserve fund to offset revenue effects of economic downturns; it came under substantial pressure during the current recession and ultimately was inadequate to offset the particularly severe ongoing drop in revenues. Whether lawmakers can devise mechanisms in the future to resist spending pressures on such "rainy day" funds remains to be seen.

Whither the Property Tax?

Proposition 13 rolled back property tax rates to their 1975 levels, placed a cap on rates, and limited their annual increase to at most 2 percent. However, when a property is sold, its assessed value is based on the sale price. One might argue that the effects of Proposition 13 will mitigate with time as properties turn over and as new assessments come into effect. Since the 2 percent cap in the annual rate of tax increase applies to transferred properties, however, the effects of the initiative will continue to be felt, especially if real estate values or inflation increases.

Thus, Proposition 13's limit on the rate of increase in property taxes seems certain to hold them down as a share of local revenues. Despite the dramatic increases in construction and property values in Los Angeles during the 1980s, property taxes only held even at their real 1977 levels, and they declined as a share of the city's general budget.

But repeal or reform of Proposition 13 seems unlikely. The recent U.S. Supreme Court decision in *Nordlinger v. Hahn* (1991) held that Proposition 13 is constitutional, thus dealing a severe blow to opponents of the initiative. In addition, although a proposition on the ballot this fall would raise the tax levy on business properties, it would not affect residences.

In sum, although the property tax will continue to be with us, it seems unlikely to resume its preeminent role in California local finance, and continued reliance on procyclical sales and income taxes seems likely, despite their drawbacks.

Greater Reliance on Marketlike Mechanisms?

It is clear that either reductions in current service levels or tax increases will be hard to enact. Current service levels in Los Angeles are experiencing upward pressure brought on by continued demographic change and the weak economic recovery. At the same time, there is downward pressure on current tax levels, or at least a solid ceiling above these levels. Political resistance to increased personal or business taxes is substantial, and there is a growing sentiment within the state that the tax burden is damaging California's ability to attract new jobs. [3]

With these realities in mind, it is not difficult to understand why user fees and charges have grown more rapidly than other revenue sources in the city of Los Angeles. Moreover, the rise in wholly or partially self-financing single-function agencies or special districts is consistent with this trend.

In general, many applaud the introduction of marketlike mechanisms into government finance since they provide better signals of the demand for services and promote efficient allocation of resources. However, a major drawback to this approach is its disproportionate impact on lower-income individuals for many types of public service usage. That is, all users of these services pay the same fee, and the fee thus amounts to a greater fraction of a poor household's income. Hence, if all households can reasonably be expected to use the service and especially if usage is concentrated among lower-income households, concerns about equity may ultimately limit the role of marketlike mechanisms.

Prospects for Increased Federal Aid

A final and often heard solution to the fiscal dilemmas facing the nation's cities and counties is a return to a greater federal role in financing local public services, especially now that the Cold War has ended and cuts in defense spending loom. It would be wrong to draw too many parallels between the "fiscal dividend" debate that accompanied the end of the war in Vietnam and ongoing calls for a "peace dividend," not least of all because the federal budget deficit has grown substantially in the interim. Nonetheless, the historical basis for increased federal grants is in place.

As Figure 15 shows, and as a forthcoming RAND report will argue in detail, [4] about 75 percent of the federal budget is concentrated in only five spending categories: defense and grants-in-aid to states and localities, which are both relatively discretionary and are hence aggregated in the figure; and the less-discretionary categories of retirement benefits, Medicare payments, and net interest payments on the federal debt. (Here, retirement benefits include the Old-Age and

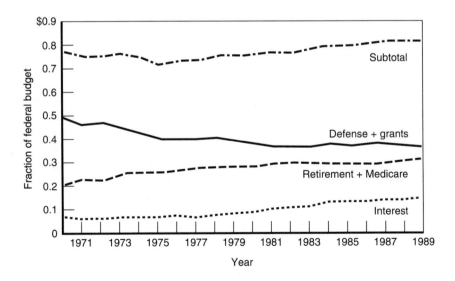

Figure 15—Major Categories of Federal Expenditures, 1970–1989

Survivors' Insurance component of Social Security, federal civilian and military retirement benefits, and railroad retirement benefits.) All other activities of the federal government make up the remaining 25 percent, with no one activity accounting for more than 3 percent of the federal budget in 1989. Taken together, these categories have been stable at around 75 percent of the budget since 1970.

This stability masks several important underlying shifts, however. In particular, the increase in net interest payments, retirement benefits, and Medicare payments provides the long-term backdrop against which recent federal fiscal history has been played out. As these categories have grown, the total of defense spending and grants has declined, with other categories of federal spending adjusting themselves within the near-constant 25 percent of the budget.

However, Figure 16 shows that the decline in this total has not been shared equally across defense spending and grants. Indeed, grants have tended to rise just when defense spending has fallen. Thus, between 1970 and 1978, during the conclusion of the Vietnam War and after, grants rose and *partially* offset the fall of defense spending as a share of the federal budget. Between 1978 and 1987, during the Carter-Reagan defense buildup, the opposite occurred: grants declined, while defense spending rose as a partial offset. Finally, since 1987, with the conclusion of the Cold War, defense spending has begun to fall, and grants have risen weakly.

The reasons behind the trade-off between grants and defense spending are complex, but we would not go far wrong to think of the federal government as subcontracting out many of its responsibilities to state and local governments and paying for the services that these governments provide with grants-in-aid. [4] Some services, particularly those connected with defense, social insurance, and finance, the federal government provides itself. If it reduces outlays for these functions, however, the federal government "buys" more of the subcontracted services for its citizenry from state and local governments, the actual providers of most services. Since national defense is the only large federal function that has fallen in recent decades as perceptions of the external threat have periodically waned, it has tended to trade against grants in the federal budget.

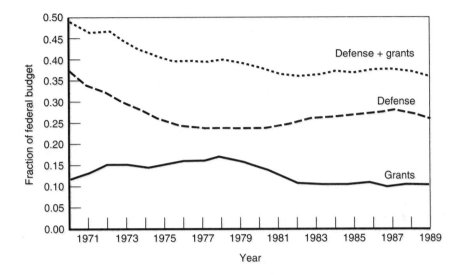

Figure 16—Defense Spending and Federal Grants, 1970–1989

The implications of this metaphor for the future are difficult to assess because of calls for reduced federal expenditures and, hence, reduced deficits. In particular, it is always possible that the passing of the Soviet threat will lead to reduced federal expenditures rather than to redirection of federal funds toward states and localities. More to the point, grants are discretionary, and federal expenditures for retirement, Medicare, and interest are less discretionary and are growing. Hence, in the future it may be hard for grants to expand or even to hold their own against these other categories, regardless of what past spending trends suggest.

The state budget finally approved on the second of September dramatically affected local governments. Property and other tax revenues were taken from local governments to balance the state's budget. The city of Los Angeles will lose an estimated $53 million and the county some $586 million. Health and welfare services will be most severely cut, but other functions will be affected as well. Notably, primary and secondary education will suffer a cutback in real terms. Renewed economic growth will certainly alleviate some of the pressures on the fiscal situation in the city and county of Los Angeles, but without a very strong recovery, more cutbacks in state aid are anticipated next fiscal year.

Increasingly, California's local governments will have to turn to their own resources to finance services. So far, as the city has demonstrated, they have been able to maintain service levels, even in the face of lower property taxes and reduced intergovernmental aid. The next few years will test their ability to continue to fund basic public services out of their own pockets. Moreover, other services that have been largely the financial responsibility of the state, such as schools and health programs, may now fall to local governments. A basic realignment of responsibility for funding local services is underway, and Los Angeles is one of the laboratories in which the experiment is being conducted.

SOURCES

The authors gratefully acknowledge the comments they received from Edward Keating and John J. Kirlin. The especially penetrating reviews of Thomas K. Glennan, Jr., improved the chapter substantially. Any errors of fact or interpretation that may remain are the sole responsibility of the authors.

All state and local spending and revenue data presented in this chapter are drawn from the Census Bureau's annual government finances publications for the various years discussed. These publications are *Government Finances*; *State Government Finances*; *City Government Finances*; and *County Government Finances*.

Data for Figures 15 and 16 are drawn from Table 3.15 in the U.S. National Income and Product Accounts for the years discussed.

REFERENCES

1. Odden, Allan, "Financing Public Schools," in John J. Kirlin and Donald R. Winkler, eds., *California Policy Choices, Volume 7,*

Los Angeles: University of Southern California School of Public Administration, 1991.

2. *California's Growing Taxpayer Squeeze*, Sacramento: California Department of Finance, November 1991, p. 5.

3. Romero, Philip J., and Steve Arthur, *Keeping California Competitive, or, The Self-Inflicted Wounds of Raising Taxes*, Sacramento: Governor's Office of Planning and Research, 1992.

4. Dawson, John E., and Peter J.E. Stan, *Public Expenditures in the United States Since 1952*, Unpublished Research.

Chapter Eleven

Needed: A Federal Role in Helping Communities Cope with Immigration

Georges Vernez

Over the last decade, Los Angeles, along with a half dozen other large metropolitan areas, has experienced an unprecedented growth in international immigration. Immigrants accounted for more than 60 percent of the three million population growth in the Los Angeles consolidated metropolitan area, and similar or larger effects have been felt in other areas.

Immigrants have contributed to the nation's economic growth, primarily by providing a growing and relatively cheap and eager labor pool. They have also enriched the nation's already unique cultural diversity. At the same time, their sheer numbers, relatively high fertility rates, relatively low wages, and competition for jobs and public benefits place considerable demands on state and local jurisdictions and may stress the sociopolitical fabric of the communities in which immigrants are concentrated.

In the context of a steadily growing economy, these demands can usually be accommodated. But they become more visible and intense during periods of economic slowdown or stagnation. During such periods, demands for public services by immigrants *and* their children continue to grow while the local revenues to meet the demands decline. At the same time, competition for jobs and public services among immigrants and other groups may also intensify. At worst, immigrants may become the symbol of an area's problems and the target of recrimination and occasional violence.

In the past, federal immigration policy-making, which is the exclusive prerogative of the federal government, has not been sensitive to the costs that concentrated flows of immigrants impose at the state and local levels. Now, however, since immigration is expected to continue at peak levels throughout the 1990s, the local effects of immigration and the fiscal capacity of local areas and of individual communities to integrate successive waves of immigrants have emerged as significant policy issues. This essay outlines the key dimensions of these issues and argues for the development of a federal immigrant policy* in which the federal government would assume some of the cost burden of public services to immigrants that states and localities now shoulder by themselves. Requiring the federal government to "internalize" the costs of its choices should assure that the trade-offs made serve the broader national interest.

FEDERAL POLICY: REOPENING THE DOOR TO IMMIGRANTS

The decade of the 1980s was marked by a wave of immigrants nearly equal to the peak number who arrived in the first decade of the century (see Figure 1). At that time, the surge of entrants eventually sparked nativist feeling that led Congress to close the door to immigration in the mid-1920s. The door remained closed for more than a generation, allowing for the progressive intergenerational integration of that earlier wave of immigrants and their children. During that period, the foreign-born population in the country declined threefold, from a high of 13 percent in the 1910s to less than 5 percent in the 1960s (Figure 2).

With the accelerated resumption of immigration since then, the proportion of immigrants in the total population has once again increased, reaching 8 percent in 1990. Nearly one of every two foreign-born persons now residing in the country entered within the last decade. They account for 40 percent of the 22 million 1980–1990 population growth in the nation and for more than half of that growth if the U.S.-born children of immigrants are included.

Policy Changes Will Increase and Diversify Immigration

The 1980s were remarkable not only for welcoming the largest and most diverse group of immigrants since the beginning of the century but also for witnessing a comprehensive redesign of U.S. policy toward refugees, undocumented immigrants, temporary immigrants, and those gaining permanent immigrant status.   Three new statutes—the Refugee Act of 1980, the Immigration Control and

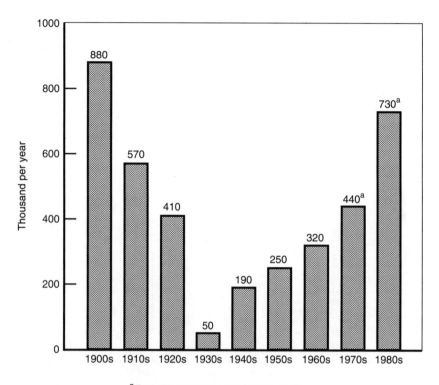

^aExcludes undocumented immigrants.

SOURCE: INS.

Figure 1—Immigration in 1980s Rivals Levels of 1900s

Reform Act of 1986 (IRCA), and the Immigration Act of 1990—are the most important components of this redesign.[†] Taken together, they will increase the number of immigrants coming into the United States. The key expansionary provisions include the following:

- The number of legal immigrants allowed to enter the United States each year will increase from about 500,000 in the 1980s to 675,000 or more between 1992 and the year 2000.

- Refugees and asylees will remain outside that limit and can be expected conservatively to add from 150,000 to 200,000 entries every year, up from an average of about 100,000 in the 1980s.

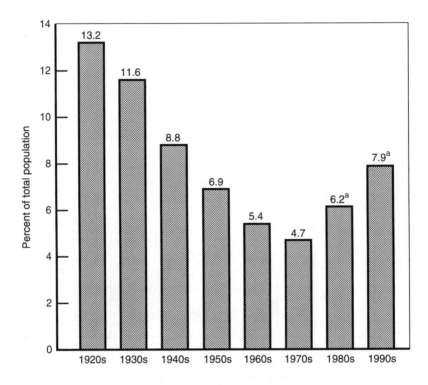

^aIncludes undocumented immigrants.
SOURCE: U.S. Census of Population.

**Figure 2—Foreign-Born Population in
the U.S. as a Percent of Total Population**

The number of refugees to be admitted each year is set annually by Congress and the executive branch, and that ceiling has been exceeded and increased every year since 1988 under the pressures of international events and regional conflicts. In 1992 the ceiling for refugees alone was set at 141,000. More than 60,000 asylees were added to that number. In light of the profound international geopolitical changes and growing incidence of regional conflicts throughout the world, we expect these pressures to continue, if not increase. [1]

In addition, the new laws provide for four new categories of immigrants that, over the long run, will significantly affect the size and composition of immigration in the United States:

1. The largest amnesty program for undocumented immigrants ever implemented by any nation, with more than 3 million applications submitted in 1987 and 1988—1.7 million under the pre-1982 program and 1.3 million under the Special Agricultural Workers (SAW) program. The majority of applicants to both programs are Mexicans (75 percent), reside in four states along the U.S.-Mexico border (84 percent), are between the prime working ages of 15 and 34 (64 percent), and are male (67 percent). Nearly half are married (41 percent). Over time, as amnestied immigrants become permanent immigrants and eventually U.S. citizens, they will be able to bring additional immigrants into the country via family reunification.

2. An increase in each individual country's quota for legal immigrants from 20,000 to about 47,000. Countries most likely to benefit are those with long waiting lists, including the Philippines (472,000), Mexico (466,000), India (254,000), China, Korea, and Vietnam.

3. The creation of a "diversity" visa (55,000 annually starting in 1995) to be granted to nationals from countries that had been sending few immigrants to the United States under existing laws favoring family reunification. This is likely to open the door to increased immigration from some European countries (e.g., Ireland and Eastern Europe) and from Africa. Over time, immigration from such countries may also be accelerated through family reunification.

4. The establishment of a "temporary protected immigration status" for a selected group of undocumented immigrants. Beneficiaries of this status are not subject to deportation and are authorized to work. Currently two groups are so covered: spouses and children of the nearly 3 million persons granted amnesty under IRCA and nationals from El Salvador and a few other countries experiencing civil strife. The new law provides the seeds for extending this protection to other groups as the need arises (e.g., undocumented nationals from war-torn countries such as Kuwait, Lebanon, Liberia, and Somalia and from repressive countries such as China). It also foreshadows the possibility of subsequent amnesty and permanent immigration for beneficiaries of that initially temporary, but legal, status. It is only a matter of time before these immigrants will have established eco-

nomic and social ties here and will not return voluntarily to their country of origin, regardless of whether the conditions that pushed them out have changed. In other words, these "temporary immigrants" should be considered permanently settled here and will soon meet the conditions that prompted congressional passage of IRCA's amnesty programs in the first place.

Undocumented Immigration Continues

While Congress has increased the range of opportunities for legal immigration, it has also sought to stem undocumented immigration by making it illegal for employers to hire undocumented immigrants, a path taken earlier by most European nations. Although IRCA's employer sanctions have been in effect for more than four years, analysts generally agree that the sanctions have only modestly reduced entries of undocumented immigrants. [2,3,4,5] There was a brief decline in that flow in 1987 immediately after the passage of the law, but over time undocumented immigration seems to have regained its pre-IRCA levels. This modest effect of the new law is due primarily to two factors:

1. A low level of enforcement activity as initial governmental efforts have focused on educating employers about the new law and on seeking voluntary compliance.

2. The ease with which one or more of the 19 different acceptable proofs of "work authorization" can be falsified and obtained on the black market.

In the end, reducing undocumented immigration will depend largely on the handling of three issues: whether an enforceable and relatively fraud-proof documentation system can be developed and approved by Congress; whether enforcement of IRCA's employer prohibition against hiring undocumented immigrants is eventually coordinated with the enforcement of other labor laws; and whether additional funding will be allocated for more aggressive enforcement of the new law. Widespread concerns about protecting individual civil rights and liberties and growing pressures to reduce the federal budget deficit have put enforcement low on the scale of the nation's priorities. It is likely to remain there for the foreseeable future. [6]

Expected: 10 Million Immigrants in the 1990s

The current statutes assure the expansion of opportunities for immigration, and undocumented immigration is likely to continue unchecked. As a consequence, we can expect immigration to reach one million a year or more during the 1990s. Arguably the current economic recession might curtail this growth. However, family reunification and humanitarian immigration will continue to constitute 80 to 90 percent of legal entries, and this type of immigration is not likely to be sensitive to economic fluctuations, at least in the short and medium run. Other pressures that could reduce immigration include public backlash generated by continuing pressures at the local and community levels. As we will see later in this discussion, such pressures are growing, but may be alleviated either by renewed economic and job growth and/or by federal policy actions. Undocumented immigration is potentially most affected by a prolonged recession. Yet even in this case, a sizable portion of the immigration is family related or otherwise linked to social support networks, whose response may lag behind economic fluctuations in the United States.

FROM NATIONAL POLICY TO LOCALIZED EFFECTS

For more than a century, formulating and enforcing immigration policy have been the exclusive prerogative of the Congress and the federal executive branch. But today, as in the past, the effects of immigration policy are felt mainly at the local level, a fact that has yet to be fully recognized by Congress, by immigration advocacy groups, or even by analysts. The latter have typically taken a national perspective on how immigration affects the nation's economic growth and whether immigrants take jobs from other groups of workers. Analysts have also tended to take the long-term view, neglecting the significant geographic concentration of immigrants in specific areas of the nation and the consequent short- and medium-term strains on those affected areas. [6] In fact, as we shall see below, the geographic concentration of immigrants is increasing over time, and their socioeconomic characteristics distinguish them in important ways from native residents.

Concentration of Immigrants Is Increasing

Between 1980 and 1990, 8.7 million new immigrants (legal and un-documented) entered and remained in the country. Seventy-one percent of these immigrants reside in just five states: California, New York, Illinois, Florida, and Texas (Table 1). These new immigrants joined 11 million earlier immigrants, 66 percent of whom also live in these five states. Because of the now well-documented self-reinforcing development of social networks of immigrants, [7,8] we can expect the trend toward geographic concentration to continue throughout the 1990s.

Table 1

Foreign-Born Population by State, 1980–1990

State	Foreign Born, 1990 (in thousands)	Foreign Born in Total Population, 1990 (%)	Foreign Born Entering, 1980–1990 (%)	Contribution of Immigration to 1980–1990 Population Growth (%)
California	6,459	22	50	54
Florida	1,506	12	44	26
Illinois	952	8	39	908[a]
New York	2,859	16	42	275[a]
Texas	1,245	7	58	26
United States	19,767	8	44	39

[a]Values in excess of 100 percent mean international immigration has substituted for a decline in native-born population.

SOURCE: Calculated from Census of Population and Housing, 1990, STF-3.

Relative Concentration Increases as Size of Jurisdiction Decreases

The relative concentration of immigrants increases as the size of the jurisdiction decreases. Within a state, about 80 percent of immigrants are concentrated in the largest metropolitan areas. With the exception of New York and Chicago, these metropolitan areas have been among the fastest-growing areas in the country, expanding at rates two to three times the national average. In these areas, international immigrants in the last decade have accounted for 60 to 100 percent of population growth (Table 2). In New York and Chicago,

Table 2

Population and International Immigration in
Selected Large Metropolitan Areas, 1980–1990

Consolidated Metropolitan Statistical Area (CMSA)	1980 Population (in millions)	1980 Foreign Born (%)	1990 Population (in millions)	1990 Foreign Born (%)	1980–1990 Population Growth (%)
Los Angeles	11.5	18	14.5	27	26
New York	17.5	15	18.0	15	3
Chicago	7.9	8	9.9	11	25
San Francisco	5.1	14	6.3	20	21
Dallas	2.9	4	3.9	18	33
Houston	3.1	7	3.7	12	20
Miami	2.6	26	3.2	34	23
United States	226.5	6	248.7	8	10

SOURCE: U.S. Bureau of the Census, CB 91-66, February 21, 1991; *New York Times*, August 1, 1992.

international immigrants have offset an otherwise large out-migration from these areas, with the net effect of maintaining a relatively stable population.

The inverse relationship between concentration of immigrants and size of jurisdiction is further illustrated in Table 3, which shows the proportion of foreign born for various jurisdictions within the Los Angeles metropolitan area. In many of these jurisdictions, immigrants account for all growth or have replaced a previously black or white population. As Sam Roberts of the *New York Times* noted (August 1, 1992, p. 7), if metropolitan areas and cities within those metropolitan areas seem foreign to the rest of America, and for that matter to the natives remaining in those cities and surrounding areas, it is because they are.

The most visible effect of this concentration is growing ethnic diversity. Already no one ethnic group is a majority group for most central cities in these areas. As Peter Morrison puts it, "the term 'minority' is becoming increasingly obsolete." [9]

Socioeconomic Characteristics of Immigrants

Increasing numbers and increasing concentration are not the only salient characteristics of recent immigrants. The demand for public services and the income from tax revenues in a jurisdiction are in part determined by the socioeconomic characteristics of its population, including its growth, age, sex, education, and income distribution. For immigrants, these characteristics—and how they differ from those of native-born residents—have been relatively well documented, although their implications have yet to be fully recognized in federal, state, and even local public policies.

Age and sex. As in the past, newly arrived immigrants are generally younger than the native population, evenly distributed between males and females, and just as likely to be already married (or to marry) as the native population. There are, of course, variations depending on the country of origin and on the category of immigrant. For instance, Mexican immigrants, who constitute the largest group of new immigrants (about one-third), are somewhat more likely to be

Table 3
Foreign-Born Population in Selected Areas
of California and Los Angeles, 1980–1990

Area of California	Foreign Born, 1990 (in thousands)	Foreign Born in Total Population (%)	Foreign Born, 1980–1990 (in thousands)	Foreign Who Entered, 1980–1990 (%)
California	6,459	22	3,255	50
LA (consolidated metropolitan area)	3,938	27	NA[a]	NA[a]
LA (county)	2,895	33	1,526	53
LA (city)	1,337	38	754	56
South Central LA	164	31	97	59

[a]NA means not available.

SOURCE: Census of Population and Housing, 1990, STF-3A.

males than are other immigrants. But in general, this broad-brush portrait is valid. [10,11]

In addition, most groups of immigrants have higher fertility rates than native women. Jasso and Rosenzweig show that the number of children born to immigrant women who entered the country between the ages of 15 and 24 in 1970 exceeds that for native-born women of the same age by 27 percent for Western Hemisphere women, by 5 percent for European women, and by 1 percent for Asian women. [12] They also show that fertility rates of the more recent female immigrants have been increasing. This trend is occurring at the same time that there are more female immigrants who are younger, particularly if they come from the Western Hemisphere. This combination of higher fertility rates and younger population implies higher demand for elementary, secondary, and adult education and some health services, particularly those associated with prenatal and postnatal care.

Education. The new wave of immigrants has relatively low levels of education, and the educational gap between native-born persons and newly arrived immigrants has been increasing since the 1960s. [10,11,13] This is best illustrated by examining the school deficit of male Mexican immigrants who entered the country within the five years preceding the various decennial censuses. The ratio of Mexican immigrants completing eight years or less of schooling to other immigrants and to natives has increased from 1.5 to 3.2 and from 2.5 to 5.1, respectively, between 1960 and 1980 (Table 4).

Data for the period from 1980–1990 are not yet available, but there are indications that these trends may have been magnified by the Refugee Act of 1980 and IRCA. The average schooling completed by the amnesty population in their country of origin is 5.6 years. [14]

Economic status and mobility. In part because they have less education, immigrants command lower earnings and experience higher unemployment rates than the native born; thus they are at somewhat greater risk for needing publicly supported services such as medical care and income transfers. In 1980 immigrant households were only slightly more likely than native households to receive welfare, 9 percent versus 8 percent, respectively. However, Mexican immigrants

Table 4

Schooling of Natives, Immigrants, and Mexican-Born Immigrants Aged 18 or Older, 1960 and 1980

Schooling	1950–1960 Cohorts (%)			1970–1980 Cohorts (%)		
	Native, 1960	Immi-grants[a]	Mexican-born	Native, 1980	Immi-grants[a]	Mexican-born
8 years or less	32	52	80	13	21	67
2 or more years college	15	13	4	28	40	7

[a]Includes foreign born from all countries except Mexico.

SOURCE: Author's tabulations from the 1960 and 1980 Public Use Sample of the U.S. Bureau of the Census.

were nearly twice (12 percent) as likely as the native born and other immigrants to receive welfare. [11]

Low levels of education also imply that most immigrants enter with little or no knowledge of English, which places pressure on the adult education system to provide English as a second language (ESL) classes and basic literacy instruction.

The prevalence of relatively low levels of education and resulting low wages is related to a third well-documented characteristic: economic mobility and sociocultural integration occur primarily *across* generations, not *within* the first generation of immigrants. Although the literature is replete with anecdotes of immigrants who have made it big in America, the average adult immigrant experiences little if any economic mobility relative to the native born throughout his lifetime. Put another way, the wage differential at which an immigrant starts a career in the United States is the wage differential at which he retires. However, the wage differential is significantly smaller for children of immigrants born here and for immigrants who entered as children or adolescents and hence received part or all of their schooling in the United States. [13,15] These findings underscore the vital role U.S. education has played in the mobility of immigrants' children and the vital role it is once again being called on to play for millions of children of immigrants and immigrant children who will be pouring into the school systems of the country's largest metropolitan areas.

EFFECTS OF INTERNATIONAL IMMIGRATION ON LOCAL JURISDICTIONS

How do immigrants affect local jurisdictions? To answer this question, we need to know how immigrants affect the demand for the full range of public services primarily funded by state and local governments and how immigrants affect the jurisdictions' ability to pay for these services. Neither of these questions has been systematically and fully addressed in past research. But an examination of the available studies, coupled with the socioeconomic characteristics we have just described, suggests the following pattern:

- A few states and counties bear a disproportionate share of the costs of the socialization, education, and social support of immigrants.

- As immigration has increased over the last decade, these jurisdictions are increasingly unable to meet the demand for public services—not only from immigrants, but from all segments of their population.

Implications for Local Jurisdictions: Demand for Services

Education. Immigrants make their largest service demand in education. Education also represents the largest component of states' budgets and constitutes a significant portion of local county and/or city budgets. In California, for instance, education constitutes 40 percent of the state budget. There, the state covers 61 percent of K–12 expenditures, local districts provide 21 percent, and the federal government funds 7 percent. This pattern generally holds nationwide, with a long-term trend toward increased state and local participation and declining federal participation. In addition, two recent U.S. Supreme Court rulings have broadened state/local responsibility in this area, first by mandating equal access to K–12 education for the children of undocumented immigrants (*Plyler v. Doe*, 1982), and second by requiring greater state and local attention to language-minority students (*Lau v. Nichols*, 1974).

Concentrated immigration has significantly increased school enrollments in the districts most affected. Nearly four out of five recent immigrant students (those who have lived in the United States for three years or less) attend schools in California, New York, Illinois, Florida, and Texas, and a startling 45 percent of them are enrolled in California. In that state alone, new schools and classrooms must be built or otherwise created to accommodate from 180,000 to 200,000 new pupils every year throughout the 1990s. Schools in the same five states serve two out of every three students of limited English proficiency (LEP). [16]

For the largest school districts in these states, recent immigrant students represent from 5 percent of total enrollment (Chicago and Houston) up to 15 percent or more (San Francisco and Miami), with New York and Los Angeles in between with 8 and 10 percent, respectively. Should recent trends continue, as they are expected to do, the number of these student immigrants will increase by about 10 percent a year. [16]

In addition to coping with the sheer numbers, the states and school districts most affected are confronted by a number of additional funding, educational, and logistical problems that are uniquely stimulated by the immigrants' linguistic diversity and by special needs stemming from the rigors of immigration and adjustment to a new environment. A recent study of school districts most affected by immigration by Hill and McDonnell [16] and a review of the literature in Vernez and McCarthy [6] identified a broad range of coping difficulties, including continuing problems with instructing students with limited English proficiency; inadequate academic preparation, particularly pronounced among children of junior high and high school age; high turnover and high absenteeism among immigrant students and children of immigrants; lack of materials in students' primary language and shortages of trained bilingual teachers and aides; and adjustment problems for some immigrants, particularly refugees, who suffer from severe emotional stress due to violence they have witnessed, deprivation they have experienced, or simply long separations from one or both of their parents.

All of these add to the budgetary needs of those school districts that by all accounts (see Chapter Five) already lag in local capacity to meet the educational and social needs of their students, a majority of whom are minorities (Table 5).

Table 5

High Immigration Central Cities or Counties
with a Majority of Minorities, 1990

Central City or County	Total Population (in thousands)	White (%)	Hispanic (%)	Asian (%)	Black (%)
New York	7,322	43	24	7	26
Chicago	2,783	38	20	4	39
Los Angeles	3,485	37	40	9	13
San Francisco	724	47	14	28	11
Miami (Dade Co.)	1,937	30	49	1	19
United States	248,710	NA[a]	9	3	12

[a]NA means not available.

SOURCE: Census of Population and Housing, 1990, STF-3A.

Adult education (for basic literacy, ESL, and vocational education) is another service for which demand by immigrant adults may be outstripping the ability of the states and districts to provide. Although the fifth national education goal, driving ongoing national efforts to reform schools, states that "Every adult in America will be literate and will possess the knowledge and skills necessary to compete in a global economy and exercise the rights and responsibilities of citizenship," adult education has been, and continues to be, the most-neglected area of education, not only for immigrants but for all adults. Two recent studies that focused on the use of adult education by the 2.7 million IRCA amnestied population are suggestive of this latent demand. [14,17] In 1987 states offered ESL/citizenship classes to amnestied immigrants: the size of the demand exceeded by 100 percent the highest state estimates. In California statewide enrollment (in 1988 and 1989) in these classes doubled, and the entire adult education enrollment increased by one-third.

This group's future economic prospects depend on access to basic adult education: about two-thirds attended six or fewer years of school in their native countries; more than one-third are not literate in their native language; and nearly two-thirds have such low proficiency in English that they would have difficulties functioning in other than entry-level jobs, in most job training programs, and in the community. [14]

Demand for other services. In general, we lack definitive, aggregate information about how immigration affects the demand for or use of other public services. Generally, rapid population growth—fed primarily by immigration—places disproportionate demands on those services that are primarily the responsibility of state and local governments, including public infrastructure (roadways and highways, water and sewerage), public safety (police and fire), social and cultural services (parks and recreation, libraries), and public health. Recent immigrants may be especially heavy users of some services, not because they are immigrants per se, but because, hampered by poor education and inadequate English, they have lower incomes. As a consequence, they must turn to public rather than private services when in need. For instance, 39 percent of Hispanics, a large percentage of whom are recent immigrants, and 22 percent of Asians lack health insurance compared with 14 percent for whites. For Hispanics, this proportion has increased by more than 50 percent in the last 20 years. [18] Again, California, Texas, Illinois, New York, and Florida, the magnet states for immigration, have the largest incidence of uninsured among the Hispanic population—about 40 percent.

Implications for Local Jurisdictions: Ability to Pay for Public Services

The available evidence suggests three reasons why the states and localities most affected by international immigration are feeling financially pinched:

1. Tax revenues from immigrants do not fully cover the costs of the state and local services they use, at least in the short run.

2. Jurisdictions are vulnerable to economic fluctuations.

3. There are conflicting priorities among population groups.

Paying for services to immigrants. Whether immigrants "pay their way" for the public services they receive is possibly the most controversial issue pertaining to immigration. Estimates can be found to support either side of the argument, and all suffer from serious methodological deficiencies. Still, with the growing attention given this issue and as studies at all levels of government become more numerous, a pattern begins to emerge: *the fiscal burden of immi-*

grants increases as the size of the jurisdiction decreases, ranging from neutral or even positive at the national level, to neutral to negative at the state level, to negative at the local (county/city) level. [15,19,20,21,22,23,24,25]

This sliding scale of fiscal effects appears to stem from the complex interplay between the sources of federal, state, and local revenues and variations in the level of government responsible for funding the services that immigrants most use. Recent estimates of the county costs of services to immigrants in such places as San Diego and Los Angeles suggest that these services may represent a sizable portion of the current budgets in those counties, even adjusting for politically motivated upward biases in the estimates.

Counties and states not only bear a disproportionate share of the costs of the socialization, education, and social support of immigrants, they are also constrained by their constitutional requirement to balance their *operational* budgets on a yearly basis. This requirement seriously reduces a jurisdiction's ability to respond flexibly to demands for services. For example, education—the service most demanded by immigrants—is both a consumption good and an investment in the future. But states and locals cannot borrow against their future revenue to finance the operating costs of providing it.

Vulnerability to economic fluctuations. Even without further immigration, demand for the services we have discussed above will grow. This is particularly to be expected from the three million amnestied population, whose eligibility exclusion from certain services will expire in 1992 and whose newly gained permanent status is expected to result in increased demand over time. [11] And, for the reasons we discussed earlier, immigration will almost surely grow at an increasing rate throughout the 1990s, thus intensifying the demands placed on the affected communities. But in the current environment of sluggish economic growth and high unemployment, the funding ability of these states, counties, cities, and school districts to meet the growing demand diminishes. The gap between demand and capability is even wider in jurisdictions experiencing continuing and growing immigration: most experts agree that the one group whose job opportunities and wages are consistently reduced by successive waves of immigrants are the immigrants themselves, both the newcomers and those already here. [11] As more immigrants try to enter the job market, incomes and employment fall; the result is increased demand for public services and decreased contributions through taxes to cover the costs.

The results of this service pinch are dramatically illustrated by the plight of affected school districts:

> Los Angeles' total funding fell nearly 20 percent between September 1990 and January 1992. Chicago anticipates a $220 million deficit in 1991–1992, on a $2.4 billion budget. Chicago's annual deficit is expected to exceed $500 million within 5 years; New York City and Dade County face years of deficits approaching 10 percent of their prolonged budgets.

> All the districts are suspending or abandoning activities that their boards had considered essential elements of program quality. The cuts have immediate effects on student services. Los Angeles, Houston, and New York have increased pupil-teacher ratios and New York has cut costs by furloughing teachers and students for periods during the school year. Miami has slowed the construction of schools in overflow areas, and all have cut back on maintenance and repairs. Chicago's central office, already cut by a school-centered reform movement, will face even deeper reductions due to the budget deficit. Chicago will also further defer an estimated $1 billion in critically needed maintenance and repairs, continue a freeze on teacher hiring, and increase class size in all schools. All districts have reduced extracurricular activities and supportive after-school services. Most Los Angeles schools have gone to year-round schools. New York has suspended special training programs designed to help immigrant professionals become bilingual and ESL teachers, and all districts have curtailed the hiring of replacement teachers. [16, p. 18]

This budgetary crisis is being repeated in Sacramento and Los Angeles (county and city), in Albany and New York City, in Springfield and Cooke County, and in Tallahassee and Dade County. The 1992 budgetary deadlock first in Albany and then in Sacramento are only symptoms of the difficult trade-offs that must be made when demand for public expenditures badly outstrips public revenues.

Conflicting priorities. Many have observed that increased fragmentation among subgroups of the population may be eroding the country's ability to reach consensus on vital domestic and international issues (i.e., the development of a policy-making "gridlock" at all levels of government). Increased immigration itself is fueling intense debate that pits the needs for education, training, and other services for the younger age groups—in which immigrants are currently disproportionately represented—against the needs of the growing elderly population, which is disproportionately native born, the natives' desires to control growth and preserve the environment against the need to create jobs for the newcomers, and the rights and entitlements of the native born against the targeted benefits and entitlements of immigrants. This growing political pluralism is highly visible in those jurisdictions experiencing immigration, but it is also emerging as an issue across the nation. It is at the heart of the fights over local decennial redistricting and drives the debate about how immigrants, who cannot voice their priorities on public issues because they have not yet acquired citizenship, should be represented in the public dialogue.

TOWARDS A NEW FEDERAL ROLE

We have argued that the costs of the federal government's open door policy and its inability or unwillingness to effectively stem undocumented immigration fall primarily on a few state and local jurisdictions and that these jurisdictions experience increasing difficulties in meeting those costs. Until now the federal government has had little or no incentive to cover these costs for several reasons:

1. Immigration is perceived as having long-term positive socioeconomic benefits for the nation as a whole, and research generally supports this view.

2. The costs of immigration are concentrated in a few jurisdictions, making it difficult in our federal system to muster political support for federal intervention.

3. The phenomenon we are observing today is barely a decade old, and it has taken an unusually long and deep recession to make the "problem" visible and urgent.

Why should the federal government bear some of the costs of its immigration policies now?

- Only the federal government can effectively intervene to control the number of immigrants entering the country. Shifting to the federal government responsibility for the public costs of providing services to immigrants would have a moderating influence on federal immigration policy.

- A finite number of states and local jurisdictions do not have the resources to meet the current demand for services by immigrants and are constitutionally prevented from borrowing from future revenues to cover the operational costs of providing these services. The nation's long-term economic growth and competitiveness as well as the attainment of its national educational goals will be threatened if those areas of the country most affected by immigration falter, as they are giving signs of doing.

To address these issues, federal immigration policy should shift to the federal government a portion of the incremental costs currently being borne by a few states and localities for the services they provide to immigrants. This objective could be achieved by means of one or a combination of the following:

First, targeted federal funds should be made available to the local institutions funded primarily with state and local funds that are most affected by the influx of immigrants and their children. As we have discussed, these are primarily educational institutions ranging from early childhood to K–12, adult education, and community colleges. However the purpose of this assistance should be to improve and sustain the capacity of these affected institutions to serve all students, the majority of whom are minorities, whether immigrants or native born.

Second, general assistance should be provided to partly compensate localities for costs they incur as providers of social and health services of last resort as well as for general services. This assistance could be augmented during recessionary times and reduced or phased out during periods of local economic growth.

Third, the federal government should standardize the requirements for existing federal, social, and other entitlement programs for which immigrants are eligible. Currently, eligibility for federally funded programs varies across categories of immigrants. Although the federal government has legitimate foreign and domestic policy reasons to set different standards of entry for different types of immigrants, at the local level these distinctions are irrelevant. A public hospital emergency room is compelled to provide service to an undocumented immigrant just as it is to a legal immigrant. The latter may be eligible for Medicaid; the former is not. A legal immigrant temporarily without a job is just as needy as a refugee without a job. Yet the latter is eligible for some federal benefits, while the former is not.

We recognize that whether to provide eligibility for federal programs to undocumented immigrants is a thorny question. Arguably, extending federal program benefits to undocumented immigrants may be an additional incentive for them to come to and stay in the United States. But this argument carries little weight because it ignores the fact that immigration status makes no difference to many local service providers who usually lack the legal authority to ask about status or to deny service because of it. Pragmatic federal recognition of state (and by derivation local) constitutional obligations to serve all immigrants, regardless of status, is long overdue. The intent here is less to broaden eligibility for services not currently being provided to immigrants, including undocumented immigrants, than to restore an appropriate balance in regard to who pays for the services.

Developing an effective and equitable federal immigration policy along the principles outlined above cannot be done in an information vacuum. We lack systematic information about the pattern of public services used by different groups of immigrants; the effects of public service use on the nature and speed of immigrants' linguistic, economic, and social integration and that of their children; and the budgetary, institutional, and community relations effects of sustained cumulative waves of immigrants on local jurisdictions. We particularly need to understand this last set of issues to help define what is meant by the concept of "local community absorptive capacity" (i.e., the ability of a given area to absorb large numbers of immigrants effectively). The term "absorptive (or carrying) capacity" is often used to suggest that there is a limit to the number of immigrants a community can assimilate without threatening national and local values, generating a political backlash, and placing unmanageable demands on resources and existing institutions. We simply do not know where this limit is, or how it is delineated under various circumstances, but we can and should try to find out.

These proposals, although individually not new, remain controversial. They overlap current efforts to redefine national domestic policies in the areas of education, health, and entitlement programs.

And, most important, they interact with immigration policy. The federal government has the power and the means to regulate the flow of refugees and of legal and undocumented immigrants to levels of its choosing. Internalizing the costs of its choices should help ensure that the trade-offs it makes serve the broader national interest.

NOTES

*Although they are related, we make an important distinction between immigration and immigrant policies. Immigration policy is the set of laws, regulations, and programs that determine and enforce the number and characteristics of immigrants allowed to enter and work in the United States. By contrast, immigrant policy is the set of laws, regulations, and programs that facilitate the social adjustment and entry into the work force of immigrants once they have come to the United States.

†See Rolph, Elizabeth J., *Immigration Policies: Legacy from the 1980s and Issues for the 1990s*, Santa Monica, Calif.: RAND, R-4184-FF, 1992, for a comprehensive review of how these three pieces of legislation have altered the rules governing eligibility for legal status, the benefits available to immigrants, and enforcement strategies.

REFERENCES

1. Vernez, Georges, *After Amnesty: The New Migratory Movement in the United States*, Santa Monica, Calif.: RAND, P-7786, 1992.

2. Fix, Michael, and Paul T. Hill, *Enforcing Employer Sanctions: Challenges and Strategies*, Santa Monica, Calif.: RAND and the Urban Institute, JRI-04, 1990.

3. Crane, Keith, Beth J. Asch, Joanna Zorn Heilbrunn, and Danielle C. Cullinane, *The Effect of Employer Sanctions on the Flow of Undocumented Immigrants to the United States*, Santa Monica, Calif.: RAND and the Urban Institute, 1990, JRI-03, 1990.

4. Bean, Frank D., et al., *Undocumented Migration to the United States: IRCA and the Experience of the 1980s,* Washington, D.C.: The Urban Institute and RAND, JRI-07, 1990.

5. Donato, Katherine, M., Jorge Durand, Douglas S. Massey, "Stemming the Tide? Assessing the Deterrent Effects of the Immigration Reform and Control Act," *Demography,* Vol. 29, No. 2, May 1992, pp. 139–157.

6. Vernez, Georges, and Kevin McCarthy, *Meeting the Economy's Labor Needs Through Immigration: Rationale and Challenges,* Santa Monica, Calif.: RAND, N-3052-FF, 1990.

7. Massey, Douglas S., and F. Garcia-Espana, "The Social Process of International Migration," *Science,* Vol. 237, pp. 733–738.

8. Sassen, Saskia, *The Mobility of Labor and Capital,* New York: Cambridge University Press, 1988.

9. Morrison, Peter A., *Testimony Before the House Subcommittee on Census and Population,* Santa Monica, Calif.: RAND, P-7784, 1992.

10. Borjas, George T., *Friends or Strangers? The Impact of Immigrants on the U.S. Economy,* New York: Basic Books Inc., 1990.

11. Vernez, Georges, and David Ronfeldt, "The Current Situation in Mexican Immigration," *Science,* Vol. 251, March 1991, pp. 1189–1193.

12. Jasso, Guillermina, and Mark R. Rosenzweig, *The New Chosen People: Immigrants in the United States,* New York: Russell Sage Foundation, 1990.

13. Smith, James P., *Hispanics and the American Dream.* Book manuscript in preparation.

14. Comprehensive Adult Student Assessment System (CASAS), *Three Years of Amnesty Education in California,* Prepared for the California Department of Education, Amnesty Education Office, 1992.

15. McCarthy, Kevin, and R. Burciaga Valdez, *Current and Future Effects of Mexican Immigration in California*, Santa Monica, Calif.: RAND, R-3365-CR, 1986.

16. Hill, Paul T., and Lorraine M. McDonnell, *Schooling for Immigrant Youth*, Paper Presented at Teachers College Conference on Urban Education, July 9, 1992.

17. Ramsey, Kimberly, and Abby Robyn, *Preparing Adult Immigrants for Work: The Educational Response in Two Communities*, Santa Monica, Calif.: RAND, N-3586-NCRVE/UCB/RC, 1992.

18. Valdez, R. Burciaga, *Insuring Latinos Against the Costs of Illness*, Santa Monica, Calif.: RAND, P-7750, 1991.

19. North, David, and Marion Houston, *The Characteristics and Role of Illegal Aliens in the U.S. Labor Market: An Exploratory Study*, Washington, D.C.: Linton & Lo, 1976.

20. Blau, Francine, "The Use of Transfer Payments by Immigrants," *Industrial and Labor Relations Review*, Vol. 37, No. 2, pp. 222–239.

21. Mueller, Thomas and Thomas Espenshade, *The Fourth Wave: California's Newest Immigrants*, Washington, D.C.: Urban Institute Press, 1985.

22. Collins, Nancy, *Do Immigrants Place a Tax Burden on New Jersey Residents?* Unpublished Senior Thesis, Princeton University: Department of Economics, 1991.

23. Community Research Associates, *Undocumented Immigrants: Their Impact on the County of San Diego*, San Diego, 1980.

24. "Study Reports Illegal Aliens Cost in Services," *Los Angeles Times*, August 6, 1992.

25. Los Angeles County, Chief Administrative Office, *Updated Revenues and Costs Attributable to Undocumented Aliens*, 1991.

Chapter Twelve

Providing Health Care for the Uninsured and Underinsured in Los Angeles County

Robert E. Tranquada and Peter A. Glassman

INTRODUCTION

Los Angeles County, like many local governments, plays an important role in providing medical care to people who cannot afford to pay for it. These people, primarily the uninsured and "underinsured," use the county-operated health care system primarily because they cannot readily pay for their care in the private health sector.

The uninsured are often in poverty or near poverty. They do not have medical insurance because they are unemployed, have jobs that do not offer health benefits, are dependents of those whose jobs do not offer health benefits, and are not eligible for public health insurance. In some instances, some of the uninsured work in firms that offer health insurance, but they do not take the offer. The uninsured depend on charity care from private providers or, for the most part, on county-operated hospitals and clinics which are required by law to act as providers of the last resort, serving all regardless of their ability to pay.

The underinsured are individuals and families whose insurance does not cover all their health expenses (including costs incurred for pre-existing conditions) or who cannot meet their deductibles or copayment costs. Moreover, the underinsured population includes those Medicaid beneficiaries whose insurance is not readily accepted by private providers.

Both the uninsured and underinsured receive care from a variety of sources for their health needs. These sources include the county-operated health care system, university hospitals (some of which are associated with county health services), and community hospitals;

the Veterans Affairs Medical Centers provide care to a number of veterans who are poor and who have no other health insurance coverage. The county system, which provides a substantial amount of outpatient and inpatient care to those without adequate insurance, includes six county hospitals (four with emergency departments), 41 public health clinics, and six comprehensive health centers. In addition, there are about 70 privately operated free and community clinics in Los Angeles County. The uninsured and underinsured also use those private physicians or hospitals who treat the uninsured for low or no cost or who readily accept Medicaid (known as Medi-Cal in California) payments.

Although the county-operated health care system receives funds when it serves insured persons (primarily Medicaid eligibles as well as small numbers of Medicare recipients and privately insured individuals) and through direct grants from the state, the county itself must cover the remaining costs. The county devotes substantial resources to health care, but these funds are inadequate to prevent overcrowding and long delays for both inpatient and outpatient care.

National or statewide reforms, such as universal health insurance or broader employer coverage, could ease the burden on county finances by providing new sources of revenue to pay for the care of the currently uninsured and underinsured. But the prospects for broad-ranging reform are uncertain, and in the current fiscal climate, Los Angeles is unlikely to receive increased assistance from the state; if anything, the prospects in the near term are for further cuts in state aid to local governments. As a result, it is more important than ever that the county make the best use possible of existing resources, public and private.

In the following discussion, we identify who turns to the county for care; then we describe the county health care delivery system and where it falls short of meeting the needs of those who use it. Finally, within the limits of the existing mix of public and private resources, we suggest some steps to improve health care in Los Angeles County for the population in need.

WHO ARE THE UNINSURED AND UNDERINSURED?

The private health care system is designed to meet the needs of individuals and families who have private health insurance or who belong to health maintenance organizations (HMOs); with some exceptions discussed below, these groups are able to obtain needed health care from private providers. However, although the private sector also provides some care to the uninsured and a significant amount of care to the Medi-Cal population, it does not effectively serve all the uninsured and underinsured. These are the individuals who rely primarily on the county-operated health care system and on privately operated clinics.

The Uninsured

The uninsured use the public health system because they cannot often afford the out-of-pocket expenses necessary to pay for care without support from health insurance. In Los Angeles County, this group primarily consists of the unemployed, the poor, and non-covered workers and their families, who are not eligible for public health insurance programs.

A UCLA School of Public Health Report estimated Los Angeles County's uninsured population in 1989 at about 2.7 million people, roughly one-third of the county's 8.9 million 1989 population. According to the study, Los Angeles County had the highest uninsured rate among the 30 largest metropolitan statistical areas in the country. [1]

Nationally, the uninsured are disproportionately young, male, black, and Hispanic, below or slightly above the poverty line, and unemployed. [2,3,4,5] Some of the poorest, as well as other eligible persons (such as pregnant women), do receive coverage under Medi-Cal. The poor aged are almost always covered by health insurance, such as Medicare. Medicare, which is readily accepted by most hospitals and physicians, covers about 99 percent of persons 65 years and older. [6]

In Los Angeles County, the number of uninsured persons is swelled by three factors: the relatively high percentage of workers without health insurance, the large number of undocumented immigrants and homeless, and more recently, the unemployed, whose numbers have increased due to the recession.

Workers without health insurance. Although reliable data is not available for Los Angeles County, proportionately fewer California workers receive health insurance from employers than the national average; only 56 percent of working Californians receive insurance from their employers, compared with 64 percent elsewhere in the United States. [1] The problem is especially acute for working Hispanics (40 percent with work-related coverage) and blacks (52 percent with work-related coverage). Eighty-seven percent of the uninsured in California have jobs or are in a family headed by at least one working person; 65 percent of the uninsured are full-time employees or dependents of full-time employees.

Companies that do not offer health insurance are typically small (under 25 employees). [7] Workers' health insurance is particularly expensive for small employers because of high administrative, underwriting, and sales costs, which can amount to 30 percent of premiums. [8] For-low income workers who do not have work-based group health insurance, the cost of individual coverage is often prohibitive.

Undocumented immigrants and the homeless. Los Angeles County has a large population of undocumented immigrants, estimated somewhere between 660,000 and 770,000. [9,10] Many, except pregnant women, are ineligible for Medi-Cal because federal legislation specifically bans spending federal funds for this group except for emergency conditions and pregnancy-related care. Most are believed not to have other health insurance and some who are eligible for Medi-Cal are afraid to apply for fear that it will lead to deportation.

The homeless, numbering around 35,000 to 50,000, [11] also have difficulty obtaining Medi-Cal; in many cases because they are ineligible unless they are also disabled, blind, or have dependent children.

The unemployed. The recession helps swell the number of uninsured because economic pressures cause some firms to drop workers' health insurance and some people lose insurance when they become unemployed. Although Congress sought to help laid-off workers through a 1985 law designed to let them continue their health insurance coverage after a layoff, many of the unemployed cannot afford the monthly premium they are required to pay. Moreover, this law does not benefit those who had no health insurance while employed. [12]

The Underinsured

This group includes Medi-Cal recipients who cannot always depend on private practitioners and hospitals because Medicaid has limited acceptance among many providers. Also within this group are individuals with medical problems (such as pre-existing conditions) not covered by their insurance, those who have exhausted their insurance benefits, or those who cannot meet their deductibles or copayments. Although data is not available for Los Angeles or California specifically, national data suggest that as many as 26 percent of nonelderly Americans are underinsured. [2]

Medi-Cal, whose recipients account for a large number of the underinsured, covers families who receive welfare, the disabled poor, and adults with incomes below or near the poverty line. Medi-Cal eligibles in California comprise about 9 percent of the state population [1] and roughly 10 percent of the population in Los Angeles County. [13]

Medi-Cal patients use both the private sector and county facilities for their health care. A number of private as well as county hospitals contract with the state government to care for Medi-Cal recipients. But the proportion of Medi-Cal eligibles using county hospitals is disproportionately high: the county system has 9 percent of the total acute hospital beds (see below) but accounts for 30 percent of all Medi-Cal inpatient days in Los Angeles County. [3]

THE LOS ANGELES COUNTY HEALTH CARE SYSTEM

The county health system is, by law, responsible for those persons who cannot find health care from other providers or facilities. In 1937 section 2500 of California's Welfare and Institutions Code formalized the obligation of the counties to provide access to health care for the medically indigent now found in section 17000 of the

1965 code: each county is charged, by law, to "relieve and support all . . . poor, indigent persons, and those incapacitated by age, disease or accident," when these persons are not "supported and relieved by their own means, or by state hospitals or private institutions."

Historical Background

Los Angeles County has operated its own hospital system since 1878, when Los Angeles County General Hospital was founded. The Department of Health Services (DHS), created in 1972 by combining the departments of Hospitals, Mental Health, Public Health, and Veterinary Services, currently oversees the county's hospitals as well as its health clinics and centers. The county system in 1992 included six county hospitals, six comprehensive health centers, and 41 public health clinics.

The county system has, over the past 25 years, attempted to address the inequitable geographic distribution of hospital beds and medical care noted in the aftermath of the 1965 Watts civil disturbances. The opening of Martin Luther King Hospital (now King/Drew Medical Center) in South Central Los Angeles in 1972 and the opening of Olive View Hospital in the San Fernando Valley in 1982 have alleviated some of the inequality in access, but the population in need has substantially increased. The county has announced plans to build another hospital to serve the East San Gabriel Valley, and if constructed, that facility will complete the planned redistribution of county beds.

Financing the County System

The county's health services and facilities are financed by revenues from a number of sources, including property tax dollars (covering about 20 percent of costs), private funds and insurance, Medicaid and Medicare, and state and federal grants. All of these sources together do not provide sufficient funds to meet all of the county's health needs. In fiscal year 1991–1992, the Los Angeles County system provided approximately 3.5 million outpatient visits and 178,000 inpatient admissions at a total budget (from all sources) approaching $2.2 billion. Over $300 million was provided by the county for uncompensated care. [14,15] County hospitals' revenue for inpatients was derived from Medicare patients (3 percent of total revenue), Medi-Cal (60 percent), self-paying or uninsured patients (27 percent), and private insurance, including workers' compensation (10 percent). [14].

The county has not increased its health care subsidy in parallel with increased health needs and costs: while the county population rose from 7.5 million in 1980 to 8.9 million in 1990 and while the population in poverty increased from 980,000 (13 percent) to 1,308,000 (15 percent), the Los Angeles County health care subsidy, adjusted for consumer price inflation, fell from $384 million to $316 million. Per capita health care expenditures for persons in poverty also fell, from $390 in 1980 to $242 in 1990 (all figures in constant 1990 dollars). [16] This has occurred during a 10-year period when health care expenditures throughout the United States have risen at roughly twice the yearly rate of inflation. [17]

Medi-Cal payments, which support a great deal of the county's health care, have at best kept pace with the growing Medi-Cal patient load in California. In 1990 the average monthly number of eligibles was about 3.5 million, up from 2.8 million in 1980. Total Medi-Cal spending (in constant 1990 dollars) rose from about $5.3 billion to $6.6 billion over that time, but the average per capita real monthly expenditure stayed at about $155 per recipient. [13]

In recent years, the county received new revenues from the California Tobacco Tax Initiative, federal immigration reform legislation, and non–Medi-Cal state funds. In spite of these added revenues, county expenditures per inpatient day have declined significantly when compared with other noncounty hospitals in California. In 1980 the average expenditure by Los Angeles County hospitals per inpatient day exceeded the average reported expenditure per inpatient day for all California hospitals. In 1992, however, county expenditures had dropped to 75 percent of the statewide average per inpatient day. [18] This relative decline (which may be due to a number of causes, including inflationary pressures in the private health sector and/or to decreased county health expenditures) points to an inability of the county to keep pace with expenditures at other hospitals.

County Hospital Resources

Taking the private and public health care systems together, Los Angeles County has substantial resources for meeting the hospital needs of its population. In 1991 the county had a total of 34,000 licensed acute private and public hospital beds (although low staffing levels permitted the use of only 28,000 beds). [19] Yet, between the private and county hospital sectors, there are significant differences in the number and use of beds (occupancy rates). The county has 4,300 licensed hospital beds, of which only 2,700 are available as acute hospital beds, representing only 9 percent of the available acute hospital beds in Los Angeles County. [14] According to the Los Angeles County DHS, occupancy rates in county hospitals average 96 percent, while in private hospitals the rate is about 53 percent. [15] This indicates that, while private hospitals are much more numerous and have a significant number of empty beds at any given time, the medically indigent in Los Angeles County depend predominantly on a public hospital sector which is consistently near full capacity.

County hospitals offer both inpatient and full-service outpatient care (primary care, obstetric care, and most medical and surgical subspecialties), although only four of the hospitals have emergency departments. The health centers, which do not have inpatient or emergency facilities, offer a wide variety of services, including general medical and subspecialty care; some minor surgery; mental health facilities; prenatal care; well-baby care; public health services, such as immunizations and diagnosis and treatment for sexually transmitted diseases and other infectious diseases (e.g., tuberculosis). The public health clinics offer a modest amount of primary care, but their main function is to provide prenatal care, immunizations, well-baby clinics, and public health care. Although the public health clinics and comprehensive care clinics, which are mostly located in low-income areas and are staffed by county-paid physicans and ancillary staff, do see many patients needing primary care, a substantial burden falls on the outpatient and emergency services at the county hospitals.

The county's outpatient services are heavily used by the uninsured. In fiscal year 1990–1991, the breakdown of outpatient visits were as follows: hospital-based clinics, 1.1 million; comprehensive health centers, 1.1 million; and public health clinics, 1.3 million. [15]

Current estimates indicate that approximately three-quarters of these visits were for uninsured individuals. [20]

Community Clinics and Other Sources of Care

There are about 70 community and free clinics in Los Angeles, which provided about 1.1 million outpatient visits in 1990. About 350,000 of those visits were provided to the uninsured. Private hospital–based outpatient clinics provided the equivalent of about 200,000 uncompensated visits in 1990 to the uninsured. [21] In addition, private physicians serve a number of nonpaying patients: although exact data for Los Angeles are unavailable, applying national rates of physician services to nonpaying patients suggests that Los Angeles–area physicians may provide as many as one million free visits per year.

STRAINS ON THE COUNTY SYSTEM

There are numerous signs of stress on Los Angeles County's current health care system. These include:

1. The county-operated system with 2,700 available acute beds cannot adequately care for nearly 3 million uninsured people, even with some assistance from private charity care. The nearly 100 percent occupancy rate in county hospitals means that sick patients must often be kept in emergency rooms and in walk-in clinics until beds become available; this adds to the crowding in emergency departments, delays inpatient treatment, and ties up hospital staff that work in outpatient areas.

2. As the county has tried to maintain essential inpatient services, the funding squeeze has forced the county to reduce staff for county hospital outpatient clinics and for public health and comprehensive care centers. This has led to increasing shortages of ambulatory care at county facilities and has increased dependence on county emergency rooms and urgent care centers for providing primary care to those who use the county system. A 1990 study found that overcrowding at Los Angeles County Harbor–UCLA Medical Center emergency room prompted many patients to leave before being seen by a physician. [22] The average waiting time for those who saw a

physician was 6.2 hours. Patients who left the emergency department without being seen by a physician waited an average of 6.4
hours: of those patients, 46 percent were judged to have needed urgent medical care. Other county and private emergency rooms that
serve large numbers of uninsured in Los Angeles County face similar
problems (by law, any licensed emergency facility must evaluate all
patients who present themselves). [23]

3. Financial difficulties caused by the large number of uninsured
have forced the emergency departments in some private hospitals to
close. Since 1982, the number of licensed hospital emergency
departments in the county has fallen from 103 to 85. The primary
reason for the reduction in services is financial losses from growing
proportions of uncompensated care exacerbated by problems in
obtaining certification of eligible persons for Medi-Cal and by delays
in receiving expected Medi-Cal payments. [24]

4. Private emergency departments have had difficulty recruiting sufficient emergency on-call physician coverage primarily because of
problems associated with the large proportion of uncompensated
care cases. A comprehensive survey of these emergency facilities by
the Hospital Council of Southern California and Los Angeles County
Medical Association found that on-call coverage was deficient at a
number of private emergency departments in the county. Finding
physician coverage for neurosurgical trauma, obstetrics and gyne-
cology, and psychiatry was particularly difficult. According to the
survey, the major reasons for the breakdown in care included (a) low
payments to covering physicians because of the uninsured and underinsured, (b) concerns over malpractice liability, and (c) difficulties
in transferring indigent patients to county facilities. [25] The effect of
this problem is to shunt patients away from emergency rooms that
are "closed" because of reduced physician coverage. This increases
transport time for patients, crowds other "open" emergency rooms,
and ties up ambulances while they search for a hospital that will care
for the patient.

5. The trauma system has faltered since it was inaugurated in 1983,
when 23 centers were initially designated as level 1, 2, or rural trauma
facilities. At that time, many hospitals hoped that designation as a
trauma center would enhance their prestige, increase admissions,
and boost revenues. Instead, the proportion of uncompensated care

from traffic, gunshot, and other traumas escalated, reaching as high as 57 percent in 1990; moreover, Medi-Cal, which paid only a part of actual costs, accounted for another 21 percent of patients. These finance problems caused significant operating losses, while physicians and facilities remained liable for problems associated with difficult trauma cases. The effect has been to decrease the number of trauma centers to 13 and to increase both transport time and waiting time for trauma victims. [26,27] This situation puts at risk not just the medically underserved, who are often victims of violent assault and accidents, but every victim of trauma in Los Angeles County.

The county, facing significant revenue limitations because of Californians' decision to keep taxes low (Proposition 13), reduced payments to trauma centers for uncompensated care. The net effect was to increase the pressure for trauma hospitals to leave the network. The enactment of the Tobacco Tax Initiative (Proposition 99) has helped the county pay for uncompensated trauma care and stabilize the number of trauma centers at 13. [26] However, those that remain are overused and overstressed, adding to the overcrowding in emergency care.

6. The private sector is playing a smaller role in bearing the costs of uncompensated care. There are several reasons for this development. First, large firms providing health benefits have responded to rising insurance premiums and health care costs by self-insuring and by arranging discounted health plans with hospitals, physician groups, and managed care organizations. This has reduced hospital revenues significantly and, in turn, decreased surplus hospital income previously used to cover uncompensated care for the uninsured and medically indigent. The private sector's reduced ability to "cost shift" increases the pressure for it to "patient shift" by shunting the uninsured to the public hospital system. [28,29,30]

Second, managed care plans, which are designed to contain health care costs, have had the unwanted side effect of curtailing access for the uninsured. The managed care industry originated in Los Angeles with the formation in 1928 of the Ross-Loos Clinic, a prepaid plan that delivered health services exclusively to teachers in the Los Angeles Unified School District. After 1945, the Kaiser Permanente system began operation and now provides care to approximately 2.3 million Southern Californians. By 1989, there were 28 HMOs serving

32 percent of the Southern California health market compared with a national average of 15 percent. [31,32] The industry's expansion has meant the withdrawal of health care resources potentially available to meet the medical needs of the uninsured and underinsured. Twenty years ago, nearly all private physicians and beds in Los Angeles County were potentially available for charity care. Now, however, in staff and group model HMOs, such as Kaiser Permanente, or FHP, neither physician nor hospital care is normally available to nonmembers.

Finally, private hospitals are also receiving reduced revenues from Medicare, which further limits their ability to absorb the costs of uncompensated care. [33]

7. As the county has increasingly struggled to meet its responsibility for supplying acute and inpatient care, emergency and ambulatory services, and public and mental health services, its centralized administrative structure has not changed to meet new demands. County hospitals and public health outpatient services are not effectively coordinated. Moreover, the county has failed to play a significant leadership role in coordinating county services with services provided by the more than 70 community and private clinics that serve the uninsured and underinsured.

THE HEALTH CONSEQUENCES OF
DECREASED ACCESS TO CARE

Shortfalls in health insurance coverage and the limited availability of uncompensated care in Los Angeles County and throughout the United States have a demonstrable adverse impact. Although it is difficult to give a systematic account of the health effects of the current system, a number of recent studies illustrate the problem. Lack of adequate insurance makes it more difficult for individuals to get reasonable, timely, and dependable private health care. [34,35] For instance, a 1992 survey by the Kaiser Family Foundation indicated that 1.3 million Californians could not find needed medical care because they were uninsured or poor.

Lurie and colleagues noted that ill adults who lost Medi-Cal benefits experienced worsening in control of high blood pressure and diabetes. [36] Adults without health insurance are less likely to receive cancer and preventive screening: for instance, the number of in-sured women receiving a cervical smear and breast examination increased between 1976 to 1982, while over the same period the number of uninsured poor women who received these preventive procedures decreased. Uninsured women were also less likely to receive blood pressure or glaucoma screening. [37] The uninsured receive less care dedicated to early detection of potentially curable or controllable cancers or other medical problems. [38]

Compared with high-income populations within the county, low-income black and Hispanic communities have, according to a 1991 study published by the Tomas Rivera Center, [34] "excessively high rates of admission for medical conditions that often would not re-quire hospitalization if adequate outpatient care was available." Further, the study indicated that these communities have lower rates of hysterectomies, major joint operations, and coronary heart bypass operations. Although this does not in itself imply poor care or out-comes, it is indicative of the uninsured's limited access to complex medical and surgical care—a finding that has been noted in other cities as well. [39]

Finally, as of 1990, immunization levels among children in California were lower than the national average. Particularly disturbing is the increase in incidence of and deaths from measles in Los Angeles, a trend especially prevalent among Hispanic children. Moreover, studies note that there is a significant disparity between vaccination rates in the private and public health sectors and that various barri-ers to access are at least partly responsible for low immunization lev-els. [40,41]

WHAT CAN BE DONE?

We have described the dimensions of the problem facing the county health system: too many people with no or inadequate health insur-ance are crowding into county facilities. The problem is most visible at county emergency departments, but problems exist at all levels of the county health care system.

What then can be done to provide adequate care to the uninsured and underinsured at an affordable cost to the county? State or na-tional legislation expanding public or private health insurance coverage would contribute to meeting individuals' ability to pay for their health care needs while easing the financial burden on the county. At present, however, legislation to provide universal coverage or mandated employer-based health insurance is stalled at both the state and national levels.

In the absence of new health insurance initiatives, there are other options for state legislative action. For instance, the state could require all licensed hospitals to give a certain percentage of free care or face a tax to reimburse other hospitals that do give free care. Such a requirement would spread the burden of uncompensated care to all hospitals, including managed care hospitals, while opening up the underused supply of hospital beds in the private sector. Alternatively, the state could adopt a "doctor's tax," requiring licensed physicians to give a certain percentage of free care. This "tax" would spread costs and unlock a relatively untapped network of providers. However, both forms of taxes would be highly controversial and difficult to achieve.

Without state or national action, Los Angeles County must rely on its own resources for an interim solution. Given the current budgetary circumstances, Los Angeles County's support for health services in real terms will decline in the coming fiscal year, and there is little optimism that the reductions will be reversed in the near future. Political leaders and health care professionals must identify ways to redirect currently available resources—public and private—to better meet the needs of the underserved throughout the county.

In an effort to solve some of the problems associated with the uninsured and underinsured, the county government established, before the April 1992 disturbances, the Task Force on Access to Health Services in Los Angeles County. It was charged with identifying and quantifying the access problem in Los Angeles County and bringing recommendations to the Los Angeles County Board of Supervisors. The task force has focused on five major areas that would improve access for the uninsured, including (1) increasing the effectiveness of existing services; (2) supporting broadly representative community health councils as a way for planning and coordinating community-wide medical services; (3) identifying present resources that can be reoriented to better serve the underserved; (4) helping small employers obtain affordable health insurance for their workers; (5) designing new, small, low-cost community-based programs.

Although it is beyond the scope of this discussion to provide a detailed blueprint for the future of public health care in Los Angeles County as proposed by the task force, the following discussion presents potential measures that could be implemented without significantly increasing government costs.

1. The effectiveness of existing services can be improved both within the public sector itself and by coordinating (through the Department of Health Services) public and private efforts. The Los Angles County DHS should reorient its leadership to assist in public/private collaboration. At present, there is little or no coordination between the county health care system and the more than 70 private, free, and community clinics in the county. There is also little coordination between county public health clinics and county hospitals.

In order to manage care for the medically indigent and uninsured as though there were a single system incorporating both public and private elements, the DHS must take the lead in coordinating the various autonomous clinics. This would allow all such sources of care not only to share patient information and referrals but also to take advantage of economies of scale by entering, whenever possible, into joint purchasing arrangements for medical supplies, medications, and technology.

The county also needs an interactive referral system to remove relatively minor medical conditions and chronic, but stable, health problems from public and private emergency rooms. The system would list the providers willing to give free or inexpensive care and would provide a continually updated registry of both voluntary physicians and referred patients, assuring that free and volunteered services were more accessible and not oversubscribed or overwhelmed. In addition, the collaborative effort would help private physicians and hospitals refer eligible patients to other free or low-cost resources (i.e., a private subspecialty clinic) or directly to the subspecialists in the public sector; this would allow some patients to bypass county emergency rooms and walk-in centers. Such a system could be started with private foundation funds and later maintained and operated by the Los Angeles County DHS.

2. Each of the local communities in the county has different re-sources, varied populations, and specific priorities in caring for their medically indigent. Volunteer community health councils, com-prised of health care providers, social agencies, churches, parent-teacher associations, and local organizations, have already begun work in 10 areas of the county. The community health councils will serve as vehicles for planning and coordinating services in those communities and for helping in networking, priority setting, and ed-ucational programs. Such councils could, for instance, organize joint ventures between community-based health care workers (e.g., physician assistants and nurse practitioners), financed by the county, and university-based physician groups that would act as consultants and provide backup to community workers when requested.

3. A number of existing resources can and should be reoriented or supplemented to better serve the community. Unstaffed space in county clinics should be identified and made available to volunteer or paid physicians and health staff; the county should help organize a service to place volunteers, especially retired physicians and nurses (whose malpractice insurance would be provided), in county facili-ties and in free and community clinics. Physicians caring for the uninsured in the public or private system should receive assistance in purchasing malpractice coverage. Alternatively, legislation could be considered that would limit the rights of the uninsured to sue (e.g., they might be asked to sign an agreement for mandatory arbi-tration). Further possibilities for reducing the overcrowding and waiting times at county emergency departments include greater re-liance on supervised physician assistants or newly arrived foreign medical graduates (who wish to work while awaiting state licensure) in county hospital walk-in clinics.

Managed care organizations must play a greater role in providing care for the poor and indigent. To address this issue, the task force brought together a working group representing 15 managed care or-ganizations in Los Angeles County. These organizations, faced with the necessity to augment ambulatory services for the uninsured and indigent, have identified two significant contributions that they can make. These include (a) sharing expertise on managed care with the county and with the free and community clinics and (b) providing essential services, from managed care organizations and from other entities (i.e., physican groups) to existing free and community clinics.

Such resources would include voluntary staffing, accounting services, supplies, equipment, and other support measures as necessary.

With regard to county-operated services, increasing the number of Medi-Cal patients in the county-operated HMO would allow the county to maintain its revenue base while helping to alleviate overcrowding in county emergency departments and would give Medi-Cal patients better access to preventive services, to surgical care, and to long-term follow-up for chronic conditions.

4. To help small employers purchase worker health benefits, the county, in partnership with the Chamber of Commerce, should help create insurance-purchasing cooperatives among groups of small businesses. These cooperatives could negotiate less costly premiums from insurance companies or managed care organizations. A second possibility is to offer small employers a "minimum package" of health benefits for uninsured employees; this would be used for part-time workers or for small businesses who cannot find affordable health insurance. Such a package would offer basic benefits, such as vaccinations and other preventive services, primary care, and short-term (i.e., one-week) paid hospital coverage. Employees would be responsible for a portion of medical costs through deductibles or copayments.

5. The county could support small pilot projects to help find cost-effective solutions to specific problems. Examples include expanding school-based clinics in areas where child care and vaccinations are currently insufficient or offering small monthly subsidies to uninsured women who attend prenatal clinics. In areas where preventive care is deficient, it may be very beneficial to use some Medi-Cal dollars to fund such programs as hypertension and cholesterol screening, breast examinations, Pap smears, and mammography. New community clinics, funded with private or foundation funds, should be encouraged and, whenever possible, helped with start-up costs and with developing outside funding sources.

The county should continue to support a bond issue to replace the antiquated facilities of Los Angeles County–University of Southern California Medical Center with a smaller medical center at its present location and the transfer of 300 beds to a new county hospital in the East San Gabriel Valley to serve that community's medically indigent, who currently are up to an hour away by car from the nearest county hospital.

SUMMARY

Assuring adequate health care for all residents of Los Angeles County is a complex and difficult task. Many of the factors that create the need for public health care, such as unemployment, the changing mix of jobs in our economy, immigration, and demographic change, are beyond the reach of local government. New public/private insurance approaches would help alleviate the financial burden of local government and improve access to care for the uninsured and underinsured. In the interim, the county must make better use of the resources currently available and work more effectively with the private sector, including health care providers and hospitals, businesses and labor, managed care organizations, and insurers, to collaborate in addressing a problem that defies easy answers.

REFERENCES

1. Brown, E. R., R. B. Valdez, H. Morgenstern et al., *Health Insurance Coverage of Californians in 1989,* Berkeley: University of California, California Policy Seminar, 1991.

2. Friedman, E., "The Uninsured: From Dilemma to Crisis," *Journal of the American Medical Association,* Vol. 265, 1991, pp. 2491–2495.

3. Andrews, R., E. Herz, S. Dodds, and M. Ruther, "Access to Hospital Care for California and Michigan Medicaid Recipients,"*Health Care Financing Review,* Vol. 12, No. 4, 1991, pp. 99–104.

4. American Medical Association, Council on Ethical and Judicial Affairs, "Black-White Disparities in Health Care," *Journal of the American Medical Association,* Vol. 263, 1990, pp. 2344–2346.

5. Ginzburg, E., "Access to Health Care for Hispanics," *Journal of the American Medical Association*, Vol. 265, 1991, pp. 238–241.

6. Gornick, M., J. N. Greenberg, P. W. Eggers, and A. Dobson, "Twenty Years of Medicare and Medicaid: Covered Populations, Use of Benefits, and Program Expenditures," *Health Care Financing Review* [Supplement], 1985, pp. 13–59.

7. Rice, T., and C. B. Sullivan, "The Health Insurance Picture in 1990," *Health Affairs*, Summer 1991, pp. 105–115.

8. Leibowitz, A., C. Damberg, and K. Eyre, *Multiple Employer Welfare Arrangements*, Santa Monica, Calif.: RAND, N-3496-DOL, 1992.

9. *Los Angeles Times*, "Calculating the Impact of California's Immigrants," January 6, 1992, p. A1.

10. Lorey, D., ed., *United States–Mexico Border Statistics: Since 1990*, Los Angeles: UCLA, 1990.

11. Wood, D., R. B. Valdez, T. Hayashi, and A. Shen, "Homeless and Housed Families in Los Angeles: A Study Comparing Demographic, Economic, and Family Functioning Characteristics," *American Journal of Public Health*, Vol. 80, 1990, pp. 1049–1052.

12. Klerman, A. and O. Rahman, "Health Insurance for the Non-Employed," in *Health Benefits and the Workforce*, Washington, D.C.: U.S. Department of Labor, 1992, p. 21.

13. State of California, *California Statistical Abstracts*, Sacramento: Department of Finance, 1981; 1991.

14. California Association of Public Hospitals, *California's County Hospitals*, Berkeley: California Association of Public Hospitals, 1991.

15. County of Los Angeles, Department of Health Services, *Los Angeles County's Health: Uniting for a Common Goal*, Los Angeles: Department of Health Services, June 1992.

16. County of Los Angeles, Department of Health Services, personal communication, August 1992.

17. Sonnefeld, S. T., D. R. Waldo, J. A. Lemieux, and D. R. McKusick, "Projections of National Health Expenditures Through the Year 2000," *Health Care Financing Review*, Vol. 13, Fall 1991, p. 16.

18. Deputy Director, Los Angeles County Department of Health Services, personal communication, October 1992.

19. Office of Statewide Health Planning and Development, California Department of Health Services, *Quarterly Report of Hospitals*, Fourth Quarter, 1991.

20. County of Los Angeles, Department of Health Services, personal communication, October 1992.

21. Task Force on Health Care Access in Los Angeles County, 1992, Unpublished Research.

22. Baker, D. W., C. D. Stevens, and R. H. Brook, "Patients Who Leave a Public Hospital Emergency Department Without Being Seen by a Physician: Causes and Consequences," *Journal of the American Medical Association*, 1991, pp. 1085–1090.

23. Stock, L. M., G. E. Bradley, R. J. Lewis, D. W. Baker, and C. D. Stevens, "Patients Who Leave Emergency Departments Without Medical Evaluation: Magnitude of the Problem in Los Angeles County" [Abstract], *Annals of Emergency Medicine*, Vol. 20, 1991, p. 948.

24. Task Force on Health Care Access in Los Angeles County, personal communication.

25. Hospital Council of Southern California, *BRIEFS Focus* (A special Supplement to *BRIEFS* for Chief Executive Officers), Los Angeles: Hospital Council of Southern California, 1991.

26. Shekelle, P. G., D. L. Schreiger, and V. P. Hastings, "The Los Angeles County Trauma System: A Status Report," *Journal of Ambulatory Care Management*, Vol. 14, No. 4, 1991, pp. 1–9.

27. Farley, D. O., L. T. Eisenberg, and G. R. Dallek, *Assessing Emergency Medical Services in Los Angeles County: A Research Agenda*, Santa Monica, Calif: RAND, N-3306-RC, 1991.

28. Coddington, D. C., D. J. Keen, K. D. Moore, and R. L. Clarke, *The Crisis in Health Care*, San Francisco: Jossey-Bass, 1990, pp. 103–113.

29. Ginzberg, E., *The Medical Triangle*, Cambridge, Mass.: Harvard University Press, 1990, pp. 8–10.

30. Dranove, D., "Pricing by Non-Profit Institutions," *Journal of Health Economics*, 1988, pp. 48–57.

31. Gold, M., "HMOs and Managed Care," *Health Affairs*, Winter 1991, pp. 189–206.

32. Henry J. Kaiser Family Foundation, *California Minorities and Uninsured Experiencing Serious Problems Getting Health Care*, Menlo Park, Calif.: Henry J. Kaiser Family Foundation, August 19, 1992.

33. Prospective Payment Commission, *Medicare and the American Health System: Report to Congress*, June 1992.

34. Valdez, R. B., and G. Dallek, *Does the Health System Serve Black and Latino Communities in Los Angeles County?* Claremont, Calif.: Tomas Rivera Center, 1991.

35. Feder, J., J. Hadley, and R. Mullner, "Falling Through the Cracks: Poverty, Insurance Coverage, and Hospital Care for the Poor, 1980 and 1982," *Milbank Memorial Fund Quarterly*, Vol. 62, No. 4, 1984, pp. 544–566.

36. Lurie, N., N. B. Ward, M. F. Shapiro et al., "Termination of Medi-Cal Benefits: A Follow-up Study One Year Later," *New England Journal of Medicine*, Vol. 14, 1986, pp. 1266–1268.

37. Braveman, P., G. Oliva, M. G. Miller et al., "Women Without Health Insurance—Links Between Access, Poverty, Ethnicity, and Health," in *Women and Medicine* [Special Issue], *Western Journal of Medicine*, Vol. 149, December 1988, pp. 708–711.

38. Steiner, C. B., "Access to Cancer Prevention, Detection, and Treatment," *Cancer*, Vol. 67, 1991, pp. 1736–1740.

39. Weissman, J., and A. M. Epstein, "Case Mix and Resource Utilization by Uninsured Hospital Patients in the Boston

Metropolitan Area," *Journal of the American Medical Association,* Vol. 261, 1989, pp. 3572–3576.

40. Scheiber, M., and N. Halfon, "Immunizing California's Children: Effects of Current Policies on Immunization Levels," *Western Journal of Medicine,* Vol. 153, 1990, pp. 400–405.

41. Ewart, D. P., C. Thomas, L. Y. Chun et al., "Measles Vaccination Coverage Among Latino Children Aged 12 to 59 Months in Los Angeles County: A Household Survey," *American Journal of Public Health,* Vol. 81, 1991, pp. 1057–1059.

Chapter Thirteen

Getting Nowhere: Homeless People, Aimless Policy

Paul Koegel and Audrey Burnam

In 1964 when Lyndon Johnson declared an "unconditional war on poverty," no mention was made of homelessness nor did it become part of the ensuing policy agenda. This was not an oversight, for while poverty was widespread during that time, homelessness was not. The closest equivalent we had to a homeless population in the 1960s consisted largely of single, older, white, alcoholic males who were restricted to the skid row neighborhoods of our largest cities where their needs were met (at least minimally) by a network of private sector resources including missions, cubicle flophouses, and single room occupancy (SRO) hotels. Although some have estimated that there were as many as 100,000 homeless people during this period, most were stably housed; a much smaller number lived in missions or outdoors. Of an estimated 12,000 homeless people who lived in Chicago during this period, for example, only a fraction relied primarily on missions and only 110 lived on the streets. [1]

Twenty-five years later, actual homelessness is pervasive in America not only in every major urban area but in suburban and rural areas as well. On any given night, a minimum of 600,000 people bed down in temporary shelters or on the nation's streets, [2] a sixfold increase over the mainly housed skid row population of three decades past and a much larger increase over those who were literally homeless during that period. Moreover, the face of homelessness has changed. Today's homeless are younger, disproportionately nonwhite, and much more likely to be not only women but adolescents and children. While it may be hyperbole to liken current homelessness to what was seen during the Great Depression (current rates are estimated at 0.2 percent of the entire population, one-fifth the conservative rate for that earlier period), [3] not since the Great Depression have we seen such a heterogeneous, visible, and widely dispersed homeless population as we are witnessing today.

Like most large urban metropolises, Los Angeles has been hard hit by this phenomenon. Dubbed "the homeless capital of America" after the Department of Housing and Urban Development (HUD) ranked it as having the largest homeless population in the country in 1984, it has since vied with New York City for this dubious distinction. The problems inherent in enumerating the homeless make resolving this debate difficult. Whatever Los Angeles's actual rank, however, the magnitude of the problem is clear, raising serious humanitarian concerns and imposing large social costs.

Most of our response to contemporary homelessness has focused on emergency subsistence services, spearheaded by private charitable organizations but supported by public sector dollars. Although these programs have been supplemented by efforts that seek to significantly change the lives of homeless people—for example, transitional housing programs that teach skills and provide support—professionals and laypeople agree that our efforts are not having a substantial effect. The homelessness problem continues to worsen.

To understand why current efforts to solve the problem of homelessness are not working, we must first understand something about the causes of homelessness. This is because the way in which we conceptualize the causes of homelessness inevitably shapes our policy approach. If we decide, on the one hand, that homelessness is a function of the *personal characteristics* of homeless individuals, we would target our policy at individuals. Thus, if we decide that homelessness is a matter of individual choice, we might adopt policies that make homelessness a less attractive option—for example, reducing the availability of shelters and soup kitchens—in order to change the decision-making calculus. Alternatively, if we decide that homelessness is largely a function of personal problems that impair an individual's ability to function, we might pursue an approach focused on rehabilitative services. On the other hand, if we decide that *structural causes*, rather than individual characteristics, are at the root of homelessness, broader policy changes affecting housing, employment, and income distribution would be indicated.

Which of these approaches should policymakers follow? In this paper, we argue that we must synthesize the *personal* and the *structural* perspectives to understand fully why homelessness exists in its current form. To set the dimensions of the problem, we will first provide a profile of the contemporary homeless and of the experience of homelessness. Next we review what we know about the sources of homelessness, examining data bearing on the *personal limitations* explanation as well as evidence for the *structural* perspective. We then offer our synthesis of these perspectives and discuss its policy implications.

WHO ARE THE NEW HOMELESS? A PROFILE OF HOMELESSNESS IN LOS ANGELES

A national profile of contemporary homelessness has emerged from a growing number of methodologically sophisticated studies. This profile highlights the youth of today's homeless population, the disproportionate presence of minorities, the growing numbers of women (both alone and with children), the growing adolescent homeless population, and the increased prevalence of drug abuse and mental illness. [4] There is also increasing evidence to suggest that the very nature of homelessness has changed. Homelessness is less a way of life and more a relatively short but frequently repeated experience among the marginal poor. Over a year's time, only one-third of the homeless population will be continuously homeless, while the remainder will be moving from the housed population to the homeless population or vice versa. [3]

Los Angeles very neatly mirrors these national trends. Our portrait of local homelessness draws on seven local surveys of the Los Angeles homeless population, but most heavily on RAND's recent survey of 1,500 downtown and westside homeless adults conducted in 1991.*

What are the key characteristics of the Los Angeles homeless population?

- The Los Angeles adult homeless population is young, predominantly unmarried, and male. It is overwhelmingly minority, with blacks far outnumbering Hispanics (Figure 1).

- Women now represent approximately 16 percent of the population in downtown and westside areas.

- These patterns differ in the adolescent homeless population, which is 75 percent white and 40 percent female.

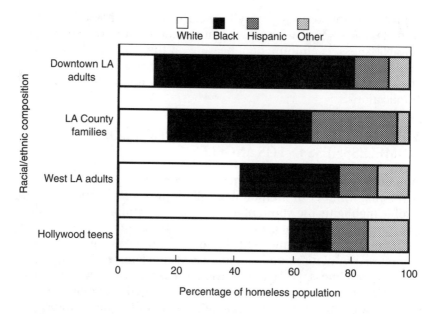

Figure 1—Majority of Homeless Persons Are Racial/Ethnic Minorities

- While at least half of the men and three-quarters of the women are parents, almost all of those with children currently in their care are mothers who, on average, are responsible for three to four children. Of those women who are mothers, approximately one-fifth currently have their children with them.

- Approximately one-third of Los Angeles's homeless adult population have had at least some college education, but fully 30 percent of single adults and 40 percent of homeless mothers have not completed high school.

- Homeless adults have little in the way of financial resources. Only one in four have worked for pay in the past month, earning a median of only $200 for a month's efforts. Even so, only half the population receives some kind of income assistance, mostly food stamps (Figure 2).

- There is considerable movement of people into and out of the condition of homelessness. Forty-four percent had been home-

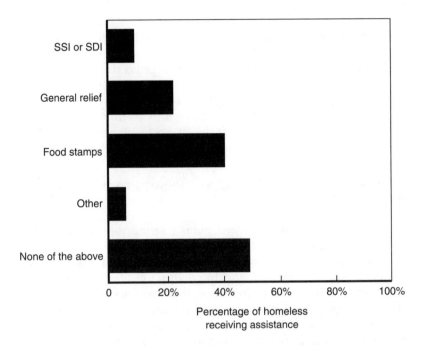

Figure 2—Many Homless Persons Receive No Income Assistance

less less than one year, counting all episodes of homelessness; 55 percent had experienced multiple episodes of homelessness, separated by periods during which they lived in conventional housing; and 60 percent had been in their *current* episode of homelessness for less than a year.

This profile of the new homeless and the new homelessness suggests that the dimensions of this policy problem have changed significantly over the last three decades. More than any other feature, it is heterogeneity that distinguishes the contemporary homeless population from the homeless of the 1960s. The ranks of the homeless now include those previously considered protected from homelessness by family and society—single women, adolescents, young adults, and mothers with young children. The threshold of vulnerability to homelessness in our society is clearly lower.

The dynamic nature of contemporary homelessness indicates that the gap between being homeless and being housed is, among poor Americans, a narrow one that is often crossed. While 600,000 are thought to be homeless on a given night across the nation, probably two to three times that many are homeless at some time over the course of a year, and many others will be homeless at some time in their lives. Our policies must look not only to those who are homeless now but to those who are at risk of, and who actually experience, homelessness during more broadly defined time periods.

PERSPECTIVES ON HOMELESSNESS: PERSONAL VERSUS STRUCTURAL

What causes homelessness? Answers to that question fall into two broad categories. Those that focus on the *human dimension* argue that homelessness results from the personal limitations of homeless people. Even those who focus on personal limitations, however, often draw opposite conclusions from this perspective. Some contend that a substantial number of homeless people, such as the mentally ill, are unable to take care of themselves and are thus homeless through no fault of their own. Indeed, there are those who argue that *most* homeless adults are innocent victims of their social and physical disability and so deserve help. Others adopt a more restrictive view of who deserves public assistance, arguing that the vast majority of homeless adults (with the exception of the chronically mentally ill and a few other deserving groups) are responsible for the personal limitations that led them to become homeless. This view assumes that substance abuse (over which individuals *should* have control), laziness, or a willful disregard for societal requirements is the underlying cause of homelessness, that the homeless do not want jobs or stable residences and would reject them if offered. They *choose* homelessness to avoid the responsibilities of a more conventional life.

A second broad explanation contends that personal limitations such as mental illness or substance abuse are irrelevant; only *structural factors* matter—for example, deindustrialization, unemployment, reductions in entitlements, a rise in poverty, and a dearth of low-cost housing. For some adherents of this perspective, a focus on individual problems merely blames the victims for society's ills or, even worse, erects a smoke screen that blinds us to the systemic social flaws that are responsible for widespread homelessness.

Let's examine the evidence for each perspective.

Individual Pathology and Problems

Consistent with profiles of the homeless across the nation, the homeless in Los Angeles have extremely high rates of mental health and substance abuse problems. Results from our 1991 survey show that approximately 20 percent of adults have chronic mental illnesses such as schizophrenia, manic depressive illness, and recurrent major depression. A little more than one-third are currently alcohol dependent; and about one-quarter are dependent on illicit drugs, predominantly "crack" cocaine. Moreover, there is overlap between these two groups, since chronically mentally ill adults are just as likely or even more likely to be alcohol or drug dependent as those without chronic mental disorders. While the proportion of homeless persons in downtown Los Angeles with chronic mental illness was lower in 1991 (19 percent) than it was in 1985 (28 percent), the rate of current cocaine dependence has grown from less than 1 percent in 1985 to 21 percent in 1991.

Serious health problems are also common among the homeless. These include not only conditions related to their homelessness (trauma, skin abnormalities, foot problems) but chronic diseases such as hypertension, hepatitis, and tuberculosis. The rates of all of these diseases are much higher among the homeless than is ordinarily found in the community, particularly considering that this is a relatively young population.

Homeless adolescents are similarly troubled. Nearly half have attempted suicide, one in four has experienced major depression, nearly half have abused alcohol, and about 40 percent have abused illegal drugs. Similarly, young children of homeless parents have extremely high rates of emotional problems, behavioral problems, and developmental delays.

Many problems of homeless adults began before they became homeless. Table 1 shows the proportion of homeless adults that acknowledge having experienced various problems during the year prior to their first becoming homeless. Nearly 90 percent report having experienced at least one, and in most cases many, of these problems—three on average. The most frequent was loss of income due to losing a job or benefits, but heavy use of alcohol or drugs was typical as well, as were problems related to health and mental health. Moreover, it is clear that a large number of the homeless experienced disruptions in relationships before their first episode of homelessness.

The childhood experiences reported by homeless individuals suggest that their problems are even more long-standing. Homelessness is often preceded by an earlier pattern of economic, social, and psychological problems. Among the homeless adults surveyed, more than half had at least one experience associated with severe financial difficulties between the ages of 6 and 18—for example, doubled up with other families or moved or were evicted because their families could not make their payments. Moreover, one in four spent time living away from parents in foster care, juvenile hall, or orphanages; and one in five was physically or sexually abused. This pattern is even more acute among homeless teens, the vast majority of whom report neglect, physical or sexual abuse by family or other adults in the household when they lived at home. More than half of homeless adolescents had been in juvenile detention, 40 percent had lived in a foster home, and nearly as many had been placed in group homes.

Table 1

Homeless Persons Experience Serious Problems the Year Before Their First Episode of Homelessness

Percentage Who:	
Had drop in income because lost a job, welfare, or disability benefits	50
Frequently got high on alcohol or drugs	47
Became separated or divorced or experienced a break in a relationship with someone else very close	42
Had someone they depended on for housing, food, or money no longer willing or able to help them out	34
Experienced a major increase in expenses, such as rent, health care, etc.	30
Spent time in a hospital, jail or prison, group care or treatment facility, or a foster home	23
Experienced serious physical or mental health problems	19

Based on this evidence, we must conclude that homeless adults, teens, and children in Los Angeles are disproportionately beset by serious economic, family, psychiatric, and physical health problems—problems that are both multiple and long-standing. Many of the homeless appear to be particularly vulnerable people whose current adaptation is shaped not only by serious mental health and substance abuse problems but by a long history of personal trouble as well. Although current studies do not allow us to tell whether problems such as mental illness and substance abuse precipitate, exacerbate, or result from homelessness, it is clear that their existence makes it much more difficult to overcome either homelessness or the extreme poverty that lies precipitously close to homelessness. These problems demand attention if these individuals' lives are to be stabilized.

Structural Causes of Contemporary Homelessness

So far, we have considered problems of homeless individuals that create vulnerability to extreme poverty and, consequently, to homelessness. This perspective suggests a policy approach that includes intensive treatment and rehabilitation interventions that could reduce individual vulnerability—for example, intensive drug and mental health treatment and job training. However, this is only part of the picture. Similarly high levels of poverty and debilitating mental health and substance abuse problems have existed in the past without the high rates of homelessness we see today. To understand better why homelessness became a major national problem in the past two decades, we must examine structural factors.

When we shift our focus to the broader social and economic climate in which contemporary homelessness has emerged, it becomes clear that the rise in homelessness over the last decade has taken place in a context characterized by two broad trends. The supply of rental housing affordable to those falling at or below the poverty level has declined steadily, precisely at the same time as the number of poor people competing for these increasingly scarce units has swelled.

The decline in low-cost housing. The nation's supply of low-cost rental housing has been shrinking for the past 20 years. The decline was especially rapid during the 1980s for several intertwined reasons.

During this period, pivotal changes in the federal tax structure, rising interest rates, and new financing practices removed incentives for private investors to build new low-cost housing, just as the federal government was dramatically scaling back the production and maintenance of public housing. Simultaneously, rising house prices made it more difficult for potential first-time buyers to purchase single-family homes; thus, more remained renters, tightening the rental market and driving up rental prices at an accelerated pace. At the same time, thousands of low-income housing units were lost to demolition and conversion, as gentrification and redevelopment reclaimed areas previously occupied by the poor. Others units were lost to arson and abandonment, as it became more fiscally prudent for owners to cease investing in, and in some cases to walk away from, low-income housing, especially in areas characterized by urban blight.

While the precise mechanics of these processes and their relative importance are open to debate, the end result is not. The national housing stock grew between 1981 and 1987, as Table 2 indicates, but not at the lower end of the housing market. The number of units renting for more than $500 per month increased by 86 percent during this period, but those renting for less than $300 *fell* by almost 9 percent, and those renting for less than $150 fell by more than 13 percent. [5] (See Figure 3.) This pattern continued a trend begun in the 1970s, when the number of units renting for less than $300 declined by 6 percent. [3] Moreover, the rental market was *tightest* among units renting for less than $300. The vacancy rate among units renting for less than $150 was 3.8 percent in 1987, well below the 5 percent threshold usually considered essential to the normal functioning of the market. [6]

The decline in low-cost housing was not limited to the stock of multi-room units typically inhabited by poor families. The number of units in SRO hotels fell even more precipitously. These units are a particularly important source of housing for poor, unattached, single persons, including the seriously mentally ill. Nationally, it has been estimated that 1,116,000 SRO hotel units, almost half of the total supply, were lost to conversion and demolition during the 1970s and early 1980s. [7] Large cities suffered proportionately higher losses. New York, for instance, lost 87 percent of its SRO housing between

Table 2

Rental Units and Vacancies Nationwide, by Monthly Rent, 1981 and 1987[a]

Monthly Contract Rent	1981			1987			1981–1987 Change in Units (%)
	Total	Vacant	Vacancy Rate (%)	Total	Vacant	Vacancy Rate (%)	
$0–150	5,045	193	3.8	4,362	165	3.8	-13.5
150–300	11,463	537	4.7	10,690	859	8.0	-6.8
300–400	6,158	307	5.0	7,483	651	8.7	+21.5
400–500	3,146	152	4.8	4,276	351	8.2	+35.9
500+	2,299	173	7.5	4,276	436	10.2	+86.0
Total	28,111	1,363	4.8	31,357	2,462	7.9	+11.5
Median Contract Rent	$281	$286	—	$304	$330	—	—

[a]Rent-specified units only, in thousands; contract rent in 1987 dollars.

SOURCE: William C. Apgar, Jr., *Recent Trends in Rental Vacancies*, Cambridge, Mass.: Joint Center for Housing Studies of Harvard University, Working Paper 89-3, 1989, Table 3.

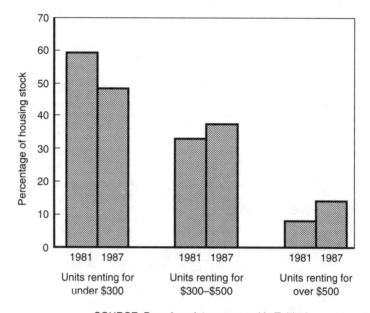

SOURCE: Based on data presented in Table 2.

Figure 3—Low-Cost Housing Across the Nation Is Declining

1970 and 1982. [8] Chicago not only experienced sharp losses in its SRO stock but also saw the complete elimination of cubicle flop-house hotels that had previously housed thousands of near-homeless individuals in its skid row area. [9, 10]

Los Angeles experienced an even more-pronounced decline in low-cost rental units. After correcting for inflation, the proportion of units renting for more than $500 in Los Angeles County grew from 14 percent in 1974 to 45 percent of the stock in 1985 at the expense of low-end units, which fell from 35 percent of the rental stock in 1974 to only 16 percent by 1985 (Figure 4). While the number of units renting for upwards of $750 per month rose by 320 percent during this time, the number of units renting for $300 or less in the county fell by 42 percent, with vacancy rates in this low-end sector hovering around 1 percent. This bleak picture continued throughout the 1980s, when there were no net additions to the public housing stock

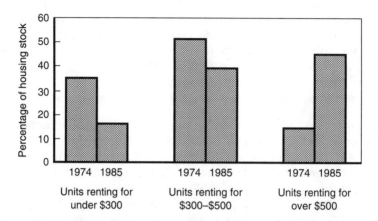

SOURCE: Based on data from Jennifer Wolch and Michael Dear, *Inside/Outside: Homelessness in Los Angeles,* Unpublished Manuscript, 1992.

**Figure 4—Los Angeles Has Lost Low-Cost Housing
at a More Precipitous Rate**

and approximately 4,000 low-cost housing units were demolished or converted annually. [11,12] By 1985 more than half the SRO housing in the downtown area that had existed in 1970 had been destroyed, [13] a process that ended only when the Community Redevelopment Agency placed a moratorium on downtown SRO demolition in the late 1980s.

The growing pool of the vulnerable poor. A decrease in the supply of low-cost housing units is not necessarily undesirable. Indeed, if the number of people in poverty were shrinking, a decline in low-end housing units could be interpreted as a normal market response to changing demand. But this has not been the case. Ironically, just as the supply of low-cost housing began decreasing, the demand for it began to grow. From 1970 to 1988, the number of poor people grew from 25.4 million to 31.9 million, an increase of almost 26 percent. [14]

One contributing factor to the growing number of poor people was undoubtedly deindustrialization—the shift in our economy's occupational structure from fewer relatively high-paying union-organized manufacturing jobs to more lower-paying, often part-time service and retail jobs that lack the same level of benefits, particularly health benefits. (See Chapter Two by Lynn Karoly for a more comprehensive discussion of labor market changes that underlie increased poverty.) This, and the failure to adjust the minimum wage between 1981 and 1989 (resulting in a 23 percent decrease in its purchasing power), meant that even full-time work would not necessarily lift a family out of poverty. [3]

A steady erosion of the real dollar value of public entitlements other than Social Security also contributed to growing poverty in the 1970s and 1980s. For instance, the average monthly purchasing power of an Aid to Families with Dependent Children (AFDC) family fell by almost a third, from $568 in 1970 to $385 in 1984, a time during which rents significantly increased, placing an added burden on households. Female-headed households at or below the poverty line increased by 16 percent during this period. In contrast, the number of elderly poor who rely on an entitlement that is indexed to the consumer price index (CPI) *decreased* by 27 percent. The federal government also tightened eligibility requirements for entitlements; this process left almost 500,000 formerly eligible recipients of AFDC without access to benefits in 1981 and an additional 300,000 with reduced benefits. It also resulted in removing almost a half million disabled individuals from the Supplemental Security Income (SSI) and Social Security Disability Income (SSDI) programs between 1981 and 1984. [3]

Deinstitutionalization of the mentally ill formerly housed in state mental hospitals also increased the numbers of those seeking cheap housing. Once back in the community, these individuals relied on public entitlements as their primary, and usually only, source of income, ensuring that most of them remained in poverty and creating a new group of competitors for the diminishing supply of affordable housing. Many former state hospital residents were placed in SRO hotels, which were sufficiently plentiful to house them during the early years of deinstitutionalization. As the SRO hotels were demolished, increasing numbers of the deinstitutionalized mentally ill adults became homeless.

Los Angeles felt all of these trends acutely. While deindustrialization was slower to hit Los Angeles than other parts of the nation, steel, rubber, and automobile plant closures and successive blows to the aerospace industry eventually ravaged the county's manufacturing base. Though the absolute number of low-skill, low-wage jobs increased between the mid-1970s and the late 1980s, the proportion of jobs appropriate to low-skill laborers decreased precisely as the region experienced a massive influx of new immigrants in need of them. Stiffening competition shut many workers, particularly those with poor educational skills, out of the work force. Moreover, the wages, benefits, job security, and opportunities for advancement associated with low-skill jobs declined. The end result was troublesome, even for those who remained employed. By 1987 the rate of male workers in Los Angeles County earning less than $10,000 had doubled relative to 1969. [11]

Those who fell out of, or never entered, the labor market, felt the full brunt of the federal restructuring of welfare and other benefits, for rather than making up for federal shortfalls, the state of California repeatedly passed most cuts through to local government and welfare recipients. Adults ineligible for AFDC were especially hard hit. They were forced to rely on general relief, which remained unchanged at $228 per month between 1981 and 1986—a period when the monthly rent for typical bottom-of-the-line SRO hotel rooms in downtown Los Angeles was $240.

The growing mismatch between available income and affordable housing. The inevitable consequence of the sharp rise in housing prices and of the parallel decrease in real wages and benefits was that poor households across the nation began spending more of their income on rent. In 1970 there was a surplus of "affordable" low-income housing units for the poorest 25 percent of renters, most of whom fell below the poverty line (an "affordable" rent is one that requires no more than 30 percent of income). By 1980 there was a shortfall of 27 percent (Figure 5). This increased to 35 percent by 1985 and to 42 percent by 1990 [3], resulting in almost two poor households for every one affordable housing unit. The end result? By 1985, 64 percent of poor-renter households across the nation were spending more than half of their limited income on rent, and households found it increasingly necessary to double and triple up, reversing a trend toward smaller households that had been in effect until 1978.

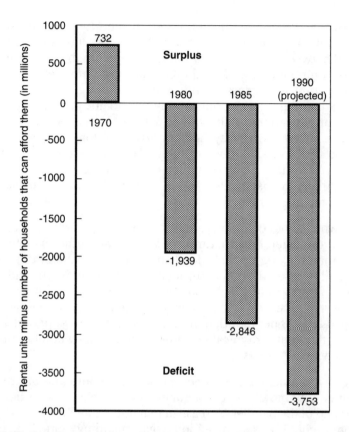

SOURCE: Based on data from Cushing Dolbeare, "Why a Housing Entitlement Program?" Paper presented at Urban Institute Housing Seminar, December 1988. Reprinted in Martha R. Burt, *Over the Edge: The Growth of Homelessness in the 1980s,* New York: Russell Sage Foundation, 1992.

Figure 5—The Gap Widens Between the Number of Households in the Bottom Quartile of the Rental Market and the Number of Rental Units Affordable to Them

So it went in Los Angeles. By 1980 there were twice as many very low-income renter households as there were units they could afford. By 1985, 74 percent of poor households were spending more than half their income on rent, dangerously stretching their ability to meet their other basic needs and seriously compromising their ability to cope with even minor financial crises. [12]

COMBINING INDIVIDUAL AND STRUCTURAL PERSPECTIVES

We are now in a position to put together the two parts of our analysis. From examining the characteristics of the homeless population, we can see that the homeless have a disproportionate number of social, psychological, and emotional problems—severe problems that would seem at first glance to explain why they have become homeless. But we also know that in the past there have been many with similar problems, yet few homeless people. This led us to look at structural problems, in particular the decline of affordable low-cost housing in the face of rising demand. But the structural analysis alone does not explain why the homeless population contains such a disproportionate number of troubled individuals.

The structural analysis helps us understand why we are witnessing pervasive homelessness *now*. Put simply, there are not enough low-cost housing units for the poor people who need them, a deepening mismatch that has left increasing numbers of people homeless. Doubling up could forestall the looming homelessness crisis for only so long. There are limits to the poor's ability to devote an increasingly greater proportion of their income to rent. Moreover, there are limits to how much overcrowding will be tolerated as a solution to this affordability problem—culturally defined limits that vary among groups of the ethnic poor and that explain, at least in part, why certain ethnic groups are more vulnerable to homelessness than others. By the early 1980s, the threshold for many of these groups had been crossed, and homelessness became an increasingly visible phenomenon throughout the decade and into the 1990s. [6]

The interaction between the structural level and the individual explains *who* becomes homeless. In any arena characterized by fierce competition for a scarce resource, those least able to compete will fall by the wayside first. It thus stands to reason that the first group to fall off the housing ladder would disproportionately include those least able to compete for housing, especially those vulnerable individuals whose traditional housing solutions—SRO hotels and the like—were fast disappearing through demolition and conversion. Seen this way, it is not surprising to find such high numbers of people with mental illness, substance abuse, and other severe adaptive problems among contemporary homeless populations. Structural factors, then, set the stage; personal problems determine who is most likely to lose out.

In a sense, this process can be likened to a variation in the game of musical chairs—one in which both the number of available seats progressively decreases and the number of people playing the game progressively increases. As hard as people may try to pile up on each others' laps to avoid standing when the music stops, inevitably a growing number of people are left without chairs. Those who are less fast and strong—especially those who find it hard to understand the rules of the game—lose out first. Later, as there are fewer and fewer chairs and more people vying for them, the losers are joined by players whose impairments are more subtle. Ultimately, as the competition gets even more fierce, even hale and hearty game players find themselves without seats.

While rates of mental illness and substance abuse are high among the homeless, these are not the only characteristics that are disproportionately present among them compared with housed people, even poor housed people. Homeless adults, as we have pointed out, are disproportionately male and have low job skills. Homeless families are disproportionately headed by single women (relative to poor households in general). These are the same groups who have experienced growing poverty over the last 20 years. Increasingly, it seems to us, the homeless population is likely to include individuals with vulnerabilities associated with economic and social standing rather than with personal pathology. As the mismatch between human needs and housing availability continues to accelerate, the threshold of what it takes to become homeless will continue to fall, forcing progressively less-impaired people onto the street and into shelters. We see evidence of this in Los Angeles already, where our research reveals a proportionate decrease in the number of chronically mentally ill individuals among the homeless.

By recognizing the critical interaction of structural context and individual vulnerability, our synthesizing framework accommodates both the perspective of analysts who highlight personal pathology as a primary cause of homelessness and those who stress structural problems. Thus the framework offers the promise of moving beyond often sterile debate, pitting those who prefer to blame homeless individuals for their plight against those who see homeless people as the innocent victims of social ills. This dispute only stalemates policy efforts. If we accept instead that homelessness occurs as a function of the personal vulnerabilities of certain individuals acting within a context set by structural pressures, we can move forward toward developing policies that address both.

TOWARD A MORE EFFECTIVE POLICY ON HOMELESSNESS

Our synthesis of individual and structural perspectives highlights the multidimensional nature of homelessness and suggests that its sources run deeply and broadly through our society. In homelessness, we see magnified the symptoms of a variety of social ills. Some of the contributing problems have gained prominence relatively recently in our history, such as the shortfall in low-income housing, the shift in the occupational base, increases in poverty, and the growing number of single-parent families. Others, such as limited opportunities for minorities, substance abuse problems, family violence, and inadequate care for the seriously mentally ill, are long-standing problems. All, however, are dauntingly difficult to solve. There will be no silver-bullet fixes to the problem of homelessness. Nor is there any hopeful sign that would lead us to expect a spontaneous decline in homelessness in the absence of dramatic policy action. If anything, the indicators point to growing numbers of homeless Americans, a trend that will continue unless we take effective steps toward arresting it.

The integrated perspective we have proposed here suggests the general contours that an effective policy response to homelessness must follow. Above all, it highlights the fact that both personal *and* structural factors are salient in explaining contemporary homelessness and that our response to homelessness must thus involve simultaneous efforts on *each* of these fronts. Our attempts to ameliorate homelessness must address the very real problems and/or disabilities that so many homeless people experience, including those that are often associated with extreme poverty, so that such people can more successfully access and maintain housing. At the same time, our policies must ensure that sufficient housing within their means exists. Partial efforts, that is, efforts that address personal vulnerabilities or housing scarcity but not both, can at best produce partial solutions. We suspect that they will fail to do even that since not addressing one can easily sabotage efforts to address the other. Our remaining comments elaborate on this central theme by suggesting why current homelessness policies are not succeeding and by further emphasizing the importance of a two-pronged prevention-oriented approach.

How do current approaches to dealing with homelessness measure up to the prescription implied by the above discussion? For the most part, not very well. While striking exceptions do exist, current homelessness policy is primarily concerned with providing emergency services—for example, food, shelter, and health care—that address immediate, basic needs. Unfortunately, these responses address only the *symptoms* of homelessness, not the causes. But short-term maintenance strategies have held sway at the expense of long-term preventive strategies. We remain so consumed by the overwhelming challenge of providing food and shelter to those who need them that we have little energy to address the more fundamental question of how to arrest the ever-increasing number of people who enter and reenter homelessness. We thus manage through our efforts to pull some people out of homelessness but not as fast as new people enter. This will continue until we focus our policy agenda on the underlying causes of homelessness.

We do not mean to imply that humanitarian assistance to those already homeless should be withdrawn. As long as there are structural pressures limiting access to affordable housing, legislating disincentives to homelessness by eliminating shelter, food, and essential treatment will not achieve their aim. In the current economic and housing environment, making it more difficult to be homeless in one community does not encourage homeless people to get jobs and rent apartments; it only pushes homeless individuals from that community to another. This might be a satisfactory solution from the perspective of the community that rids itself of its homelessness problem, but it is clearly ineffective in the broader view.

The increasing but still very limited efforts to promote rehabilitation of homeless individuals begin to attack the problems of homelessness more squarely. Programs that offer vocational training, mental health and substance abuse treatment, money management, and social skills training can reduce some people's chances of becoming homeless again. However, without simultaneous changes in the structural roots of homelessness, these programs will only enable them to compete more effectively for scarce housing, while pushing just as many new faces out onto the streets. The game of musical chairs will continue with its structural constraints unaltered. There is a further catch to providing services oriented toward helping the homeless become more self-sufficient: it is nearly impossible for people to engage in or gain any benefit from rehabilitative programs unless they first become stably housed. In a second sense, then, housing is essential to rehabilitating the homeless.

In order to reduce homelessness, therefore, it is essential that our policy approaches begin to focus more intensively on long-range preventive solutions. The aim should be to stop the move into homelessness while we continue to improve the quality of life for those currently homeless. As our synthesis of individual and structural perspectives suggests, in order to produce results, policy efforts must simultaneously attack the problems that make individuals vulnerable to homelessness and increase the access to and availability of housing. Moreover, these two policy emphases—vulnerability and housing—must be *paired* so that affordable housing is provided along with the services and supports that will allow vulnerable people to maintain it. If we succeed in increasing low-cost housing without dealing with individual vulnerabilities, we simply move poverty and other social ills indoors and out of sight. If we succeed in reducing individual vulnerabilities without improving access to housing, we set the stage for an increase in the health and diversity of the homeless population, and perhaps more turnover in the population, but not a reduction in numbers.

Implementing policies that represent long-range preventive solutions to homelessness will be very expensive. Even a relatively straightforward effort to increase the low-cost housing stock is a costly undertaking. For example, in 1988 the Los Angeles Blue Ribbon Committee for Affordable Housing estimated that the city would have to spend $200 to $400 million a year just to keep the inventory of low-cost housing from declining. Policies designed to prevent individual vulnerabilities—educational and child welfare reform, family and child care policies, better prevention and treatment of substance abuse and mental health problems—will need substantial infusions of public and private money if we are to gain significant ground.

We recognize that good policy does not flow inevitably from good analysis. Because preventive approaches are costly and are slow to produce visible results, it will be hard to generate the political will to confront these serious problems more aggressively. Reoriented priorities are a prerequisite to the efforts needed to remedy homelessness and the poverty that undergirds it. A better understanding of the causes and consequences of homelessness—consequences that impose high costs for our urban communities today and sow the seeds of social problems for future generations—may help to galvanize action.

NOTES

*Our discussion of homelessness in Los Angeles draws upon the seven most methodologically sophisticated studies of homeless populations in the Los Angeles County area. These studies were conducted between 1985 and 1991 and include two studies of homeless adults that focus on the downtown area of Los Angeles [13,15,16], one that focuses on homeless adults in Santa Monica and Venice [17,18], one on homeless teens in Hollywood [19,20] and two on homeless families across Los Angeles County [21,22]. We draw most heavily on our own baseline sample of 1,548 homeless adults, [23] two-thirds of whom were located in the downtown area of Los Angeles; the other third was located in the westside area (Santa Monica and Venice). This study, which used state-of-the-art sampling techniques and diagnostic instruments, is the most comprehensive survey of homeless individuals in Los Angeles undertaken thus far. Approximately 500 of these individuals have been followed and reinterviewed bimonthly for over a year—an extraordinarily difficult endeavor—in an attempt to determine what distinguishes those who exit homelessness from those who remain homeless and, of those who exit homelessness, what distinguishes those who remained housed from those who become homeless again. [23,24,25]

REFERENCES

1. Bogue, Donald B., *Skid Row in American Cities*, Chicago: Community and Family Study Center, University of Chicago, 1963.

2. Burt, Martha R., and Barbara E. Cohen, *America's Homeless: Numbers, Characteristics, and Programs That Serve Them*, Washington, D.C.: Urban Institute Press, 1989.

3. Burt, Martha R., *Over the Edge: The Growth of Homelessness in the 1980s*, New York: Russell Sage Foundation, 1992.

4. Institute of Medicine, Committee on Health Care for Homeless People, *Homelessness, Health, and Human Needs*, Washington, D.C.: National Academy Press, 1988.

5. Apgar, William C., Jr., *Recent Trends in Rental Vacancies*, Cambridge, Mass.: Joint Center for Housing Studies of Harvard University, Working Paper 89-3, 1989.

6. Hopper, Kim, and Jill Hamberg, "The Making of America's Homeless: From Skid Row to the New Poor, 1945–1984," in Rachel G. Bratt, Chester Hartman, and Ann Myerson, eds., *Critical Perspectives on Housing*, Philadelphia: Temple University Press, 1986, pp. 12–40.

7. Baxter, Ellen, and Kim Hopper, "Shelter and Housing for the Homeless Mentally Ill," in H. Richard Lamb, ed., *The Homeless Mentally Ill: A Task Force Report of the American Psychiatric Association*, Washington, D.C.: American Psychiatric Association Press, 1984, pp. 109–140.

8. Green, C., *Housing Single, Low-Income Individuals*, New York: Setting Municipal Priorities Project, 1982.

9. Hoch, Charles, and Robert A. Slayton, *New Homeless and Old: Community and the Skid Row Hotel*, Philadelphia: Temple University Press, 1989.

10. Rossi, Peter H., *Down and Out in America: The Origins of Homelessness*, Chicago: Univeristy of Chicago Press, 1989.

11. Wolch, Jennifer, and Michael Dear, *Inside/Outside: Homelessness in Los Angeles*, Unpublished Manuscript, 1992.

12. Research Group on the Los Angeles Economy, *The Widening Divide: Income Inequality and Poverty in Los Angeles*, Los Angeles: University of California, Los Angeles, 1989.

13. Hamilton, Rabinovitz and Alschuler Staff, *The Changing Face of Misery: Los Angeles' Skid Row Area in Transition*, Los Angeles: Hamilton, Rabinovitz and Alschuler, Inc., 1987.

14. U.S. House of Representatives, Committee on Ways and Means, *Overview of Entitlement Programs: The 1990 Green Book*, Washington, D.C.: U.S. Government Printing Office, 1990.

15. Koegel, Paul, M. Audrey Burnam, and Roger K. Farr, "The Prevalence of Specific Psychiatric Disorders Among Homeless Individuals in the Inner City of Los Angeles," *Archives of General Psychiatry*, Vol. 45, 1988, pp. 1085–1092.

16. Koegel, Paul, M. Audrey Burnam, and Roger K. Farr, "Subsistence Adaptation Among Homeless Adults in the Inner City of Los Angeles," *Journal of Social Issues*, Vol. 46, No. 4, 1990, pp. 83–107.

17. Gelberg, Lillian, Lawrence S. Linn, and Barbara D. Leake, "Mental Health, Alcohol and Drug Use, and Criminal History Among Homeless Adults," *American Journal of Psychiatry*, Vol. 145, No. 2, 1988, pp. 191–196.

18. Gelberg, Lillian, and Lawrence S. Linn, "Assessing the Physical Health of Homeless Adults," *Journal of the American Medical Association*, Vol. 262, No. 14, 1989, pp. 1973–1979.

19. Robertson, Marjorie J., Milton Greenblatt, Paul Koegel, and Peter Mundy, "Characteristics and Circumstances of Homeless Adolescents in Hollywood," Paper presented at the annual meeting of the Americn Psychological Association, Boston, Mass., August 11, 1990.

20. Robertson, Marjorie J., *Homeless Youth: Patterns of Alcohol Use*, Berkeley, Calif.: Alcohol Research Group, 1989.

21. Zima, Bonnie T., Kenneth B. Wells, and Howard E. Freeman, *Emotional and Behavioral Problems and Severe Academic Delays Among Sheltered Homeless Children in Los Angeles County*, Unpublished Manuscript, 1992.

22. Wood, David, R. Burciaga Valdez, Toshi Hayashi, and Albert Shen, "Homeless and Housed Families in Los Angeles: A Study Comparing Demographic, Economic, and Family Functioning Characteristics," *American Journal of Public Health*, Vol. 80, No. 9, 1990, pp. 1049–1052.

23. Koegel, Paul, "The Course of Homelessness Study: Aims and Design," Paper presented at the 119th annual meeting of the American Public Health Association, Atlanta, Ga., November 10–14, 1991.

24. Burnam, Audrey, "New Perspectives on the Prevalence of Specific Psychiatric Disorders Among Homeless Adults," Paper presented at the 119th annual meeting of the American Public Health Association, Atlanta, Ga., November 10-14, 1991.

25. Trude, Sally, "History of Homelessness and Its Antecedents Among Homeless Adults in Los Angeles," Paper presented at the 119th annual meeting of the American Public Health Association, Atlanta, Ga., November 10–14, 1991.

ABOUT THE CONTRIBUTORS

Audrey Burnam (Ph.D., Social Psychology, University of Texas) has extensive research experience in psychiatric epidemiology and mental health policy. She has directed a project examining the epidemiology of alcoholism among Mexican-Americans and was a principal collaborator in a study of the course of depression among outpatients in different health care systems. She has conducted several epidemiologic studies of homeless populations, including a survey of homeless persons in three California counties and a study of homeless individuals in the Los Angeles skid row area. Dr. Burnam is currently leading a five-year study to identify the kinds of things that predict exits from and reentries into homelessness and how the presence of a serious mental illness modifies these predictors. She is codirector of the RAND Drug Policy Research Center.

Julie DaVanzo (Ph.D., Economics, University of California, Los Angeles) is a senior economist at RAND and director of its Family in Economic Development Center. She has worked on research projects in Malaysia, Indonesia, Bangladesh, Jordan, The Gambia, Guatemala, Chile, and the United States, examining the effects of government programs and policies on family behavior. She is currently working on a study of Salvadoran and Filipino immigrants in Los Angeles and is also reviewing research and policies regarding American families. Dr. DaVanzo is chairperson of the Scientific Advisory Committee for the Demographic and Health Surveys Project. She has served on the National Academy of Sciences Committee on Population and also on the Population Research Committee of the National Institute of Child Health and Human Development. She has been first and second vice president of the Population Association of America.

Phyllis L. Ellickson (Ph.D., Political Science, Massachusetts Institute of Technology) is a senior behavioral scientist at RAND. A nationally recognized expert on drug prevention, her major fields of research include adolescent behavior; knowledge acquisition; and the implementation, evaluation, and dissemination of innovative intervention programs for youth. Dr. Ellickson directed Project ALERT, an internationally known smoking and drug prevention experiment tested in 30 California and Oregon schools. She has also published extensively on the patterns and antecedents of adolescent problem behavior and on the methodological issues involved in conducting large-scale field trials. She has served on advisory panels for the National Institute of Drug Abuse, the Office of Substance Abuse Prevention, and the California attorney general.

Peter A. Glassman (M.D., University of London, England) is a consultant in health policy at RAND, a clinical instructor in medicine at the University of California, Los Angeles (UCLA); and a fellow in Health Services Research at the Veterans Affairs (VA) medical center in West Los Angeles. His clinical interests include practice guidelines for outpatient care and caring for the poor and uninsured; he is an attending physician in ambulatory care at a Los Angeles county hospital and a physician-volunteer at the Venice Family Clinic in Venice, California. He is also working on a project that is examining how the threat of litigation affects physician behavior. He is the coauthor of *The Outpatient Care Handbook,* currently in press.

Peter W. Greenwood (Ph.D., Industrial Engineering/Operations Research, Stanford University) is a nationally recognized criminal justice expert. He was the first director of RAND's Criminal Justice Program and has served on the California attorney general's Research and Advisory Panel. Much of his professional career has been devoted to understanding the behavior of career criminals and identifying ways the criminal justice system can counter their future criminality. Dr. Greenwood has also worked extensively with programs designed to rehabilitate serious juvenile offenders and has directed a study of the juvenile justice system in California for the state legislature. His *Intervention Strategies for Chronic Juvenile Offenders: Some New Perspectives* (1986) was the first compelling portrait of strategies that hold promise of success after more than a decade of discouraging findings.

Paul T. Hill (Ph.D., Political Science, Ohio State University) has been a senior social scientist at RAND since 1977. He has directed RAND's Education and Human Resources Program and its Education Policy Center. He is currently leading RAND's research and analysis for the New American Schools Development Corporation. His most recent work has focused on accountability in site-managed schools, educational governance, differences in educational approaches among high schools, and immigrant education. His publications include *High Schools with Character* (1990), a report exploring the differences between effective and ineffective high schools, and *Decentralization and Accountability in Public Education* (1991), an analysis of recent efforts to reduce the burdens of regulation on teachers and principals.

James R. Hosek (Ph.D., Economics, University of Chicago) is corporate research manager of RAND's Human Capital Department and a specialist in labor economics. His research has addressed issues related to training, unemployment, income security, military recruitment and retention, civil service reform, and compensation. He has been director of RAND's Defense Manpower Research Center and also head of the Economics and Statistics Department. Dr. Hosek is currently editor of *The RAND Journal of Economics.*

Lynn A. Karoly (Ph.D., Economics, Yale University) is a labor economist who has studied topics in income distribution, employment liability, youth labor markets, and retirement. She is currently leading multiyear studies that are identifying and analyzing the demographic, economic, and technological factors underlying the changing wage structure in the United States and the growing income inequality among workers and families. Her other recent work includes studies of school-to-work transitions for youth, the effect of wrongful termination doctrines on labor markets, and the provision of health insurance in retirement. In addition to her research, Dr. Karoly teaches courses in the RAND Graduate School of Policy Studies and is the training director for RAND's postdoctoral research programs in population studies and the study of aging.

Jacob Alex Klerman (M.A., Economics, University of Chicago) is an associate economist at RAND. His major fields of interest include labor economics and econometrics. His work at RAND has focused on American labor markets and military manpower. In the area of

American labor markets, he is currently leading studies on the changing American wage structure, maternity leave, and the school-to-work transition. In the area of military manpower, he is leading studies on the relation between compensation and retention, utilization of the military health care system, and the use of surveys in manpower policy research.

Paul Koegel (Ph.D., Anthropology, University of California, Los Angeles) has been researching the adaptation of socially and economically marginal populations in urban settings for the past 15 years. Most recently, he has focused on homeless populations. His work in this area includes a nationally renowned study of homeless adults in the downtown area of Los Angeles; a longitudinal, qualitative examination of the lives of homeless mentally ill adults; and a survey of homeless adolescents. He is currently codirecting a RAND study that is examining predictors of exit from, and reentry into, homelessness. Dr. Koegel recently served as a member of the Santa Monica Task Force on Homelessness and is vice president of the Board of Directors of the West Hollywood Homeless Organization, a nonprofit agency that provides residential and rehabilitative services to homeless adults.

Robert A. Levine (Ph.D., Economics, Yale University) has planned, directed, and carried out studies in almost every area of public policy. Over the past 25 years, he has held a number of high-ranking positions in research administration: he has been president of the New York City RAND Institute, deputy director of the Congressional Budget Office, director of planning and research for the Office of Economic Opportunity, and vice president of the System Development Corporation (SDC). While with SDC, Dr. Levine was responsible for the largest evaluation ever conducted of federal compensatory education programs. He has authored several books, including *The Poor Ye Need Not Have with You: Lessons from the War on Poverty* and *Public Planning: Failure and Redirection.*

David W. Lyon (Ph.D., City and Regional Planning, University of California, Berkeley) is vice president and director of RAND's Domestic Research Division. He joined the New York City RAND Institute in 1972, and as director of research, Human and Economic Resources, and later as vice president of the institute, he was responsible for designing research projects and coordinating staff research in economic development, welfare, manpower training, housing, and education. Dr. Lyon became vice president of the Domestic Research Division in RAND's Santa Monica office in 1977. He oversees nine research programs: Criminal Justice, Education and Human Resources, Health Sciences, the Institute for Civil Justice, Labor and Population, Regulatory Policies, Other Domestic Research, and RAND's two international centers—the European-American Center for Policy Analysis and the Center for U.S.-Japan Relations.

Robert MacCoun (Ph.D., Psychology, Michigan State University) has conducted research on many civil and criminal justice issues, including illicit drug markets, compliance with laws, jury decision making, dispute resolution procedures, and citizens' evaluations of procedural and distributive justice. His work has been published widely in such journals as *Science, Law and Society Review, Crime and Delinquency,* and *Journal of Personality and Social Psychology.* Dr. MacCoun's recent publications include *Money from Crime: A Study of the Economics of Drug Dealing in Washington, D.C.* (1990) and "Drugs and the Law: A Psychological Analysis of Drug Prohibition" (*Psychological Bulletin,* in press). He is currently studying adolescent choices in impoverished urban neighborhoods.

Preston Niblack (M.A., School of Public Affairs, University of Maryland) is an associate social scientist in RAND's International Policy Department. He was executive assistant to RAND's vice president for research during 1991 and is currently working toward a Ph.D. in public finance from the University of Maryland. He has conducted research on issues relating to nuclear weapons policy and crisis management and, more recently, on state and local finance in California. His current research is focusing on the equity and distribution of tax burdens.

Joan Petersilia (Ph.D., Social Ecology/Criminology, University of California, Irvine) is the director of RAND's Criminal Justice Program and senior RAND fellow in Criminal Justice. She has been conducting research on criminal justice policy for almost 20 years, leading RAND's first study on career criminals and how they are handled within state corrections departments. She is a nationally recognized expert on intensive supervision programs and has directed a nationwide intensive supervision probation and parole demonstration project sponsored by the Bureau of Justice Assistance.

Dr. Petersilia serves in an advisory capacity to many state corrections departments. She has served as president of both the American Society of Criminology and the Association for Criminal Justice Research in California.

Peter Reuter (Ph.D., Economics, Yale University) is cofounder and codirector of the RAND Drug Policy Research Center. His early work focused on the organization of criminal activities, and his book *Disorganized Crime: The Economics of the Visible Hand* won the 1984 Leslie Wilkins Award as the outstanding study in the fields of criminology and criminal justice. Since 1983 he has worked primarily on drug policy issues. His many publications include *Sealing the Borders,* which examines the effects of increased drug interdiction, and *Money from Crime: A Study of the Economics of Drug Dealing in Washington, D.C.,* which provides the first systematic data on the characteristics and earnings of street-level drug dealers. Dr. Reuter currently is leading a major study of European drug policy.

Peter J.E. Stan (Ph.D., Economics, Harvard University) is a senior economist at RAND who works on public budgeting. A portion of this work, undertaken with Professor John E. Dawson of the Naval Postgraduate School, focuses on trends in federal, state, and local expenditures and revenues in the United States after 1952. Results of this analysis will form the basis for a study of deficits in the U.S. public sector over the past 40 years and an examination of future policy options for deficit reduction. His other work at RAND has included analysis of how informal resource transfers substitute for credit and insurance markets in developing countries. Between 1989 and 1992, Dr. Stan served as associate director of the National Security Strategies Program in Project AIR FORCE, the U.S. Air Force's federally funded research and development center at RAND.

James B. Steinberg (J.D., Yale University) is a senior analyst in RAND's International Policy Department. In addition to his writing and research on U.S. national security policy and U.S.-European relations, he has written on civil rights ("Were You Counted? Civil Rights and the 1990 Census") and public service employment programs in the 1970s. Prior to joining RAND, he was a senior fellow at the International Institute for Strategic Studies in London, minority counsel to the U.S. Senate Labor and Human Resources Committee, and a special assistant in the U.S. Department of Justice.

Robert E. Tranquada (M.D., Stanford University) is the Norman Topping/National Medical Enterprises Professor of Medicine and Public Policy at the University of Southern California (USC) and a consultant to RAND. He is a former dean of the USC School of Medicine and former chancellor of the University of Massachusetts Medical Center. As cofounder of the Watts Health Foundation in 1965, medical director of the Los Angeles County/USC Medical Center, regional director of the Los Angeles County Department of Health Services, and chair of the Department of Community Medicine and Public Health at USC, he has long been involved directly in issues of health care access. He is a member of the Institute of Medicine of the National Academy of Sciences.

Mary E. Vaiana (Ph.D., English Linguistics, Indiana University) is the founder and director of RAND's Communications Consulting Group. Members of this group work with the research staff to communicate findings of RAND studies to a wide range of audiences. Over the past 10 years, Dr. Vaiana has worked in nearly every research area at RAND, designing strategies for communicating policy results, writing synthesis documents, and assisting in the development of briefings and other high-level presentations. She has also conducted research on writing and on document format. Recently she helped design and implement a survey examining the information needs and information-gathering habits of RAND's major audiences. Following up on the survey, she assisted in redefining RAND's communications efforts and in designing new formats to meet specific audience needs.

Georges Vernez (Ph.D., Urban and Regional Development, University of California, Berkeley) is director of RAND's Program for Policy Research in Immigration and also director of the Education and Human Resources Program. His current work includes studies assessing both the domestic and international effects of immigration policies. He has recently conducted a study of programs for the homeless in California and the incidence of mental disorders in that population. In other work Dr. Vernez has examined the federal role in urban economic development and has assessed the effectiveness of alternative countercyclical policies and of alternative welfare policies. He has authored numerous publications on immigration and has served as a consultant to such organizations as the United Nations.

Barbara R. Williams (Ph.D., Sociology, University of Illinois) is vice president for research communications and deputy vice president for research at RAND. Her previous positions at RAND include seven years as director of the Criminal Justice Program, eight years as director of the domestic research programs in RAND's Washington office, and six years as director of the Urban Policy Analysis Program. In the latter capacity, Dr. Williams was responsible for overseeing research on many urban issues, including population shifts in metropolitan areas, technological innovation in municipal services and the effects of alternative pricing, and the impacts of various federal policies on metropolitan populations. She was also cofounder and for three years codirector of RAND's Drug Policy Research Center.

EDUCATION

Carroll, Stephen, and Rolla Edward Park, *The Search for Equity in School Finance*, Cambridge, Mass.: Ballinger Publishing Company, 1983.

Elmore, Richard F., and Milbrey W. McLaughlin, *Steady Work: Policy, Practice, and the Reform of American Education*, Santa Monica, Calif.: RAND, R-3574-NIE/RC, 1988.

Grubb, W. Norton, and Lorraine M. McDonnell, *Local Systems of Vocational Education and Job Training: Diversity, Interdependence, and Effectiveness*, Santa Monica, Calif.: RAND, R-4077-NCRVE/UCB, 1991.

Hill, Paul T., and Josephine Bonan, *Decentralization and Accountability in Public Education*, Santa Monica, Calif.: RAND, R-4066-MCF/IET, 1991.

Hill, Paul T., Gail E. Foster, and Tamar Gendler, *High Schools with Character*, Santa Monica, Calif.: RAND, R-3944-RC, 1990.

Hill, Paul T., Arthur E. Wise, and Leslie Shapiro, *Educational Progress: Cities Mobilize to Improve Their Schools*, Santa Monica, Calif.: RAND, R-3711-JSM/CSTP, 1989.

For information or to order RAND publications, call Customer Service (310) 393-0411, extension 6686. Order books and journal articles directly from the book or journal publisher.

Koretz, Daniel, *Trends in the Postsecondary Enrollment of Minorities*, Santa Monica, Calif.: RAND, R-3948-FF, 1990.

McDonnell, Lorraine M., and Milbrey W. McLaughlin, *Education Policy and the Role of the States*, Santa Monica, Calif.: RAND, R-2755-NIE, 1982.

Oakes, Jeannie, *Improving Inner-City Schools: Current Directions in Urban District Reform*, Santa Monica, Calif.: RAND, JNE-02, 1987.

Oakes, Jeannie, *Multiplying Inequalities: The Effects of Race, Social Class, and Tracking on Opportunities to Learn Mathematics and Science*, Santa Monica, Calif.: RAND, R-3928-NSF, 1990.

Stasz, Cathleen, David McArthur, Matthew Lewis, and Kimberly Ramsey, *Teaching and Learning Generic Skills for the Workplace*, Santa Monica, Calif.: RAND, R-4004-NCRVE/UCB, 1990.

Tan, Hong, Bruce Chapman, Christine Peterson, and Alison Booth, *Youth Training in the United States, Britain, and Australia*, Santa Monica, Calif.: RAND, R-4022-ED, 1991.

HEALTH

Brook, Robert H., and Kathleen N. Lohr, *Will We Need to Ration Effective Health Care?*, Santa Monica, Calif.: RAND, N-3375-HHS, 1991.

Dallek, Geraldine, *State Initiatives on the Medically Uninsured: A Survey*, Santa Monica, Calif.: RAND, N-3044-DOL, 1990.

Farley, Donna, Lucy Eisenberg, and Geraldine Dallek, *Assessing Emergency Medical Services in Los Angeles County: A Research Agenda*, Santa Monica, Calif.: RAND, N-3306-RC, 1991.

Kanouse, David E., Sandra H. Berry, E. Michael Gorman, Elizabeth M. Yano, Sally Carson, and Allan Abrahamse, *AIDS-Related Knowledge, Attitudes, Beliefs, and Behaviors in Los Angeles County*, Santa Monica, Calif.: RAND, R-4045-LACH, 1991.

Leibowitz, Arleen, and Joan L. Buchanan, *Setting Capitations for Medicaid: A Case Study*, Santa Monica, Calif.: RAND, N-3251-HCFA, 1990.

Pascal, Anthony, Charles L. Bennett, Marilyn Cvitanic, Michael Gorman, and Carl Serrato, *The Costs and Financing of Care for AIDS Patients: Results of a Cohort Study in Los Angeles*, Santa Monica, Calif.: RAND, N-3060-HCFA, 1990.

Vernez, Georges, M. Audrey Burnam, Elizabeth A. McGlynn, Sally Trude, and Brian S. Mittman, *Review of California's Program for the Homeless Mentally Disabled: Executive Summary*, Santa Monica, Calif.: RAND, R-3631/1-CDMH, 1988.

Zellman, Gail L., *Linking Schools and Social Services: The Case of Child Abuse Reporting*, Santa Monica, Calif.: RAND, N-3226-HHS, 1990.

Zellman, Gail L., *Report Decision-Making Patterns Among Mandated Child Abuse Reporters*, Santa Monica, Calif.: RAND, N-3225-HHS, 1990.

Zwanziger, Jack, and Glenn A. Melnick, *The Effects of Hospital Competition and the Medicare PPS Program on Hospital Cost Behavior in California*, Santa Monica, Calif.: RAND, N-3049-HHS-PMT, 1988.

JUSTICE

Chaiken, Jan M., and Marcia R. Chaiken, *Varieties of Criminal Behavior: Summary and Policy Implications*, Santa Monica, Calif.: RAND, R-2814/1-NIJ, 1982.

Ellickson, Phyllis L., and Robert M. Bell, *Prospects for Preventing Drug Use Among Young Adolescents*, Santa Monica, Calif.: RAND, R-3896-CHF, 1990.

Greenwood, Peter W., *Intervention Strategies for Chronic Juvenile Offenders*, New York, New York: Greenwood Press, 1986.

Kakalik, James S., Molly Selvin, and Nicholas M. Pace, *Adverting Gridlock: Strategies for Reducing Civil Delay in the Los Angeles Superior Court*, Santa Monica, Calif.: R-3762-ICJ, 1990.

Klein, Stephen P., Patricia Ebner, Allan Abrahamse, and Nora Fitzgerald, *Predicting Criminal Justice Outcomes: What Matters?*, Santa Monica, Calif.: RAND, R-3972-BJS, 1991.

Petersilia, Joan R., Allan F. Abrahamse, and James Q. Wilson, *Police Performance and Case Attrition*, Santa Monica, Calif.: RAND, R-3515-NIJ, 1987.

Petersilia, Joan, *Expanding Options for Criminal Sentencing*, Santa Monica, Calif.: RAND, R-3544-EMC, 1987.

Petersilia, Joan, *The Influence of Criminal Justice Research*, Santa Monica, Calif.: RAND, R-3516-NIJ, 1987.

Petersilia, Joan, and Susan Turner, *Intensive Supervision for High-Risk Probationers: Findings from Three California Experiments*, Santa Monica, Calif.: RAND, R-3936-NIJ/BJA, 1990.

Polich, J. Michael, Phyllis L. Ellickson, Peter Reuter, and James P. Kahan, *Strategies for Controlling Adolescent Drug Use*, Santa Monica, Calif.: RAND, R-3076-CHF, 1984.

Reuter, Peter, John Haaga, Patrick Murphy, and Amy Praskac, *Drug Use and Drug Problems in the Washington Metropolitan Area*, Santa Monica, Calif.: RAND, R-3655-GWRC, 1988.

Schlossman, Steven, *Studies in the History of Early 20th Century Delinquency Prevention*, Santa Monica, Calif.: N-1945-NIE, 1983.

Reuter, Peter, Robert MacCoun, and Patrick Murphy, *Money from Crime: A Study of the Economics of Drug Dealing in Washington, D.C.*, Santa Monica, Calif.: RAND, R-3894-RF, 1990.

POPULATION/IMMIGRATION

Abrahamse, Allan F., Peter A. Morrison, and Linda J. Waite, *Beyond Stereotypes: Who Becomes A Single Teenage Mother?*, Santa Monica, Calif.: RAND, R-3489-HHS/NICHD, 1988.

Goldscheider, Frances K., and Linda J. Waite, *New Families, No Families? The Transformation of the American Home*, Berkeley, Calif.: University of California Press, 1991.

McCarthy, Kevin F., and R. Burciaga Valdez, *Current and Future Effects of Mexican Immigration in California*, Santa Monica, Calif.: RAND, R-3365-CR, 1986.

Morrison, Peter A., *Demographic Factors Reshaping Ties to Family and Place*, Santa Monica, Calif.: RAND, N-3271-RC, 1990.

Rolph, Elizabeth, and Abby Robyn, *A Window on Immigration Reforms: Implementing the Immigration Reform and Control Act in Los Angeles*, Santa Monica, Calif.: RAND, JRI-06, 1990.

Smith, James P., "Children Among the Poor," *Demography*, Vol. 26, No. 2, May 1989, pp. 235–248.

Smith, James P., and Finis R. Welch, *Closing the Gap: Forty Years of Economic Progress for Blacks*, Santa Monica, Calif.: RAND, R-3330-DOL, 1986.

Stolzenberg, Ross M., *Occupational Differences Between Hispanics and Non-Hispanics*, Santa Monica, Calif.: RAND, N-1889-NCEP, 1982.

Vernez, Georges, and Kevin McCarthy, *Meeting the Economy's Labor Needs Through Immigration: Rationale and Challenges*, Santa Monica, Calif.: RAND, N-3052-FF, 1990.

Vernez, Georges, and David Ronfeldt, *The Current Situation in Mexican Immigration*, Santa Monica, Calif.: RAND, R-4099-FF, 1991.

Waite, Linda J., and Lee A. Lillard, *Children and Marital Disruption*, Santa Monica, Calif.: RAND, N-3315-NICHD, 1991.

URBAN POLICY

Berry, Sandra H., *Los Angeles Today and Tomorrow: Results of the Los Angeles 2000 Community Survey*, Santa Monica, Calif.: RAND, R-3705-LA2000, 1988.

Gurwitz, Aaron S., and G. Thomas Kingsley, *The Cleveland Metropolitan Economy: An Initial Assessment: Executive Summary*, Santa Monica, Calif., RAND, R-2883/1-CF, 1982.

Morrison, Peter A., Roger J. Vaughn, Georges Vernez, and Barbara R. Williams, *Recent Contributions to the Urban Policy Debate*, Santa Monica, Calif.: RAND, R-2394-RC, 1979.

Neels, Kevin, and Michael Caggiano, *The Entrepreneurial City: Innovations in Finance and Management for Saint Paul*, Santa Monica, Calif.: RAND, R-3123-SP/FF, 1984.

Pascal, Anthony, and Aaron Gurwitz, *Picking Winners: Industrial Strategies for Local Economic Development*, Santa Monica, Calif.: RAND, R-2932-HUD/RC, 1983.

Walker, Warren E., and Jan M. Chaiken, *The Effects of Fiscal Contraction on Innovation in the Public Sector*, Santa Monica, Calif.: RAND, P-6610, 1981.